Tolley's
Capital Allowances:
Transactions and Planning

Sixth Edition

Martin Wilson MA FCA

The Capital Allowances Partnership
www.cap-allow.com

Members of the LexisNexis Group worldwide

United Kingdom	LexisNexis UK, a Division of Reed Elsevier (UK) Ltd, Halsbury House, 35 Chancery Lane, LONDON, WC2A 1EL, and 4 Hill Street, EDINBURGH EH2 3JZ
Argentina	LexisNexis Argentina, BUENOS AIRES
Australia	LexisNexis Butterworths, CHATSWOOD, New South Wales
Austria	LexisNexis Verlag ARD Orac GmbH & Co KG, VIENNA
Canada	LexisNexis Butterworths, MARKHAM, Ontario
Chile	LexisNexis Chile Ltda, SANTIAGO DE CHILE
Czech Republic	Nakladatelství Orac sro, PRAGUE
France	Editions du Juris-Classeur SA, PARIS
Germany	LexisNexis Deutschland GmbH, FRANKFURT, MUNSTER
Hong Kong	LexisNexis Butterworths, HONG KONG
Hungary	HVG-Orac, BUDAPEST
India	LexisNexis Butterworths, NEW DELHI
Ireland	Butterworths (Ireland) Ltd, DUBLIN
Italy	Giuffrè Editore, MILAN
Malaysia	Malayan Law Journal Sdn Bhd, KUALA LUMPUR
New Zealand	LexisNexis Butterworths, WELLINGTON
Poland	Wydawnictwo Prawnicze LexisNexis, WARSAW
Singapore	LexisNexis Butterworths, SINGAPORE
South Africa	LexisNexis Butterworths, DURBAN
Switzerland	Stämpfli Verlag AG, BERNE
USA	LexisNexis, DAYTON, Ohio

© Reed Elsevier (UK) Ltd 2003

A CIP Catalogue record for this book is available from the British Library.

First Edition October 1998
Second Edition September 1999
Third Edition September 2000
Fourth Edition September 2001
Fifth Edition September 2002
Sixth Edition September 2003

ISBN 0 7545 212 14

Typeset by Columns Design Ltd, Reading, England
Printed and bound in Great Britain by Hobbs the Printers Ltd, Totton, Hampshire

Visit LexisNexis UK at www.lexisnexis.co.uk

Preface to the Sixth Edition

Beyond Capital Allowances

This work aims, above all, to save taxpayers money, by helping them to max-imise capital allowances and related tax reliefs on a wide range of commercial transactions. The opportunities to maximise capital allowances are often over-looked, and reading this book can be an easy way of getting ahead of the com-petition – to be forewarned is to be forearmed.

This book is aimed primarily at those responsible for property transactions in a corporate environment, whether they are property investors or owner-occupiers. Its unique transaction-based structure and special features such as pro forma elections and checklists make it equally useful, however, to those advising on property deals.

For the first time, this edition addresses the issues faced by a UK taxpayer claiming foreign equivalents of capital allowances, for example, in overseas subsidiaries.

Legislation is stated as at 1 August 2003. Unless otherwise stated, references are to the *Capital Allowances Act 2001* or, in Chapter 24 on Intangibles, to *Finance Act 2002, Schedule 29*. The Inland Revenue material reproduced in the book is Crown Copyright.

The views expressed are my own. Although this work aims to be comprehen-sive and practical, the availability and best use of allowances will depend on the individual circumstances of each transaction. For this reason, the reader is advised to take professional advice before proceeding with a transaction or course of action.

Martin Wilson
The Capital Allowances Partnership
www.cap-allow.com

Contents

Contents

Contents

Contents

Tolley's Table of Cases

Tolley's Table of Statutes

Chapter 1

Introduction

General

1.1   It is common practice to speak of 'preparing' a capital allowances claim. This presupposes that particular types of assets qualify automatically for particular types of allowances, and that a claim consists of no more than assembling and presenting self-evident facts. In reality, the process is much more complicated. Both tax law and building design have moved on to a new plane of complexity, and the 'grey areas' have grown — the facts are often less self-evident than they once were. In this climate, it is no longer appropriate to speak of simply 'preparing' a claim. Instead, suitable terms may be borrowed from the language of property and construction. Like the property to which it may relate, a claim for capital allowances must be *developed* and before it can be developed it must be *planned*. This clearly involves a good deal of work, and the question is often asked whether the cost (in both time and money) is justified.

1.2   One answer, which is often not understood, is that capital allowances are effectively a negative element of the total cost. Failure to exploit allowances fully will therefore effectively increase the post-tax cost of, say, a building, just as surely as if there had been a failure to identify the most competitive construction or fit-out tender. The scope for capital allowances planning extends, of course, far beyond the context of a new building development, as this work demonstrates.

1.3   A second consideration, for accounting periods ending on or after 1 July 1999, is the extension of the self-assessment regime to corporate tax-payers. Responsibility for the correctness of a capital allowances claim falls more squarely on the taxpayer than ever before, with penalties for claims proved to be incorrect as a result of negligence.

Maximising tax relief

1.4   A prime concern of any taxpayer must be to pay as little tax as possible. This, of course, must be done by legal means. This principle was enunciated by Lord Tomlin in the 1935 case *Duke of Westminster v CIR (1935) 9 TC 490*: 'Every man is entitled if he can to order his affairs so that the tax attaching … is less than it would otherwise be.' This principle has held true through a number of challenges, although with the passage of time some modification has been inevitable, and anti-avoidance schemes generally have been attacked.

1

1.5   General

1.5   In general the taxpayer should seek to claim relief for expenditure in the following order:

(1)   as land remediation expenditure or revenue expenditure on research and development, both qualifying at 150%;

(2)   as a 'normal' revenue deduction (relief at 100%);

(3)   as research and development or as an enterprise zone property (if appropriate) (relief at 100%);

(4)   as an item of plant (relieved at between 6% pa and 100%);

(5)   as an industrial or agricultural building (relief at a minimum of 4% pa).

This is not, however, a hard-and-fast rule and in some cases (eg. the purchase of some industrial buildings) the order of preference may in part be reversed.

Planning is nearly always possible and the amounts involved normally justify at least an initial examination.

Revenue deduction

1.6   The optimal tax relief will normally be obtained if it can be shown that amounts are properly deductible as revenue expenses. Most capital allowances (with the exception of 150% relief for land remediation expenditure (see Chapter 23) and 100% initial allowances for expenditure in enterprise zones (Chapter 9) and on information and communications technology (see 13.10)) are a poor alternative.

1.7   The nature of expenditure (whether it is revenue or capital) is often assumed to be a question of fact. This is far from true, although admittedly items such as buildings and machinery are usually easier to classify than some of the more esoteric subjects which have been considered by the courts, for example petrol station 'solus' agreements. In connection with the last of these, Lord Upjohn in *Strick v Regent Oil Co Ltd (1965) 43 TC 1* observed:

'no part of our law of taxation presents such almost insoluble conundrums as the decision whether a receipt or outgoing is capital or income for tax purposes'.

1.8   As a general guide, we turn to the rule put forward by Viscount Cave (in *Atherton v British Insulated and Helsby Cables Ltd (1925) 10 TC 155*) that expenditure is normally capital if it is made 'not only for once and for all, but with a view to bringing into existence an asset or an advantage for the enduring benefit of the trade'. The distinction between capital and revenue as it applies to tangible assets such as buildings and plant is often largely a question of whether an outlay represents (i) a repair or (ii) an improvement. Generally, the taxpayer will want to claim as much as possible in repairs. In this way, full tax relief will be given in the year of expenditure, rather than spread over the asset's life. However, as is to be expected, there are legal constraints.

1.9 One important case gave its name to what is generally known as the *'Law Shipping'* principle. In this case, a ship was purchased in a dilapidated state and subsequently renovated. The courts held that the need for repair was reflected in a low purchase price, and that the subsequent repair costs to the extent that they were attributable to the period prior to acquisition were therefore properly to be regarded as capital (*Law Shipping Co Ltd v CIR (1923) 12 TC 621*).

1.10 In contrast to *Law Shipping*, another case dealt with a number of cinemas purchased during and immediately after World War II. The cinemas were in need of repair, but were nonetheless capable of use (and were in fact used) before being repaired. When the repairs were eventually carried out, it was held the amounts expended were revenue and not capital (*Odeon Associated Theatres Ltd v Jones (1971) 48 TC 257*).

1.11 The distinction between capital and revenue can be equally indistinct where the expenditure is on an asset already in the ownership of the taxpayer. Any deduction from revenue will be limited to the cost of the repairs actually carried out (as distinct from repairs obviated by the improvement).

1.12 Whether expenditure is capital or revenue is a matter of law, and the accounting treatment is influential, but not conclusive. The most recent Revenue approach is that revenue expenditure is allowed only when it is charged to the profit and loss account. Where revenue expenditure is capitalised (as, say, part of the cost of a building) it may only attract a tax deduction when it is amortised. Many businesses do not depreciate buildings, in which case, no deduction is available. Companies must therefore be aware of the problems which can be brought about by accounting policies.

Refurbishment

1.13 A fundamental feature of capital expenditure is that some 'enduring benefit' must be created. However, this benefit must be of a certain kind; in particular, a new asset must be brought into existence. The *nature of the asset* is therefore important.

1.14 Where replacements are in point, another important factor is whether the replacement is of an entire asset or merely part of an asset, or whether the original asset has come to the end of its useful working life. A replacement may nonetheless be regarded as being on revenue account if it is a *like-for-like replacement*. A replacement cannot in strictness be like-for-like if there is an element of *improvement*. However, a replacement which is shown to improve overall operating efficiency, rather than simply doing the same job better, is more likely to be treated as revenue. An element of improvement is often made inevitable simply by the passage of time and associated technological progress. Some leeway is allowed by extending the scope of the term 'like-for-like' to include the *nearest modern equivalent*. Motive for incurring the expenditure is also important.

1.15 General

The nature of the asset

1.15 There is a thin line between revenue and capital items. In general terms, the distinction is not founded upon the quantum of the expenditure, nor upon the size of the assets involved. Rather, the two key principles are:

(*a*) the durability of any new asset created; and

(*b*) (in the context of replacements) whether it is the whole or merely a part of an asset which is being replaced.

1.16 There is a wealth of case law on this question. The most commonly quoted case is *Atherton v British Insulated and Helsby Cables Ltd (1925) 10 TC 155*, which speaks of capital expenditure being made with a view to bringing into existence an asset or an advantage for the enduring benefit of the trade. In *Whitehead v Tubbs (Elastics) Ltd [1984] STC 1*, it was observed that there was no single test for determining whether expenditure is revenue or capital, but one very important factor was whether, in consequence of the expenditure, an identifiable asset (tangible or intangible) of an enduring nature was acquired or produced. However Oliver LJ elaborated further, saying that capital expenditure was not evidenced by a simple enduring benefit, but rather by one of a capital nature in the sense that it enabled a company to utilise its capital assets in a way in which it could not have utilised them before. There is a distinction to be drawn here with the case of *Lothian Chemical Co Ltd v Rogers (1926) 11 TC 508*, where the cost of converting plant for use for a different process was held to be capital.

1.17 Alongside this, one needs to consider whether the item concerned is a complete asset, or merely part of an asset. This is the 'entirety' concept highlighted in the two cases *O'Grady v Bullcroft Main Collieries Ltd (1932) 17 TC 93* and *Samuel Jones & Co (Devondale) Ltd v CIR (1951) 32 TC 513*. Both concerned the replacement of chimneys. However, where the chimney was merely part of a larger building, the expenditure was treated as being in respect of repairs, whilst where the chimney constituted a complete asset in itself, the replacement cost was held to be capital.

Like-for-like expenditure

1.18 An asset which is, strictly speaking, a new part will nonetheless not be regarded as a capital item where it is a like-for-like replacement. In theory, the new asset should be identical to the old, but of course some leeway is inevitable. In the case of *Margrett v Lowestoft Water and Gas Co (1935) 19 TC 481*, it was ruled inadmissible to apportion the expenditure so as to identify the cost of repairs which would have otherwise been necessary. One key question would be — is the old asset to be replaced because the new asset could do the job better, or because the old asset used to do the job better? This was essentially the question proposed (and answered to the taxpayer's favour) in *Rhodesia Railways Ltd v Bechuanaland (1933) 12 ATC 223*.

Improvements

1.19   Expenditure on a replacement asset will generally be regarded as capital if that asset is in any way an improvement on the old. However, there is little or no guidance as to what constitutes an improvement. There are two possibilities:

(*a*)   the replacement is in some way intrinsically better than the old asset; or

(*b*)   there is an anticipated future benefit in terms of operating efficiency (of the business as a whole, rather than simply of the machine).

1.20   In the former case there would be little merit in claiming that the cost of the replacement was revenue. In the latter case, however, there is considerably more hope. As with like-for-like replacements (above), it is important to look at the reasons behind the incurring of the expenditure. What is the future benefit, and how likely is it? This illustrates an interesting comment made in *Tucker v Granada Motorway Services Ltd [1977] STC 353*, where Lord Wilberforce stated that the benefit must:

'endure in the way that fixed capital endures; not a benefit that endures in the sense for a good number of years it relieves you of a revenue payment'.

Nearest modern equivalent

1.21   Replacement parts will generally be allowed as a revenue expense where they are replacing like-for-like. With the passage of time, of course, it is increasingly unlikely that an exactly identical replacement can be found. Hence, the Revenue's policy that the 'nearest modern equivalent' is an acceptable substitute. One problem with this is that technology has generally improved over the years, and it is therefore sometimes difficult to say that there has not been an enhancement or improvement. Once again, an important consideration is motive, i.e. the reason why the expenditure was incurred. If the improvement is merely incidental, and was not instrumental in making the decision to incur the expenditure, it may be discounted.

1.22   The case of *Conn v Robins Ltd (1966) 43 TC 266* dealt with rather extreme facts, concerning as it did a business trading from 400 year-old premises. Such an extreme instance as replacing an oak floor with a concrete one was held to be a repair, rather than capital, on the grounds that this was the nearest modern equivalent. In defining the 'nearest modern equivalent', one must consider the wider context. It cannot be simply a matter of comparing technical specification or physical properties of the particular asset, one has to look also at, for example, comparative cost or changed operating requirements. A useful (but admittedly very hypothetical) question to ask is whether the purchaser of the old asset would, faced with today's circumstances, purchase the replacement that has been chosen.

Improvements obviating repairs

1.23 In the 1952 case of *William P Lawrie v CIR (1952) 34 TC 20* a new roof was added to a building. Once this work began, it became apparent that the existing roof had been in a poor state of repair. The taxpayer therefore claimed as a repair part of his expenditure on the new roof. This claim was not allowed because the amount claimed was for notional repairs obviated by the alterations, rather than for actual repairs carried out.

1.24 Prior to 1 April 2001, there was some relief in such circumstances for those taxed under Schedule A (income from interests in land, e.g. rent). ESC B4 read:

'Where maintenance and repairs of property are obviated by improvements, additions and alterations, so much of the outlay as is equal to the estimated cost of the maintenance and repairs is allowed as a deduction in computing liability in respect of rents under Schedule A. This concession does not apply where:

(i) the alterations etc. are so extensive as to amount to a reconstruction of the property, or

(ii) there is a change in the use of the property which would have made such maintenance or repairs unnecessary.'

This concession is now withdrawn, and the Inland Revenue has made it clear that no element of capital improvements may qualify as a repair (Tax Bulletin 48).

Alternative bases – renewals and wear and tear

1.25 As an alternative to claiming capital allowances on machinery and plant, it is possible to adopt instead what is generally known as the 'renewals basis'. Where this is adopted, no relief (either revenue deduction or capital allowance) is given for the original purchase of an asset, but the cost of any subsequent replacements or renewals is allowed in full as a revenue deduction. The availability of this basis as an alternative to formal capital allowances was confirmed by an early case, *Caledonian Railway Co v Banks (1880) 1 TC 487*, which has never been overturned. The renewals basis is most often applied to small items such as hotel crockery and linen but could be permitted for larger items. The renewals basis is often useful to the taxpayer where the items concerned have a short life, but do not qualify as machinery or plant.

1.26 It is possible for a taxpayer to change from the renewals basis to 'normal' capital allowances, provided that where they use more than one item of a class of machinery or plant they change from the 'renewals' basis to the capital allowances basis for all the items in that class (ESC B1). The commercial written-down value of items transferred is added to the qualifying expenditure for the pool for the period in which the change takes place. For this purpose commercial written-down value means the value arrived at by writing-down the asset from cost at a commercial rate of depreciation having regard for the age of the asset and its expected life (Inland Revenue Manual (hereafter 'CA'), para 29220). It is not possible to change to a renewals basis in respect of assets which have previously qualified for capital allowances.

A further alternative is available where a person is letting furnished living accommodation. Such landlords may claim a deduction for the wear and tear of plant, equal to 10% of rent, less council tax, water rates and other material services costs (ESC B47).

Progressing a claim

1.27   In the simplest case the negotiation process is compressed into a single letter or a few lines in a computation and, usually, its agreement by the Inspector. In a more complicated case it can be broken down into the following stages:

(*a*)   recording facts and decisions which constitute contemporaneous evidence;

(*b*)   presenting the claim;

(*c*)   settling the claim.

1.28   Sometimes these stages overlap. There is no bar on the inclusion in a claim of innovative ideas, provided the Inspector is supplied with enough information to enable him to make his own judgment. However, retention of credibility is an important factor in the negotiation and settlement of claims.

In addition, under corporation tax self-assessment, a claim may still be challenged by the Inland Revenue for a number of years after it is submitted. Negligent or reckless claims may result in penalties equal to the tax underpaid.

Recording facts and decisions

1.29   It is important to record the facts and decisions relating to the subject of the claim as they occur or are made. An increasing number of claims now depend for their success upon the ability of the claimant to demonstrate that an asset was acquired for use for a particular purpose. There can be nothing stronger than contemporaneous evidence, especially if the course of events between acquisition of the asset and the making of a claim is not particularly helpful.

1.30   A common example where this is true is partitioning, where a claim is dependent upon the partitions being not only movable but likely to be moved in the course of trade due to variations in accommodation requirements. If the circumstances leading to the adoption of the movable system are recorded, and preferably illustrated at the design or planning stage by projections of the likely movements as then perceived, it is so much easier to demonstrate them if subsequently challenged. Likewise, if the claim is to be based on the fact that a complex asset functions as a single item of plant, agreement will be facilitated if the evidence to that effect can be captured and made clear in the design brief or other similar documents. In the event of a formal appeal hearing this type of information is invaluable.

Capital allowances claims often revolve around matters of judgement, rather than simply applying hard and fast rules. However, nothing should be included in a claim unless there is a reasonable argument to support it. Under self-assessment, penalties may be imposed for negligent or fraudulent claims.

Presenting the claim

1.31   In many cases the claim will be incorporated in the corporation tax or income tax computation of the year in which the expenditure on the asset in question is incurred. This is not always the best policy. For example, it is possible for a factory or a warehouse to be constructed within a period of, say, four months. By the time the year end matters are due to be dealt with all the personnel involved in the development could have packed up and gone away. There is frequently some merit in opening negotiations with the Inspector on the basis of projected costs, agreeing the principles and then arranging for the revised costings (if necessary) to be prepared while the quantity surveyors, architects, project managers etc. are still on-site. This method seems to be particularly beneficial when there is a 'design and build' or 'turnkey' contract and there is often only minimal direct employment of the surveyors and/or architects by the claimant. If the claim is negotiated before the final costs are known the Inspector will expect (and it is good practice to provide) a complete reconciliation of the projected and final figures.

1.32   Early commencement of the negotiations will usually result in the Inspector's visit (if he makes one) being earlier. This gives the advantage of knowing his reaction at an early stage and sometimes facilitates the illustration of points of construction before they are hidden. It also facilitates early identification of the items to be costed and the incorporation of any resultant adjustments of the claim into the final analysis being produced by the surveyor or architect.

Settling the claim

1.33   A claim is usually settled by agreement, negotiation or withdrawal. If it is agreed there is nothing more to be said. A withdrawal might imply immovable resistance but this is not always so as will be seen later.

1.34   Many Inspectors now seem to adopt a more business-like approach to contentious claims. This can be for a variety of reasons. It may be that a formal hearing could go either way and the Inspector wishes to limit the Revenue's costs. It may be that the claimant has a strong case but the

Inspector does not wish to create a precedent which could give rise to a number of similar cases at considerable cost to the Exchequer. It is for the claimant to weigh up the situation. If he is aware that the Inspector has referred the point to his head office the position is more likely, although not necessarily, to be the latter.

1.35 When the technical arguments have been largely resolved it is advisable for the claimant to calculate exactly what the claim is worth. This will generally be the allowances expressed in terms of tax saved or, if there is an alternative claim (say industrial buildings instead of plant), the tax on the difference between the allowances. This cost (cost A) will need to take into account the speed at which the allowances are likely to be used bearing in mind available profits etc.

1.36 The next step is to compare this with the likely cost (cost B) of an appeal to the Commissioners. This will be an immediate outlay. If an appeal is seriously considered the likely value of the claim will therefore be reduced to A minus B. However, because no appeal is certain to succeed, the taxpayer must also assess the relative probabilities of success and failure.

1.37 If the Inspector's problem is in not having a 'feel' for the outcome of an appeal he is more likely to agree a compromise somewhere in the middle. If the claimant has prepared for the negotiations as indicated above, he is very likely to discover that he has more scope to accommodate a compromise than initially seemed apparent. If the Inspector's problem is in not wishing to create a precedent in the face of strong arguments, the claimant's position might not be entirely lost. Instances have occurred where the technical arguments (and therefore the relevant part of the claim) have been withdrawn in return for an unspecified adjustment to the remainder of the claim. The result has been entirely acceptable to both parties, and had the additional advantage of not creating a precedent and avoiding the expense and time of a formal appeal hearing.

1.38 The value of a settlement is sometimes enhanced by the fact that it can be applied for a number of years. If the claim is based on a review of, say, repetitive minor refurbishment of public houses or shops, it might be possible to agree that a percentage of that expenditure will be deemed to qualify for allowances for a number of years thereby avoiding time-consuming yearly detailed analysis. Situations of this nature can sometimes be useful trade-offs when negotiations founder upon technical problems.

Date expenditure incurred

General rules

1.39 Capital allowances are first given (subject to other requirements, for example, that an industrial building is in use) for the chargeable period in which the capital expenditure has been (or is deemed to have been) incurred. When the rate of an allowance is changed the new rate is effective in respect

1.39 *Date expenditure incurred*

of capital expenditure incurred on or after a specified date. It is clear, therefore, that the ascertainment of that date is very important.

1.40 The general rule is that expenditure (other than that which consists of an additional VAT liability — see 21.11 et seq. below) is incurred on the date *on which the obligation to pay it becomes unconditional*. This applies whether or not there is a later date on or before which the whole or any part of that amount is required to be paid. [*Sec 5(1)(2).*]

1.41 Except in the circumstances explained below, the date on which the expenditure is actually paid is generally irrelevant.

Payment within one month after accounting date

1.42 If the obligation to pay becomes unconditional within one month of the end of a chargeable accounting period as a result of the issue of a certificate or some other event, and the agreement provides that the asset becomes the property of the purchaser or is otherwise under the agreement attributed to him before the end of that period, the obligation to pay is treated as having become unconditional immediately before the end of that period. [*Sec 5(4).*] This subsection recognises the fact that extended contracts (frequently called 'milestone contracts' — see 1.49 below) usually provide for monthly payments or other periodical payments based on valuations of work done. If the work done before a year end (and therefore attributable to the purchaser) is not certified (which is generally when the obligation to pay becomes unconditional) until after the year end, this subsection treats the obligation to pay as having become unconditional before that year end. The Revenue was asked to comment on the expression 'or is otherwise under the agreement attributed to'. The reply was to the effect that although reference must be made to the contract there are generally clear alternatives — that the asset is either the property of the purchaser or is otherwise attributable to the purchaser. The construction of an asset to the purchaser's own specification would normally satisfy the latter requirement.

1.43 Satisfaction of the test in *Sec 5(4)* merely fixes the date on which the obligation to pay becomes unconditional. It is still necessary for payment to be required to be paid within a further four months if the provisions of *Sec 5(5)* (see 1.46 below) are not to apply. Furthermore, satisfaction of the condition of attribution does not obviate the requirement that the asset (if machinery or plant) or a relevant interest therein (if an industrial building) must belong to the claimant either during or at the end of the chargeable period.

1.44 For the Revenue's view on deposits paid shortly before the end of an accounting period, see 13.43 et seq. below.

1.45 *Sec 5(4)* cannot be invoked to treat expenditure certified in July 1998 as having been incurred in June of that year to take advantage of the first year allowances on plant (unless an actual chargeable period or its basis period ended in that June).

Payment after four months

1.46 Where an agreement requires any consideration to be paid on (or not later than) a date which is more than four months after the date on which the obligation to pay becomes unconditional, that consideration is treated as incurred on that later date. [*Sec 5(5)*.]

1.47 It follows that if an asset is unconditionally purchased with a four-month credit period, allowances will be available for the period in which it is purchased. However, if the credit period is longer than four months, the period in which allowances become available is determined as if the expenditure has been incurred on the last day of the credit period. In either case the actual date of payment is irrelevant. Consequently, if a credit period of three months is allowed, but actual credit of five months is taken, the 'four months rule' of *Sec 5(5)* has no effect.

1.48 For hire-purchase and similar agreements see 17.1 below.

Milestone contracts

1.49 In the case of a 'milestone' contract which requires the contract price to be paid in instalments (usually monthly), each instalment will generally be incurred when the surveyor or architect certifies that the work has been performed. The date(s) of payment can usually be ignored because each date will be only a matter of some three or four weeks later than the relevant date of certification and will not, therefore, trigger the application of *Sec 5(4)*.

1.50 The construction work under such a contract, if it is building or structure, is usually performed on-site, which in most cases will either be owned by the purchaser or be the subject of an interest in land to which he is entitled. Consequently *Sec 271(3)* (industrial buildings allowance — see 7.16 below) will be satisfied. If the contract, as will generally be the case, also includes some expenditure which can be allocated to machinery or plant, the Revenue seems generally to accept appropriate apportionment of each instalment without separate examination of the belonging test (see 13.41 below). Given that in most cases the plant, by virtue of its inclusion in a building, will be a fixture on land in which the purchaser has an interest, the question of ownership will most likely be already satisfied, but for further comment on the question of ownership, see 13.41 below.

Reservation of title to goods

1.51 The Revenue has stated that where goods which have been supplied subject to reservation of title have been delivered to the purchaser then the obligation to pay will have become unconditional for the purposes of *Sec 5(3)*. However, it also stated that *Sec 5(4)* will not apply because that subsection applies only when the goods are the property of the purchaser. In these circumstances the goods might be said to have been attributed to the purchaser as envisaged by *Sec 5(4)*. This will depend on the precise circumstances, the wording of any contracts, and so on.

Retentions

1.52   The Revenue's view is that the obligation to pay any part of the purchase price which is the subject of a retention does not become unconditional until the condition which gave rise to the retention is satisfied (CA, para 11800). The same principles will apply where money is paid into an escrow account, pending the satisfaction of any conditions.

Anti-avoidance

1.53   Where:

(*a*)   an obligation to pay becomes unconditional on a date earlier than that which accords with normal commercial usage, and

(*b*)   the sole or main benefit which might have been expected to be obtained thereby is that the expenditure would be taken to be incurred in a chargeable period which is earlier than would otherwise have been the case,

the expenditure is taken to have been incurred on the date on or before which it is required to be paid. The date on which the obligation to pay became unconditional is then ignored. [*Sec 5(6)*.]

Interaction of other provisions

1.54   Where any other provision of *CAA 2001* would cause any expenditure to be treated as incurred on a date which is later than that which would result from the application of *Sec 5(3)–(6)*, for example pre-trading expenditure (see 1.63) that other provision takes precedence. [*Sec 5(7)*.]

Date of delivery

1.55   Some Inspectors have contended that until the vendor had fulfilled all obligations imposed upon him (and that included delivery of the asset) the obligation to pay would remain conditional. An alternative legal view is that the question whether a person had incurred capital expenditure has to be looked at from the standpoint of the person who had incurred the expenditure and not that of the vendor. As a matter of general contractual law, if a purchaser and vendor entered into an agreement providing for payment to be made on a particular date, then as soon as that date arrived the purchaser would have incurred the expenditure. If that date were the date of execution of the contract then at that time the purchaser would be under an unconditional obligation to pay the amount due under the contract. If the Revenue view were correct the words in parenthesis in *Sec 5(3)* would need to refer to '(whether or not there is *an earlier* or later date ...)'.

Inland Revenue Tax Bulletin of November 1993

1.56   The following Revenue Interpretation was given at page 97:

'*Capital Allowances*

Time When Expenditure Is Incurred

Section 5(3) Capital Allowances Act 2001 contains the basic rule for determining when expenditure is incurred for the purposes of the Act. That rule may be subject to the further rules in *Section 5(4)* onwards. This note does not address those further rules: it is concerned only with the basic rule in *Section 5(3)*.

Section 5(3) states that any amount of expenditure qualifying for capital allowances "is to be taken to be incurred on the date on which the obligation to pay that amount becomes unconditional (whether or not there is a later date on or before which the whole or any part of that amount is required to be paid)".

The date on which an obligation to pay becomes unconditional will depend on the terms of the particular contract for the supply of the asset concerned. The date of the contract for supply or of the issue of an invoice does not settle the point. In many cases a person buying goods is legally required to pay for them on or within a prescribed time of delivery. In such cases, we consider the obligation to pay becomes unconditional when the asset is delivered.

All *Section 5(3)* does is fix the date expenditure is incurred for the purposes of, for example, *Section 11* (machinery or plant allowances). The successful claimant of allowances must, of course, satisfy the conditions for obtaining the particular allowance. In the case of machinery or plant allowance, for example, one of the conditions is that the asset on which expenditure is incurred "belongs or has belonged" to the claimant in consequence of incurring the expenditure.'

1.57   The all important point is contained in the penultimate paragraph of the Interpretation: 'In many cases a person buying goods is legally required to pay for them on or within a prescribed time of delivery'. If the contract contains such a provision it is very likely that the obligation to pay will not become unconditional until the date of delivery. However, if there is no such provision in the contract the delivery date is likely to be irrelevant.

1.58   *Date expenditure incurred*

Example

1.58   Jones Ltd, a manufacturer of marine engines, has an annual accounting date of 30 September. On 25 May 1998 it signs a contract for the erection of a factory extension for a total cost of £1,500,000. Progress instalments are due to be certified on the 25th of each month with payment due 14 days later. The progress payments were as follows.

Certificate	Amount (£)	Certified	Due
1	200,000	25.6.98	8.9.98
2	250,000	25.7.98	9.10.98
3	300,000	25.8.98	8.11.98
4	400,000	25.9.98	9.12.98
5	200,000	25.10.98	8.11.98
6 (retention)	175,000	25.6.99	8.10.99

1.59   The dates on which the expenditure has been certified are, in the first instance, the dates on which the expenditure was incurred. On those dates Jones would have an unconditional obligation to pay.

1.60   Payment 5 was not certified until after 30 September 1998, the end of a chargeable period, but it must have referred to work done during that year because the previous certificate was for the period to 25 September 1998. Such work would have been 'under the contract attributable to the person having that obligation [to pay]'. It therefore falls within the scope of *Sec 5(4)* (see 1.42 above) and the appropriate part of payment 5 can be treated as incurred during the year to 30 September. In such circumstances it would be advisable to have the certification of the expenditure apportioned (assuming any additional fee payable would not offset the benefit of advancing the allowances by one year).

1.61   It is impossible to invoke the assistance of *Sec 5(4)* to backdate part of the expenditure on certificate 2 to June 1998 to get the benefit of any first-year allowance on the machinery or plant content because *Sec 5(4)* applies only to expenditure straddling the end of a chargeable period.

1.62   Payment 6 is a retention payment for which the obligation to pay does not become unconditional until the retention period has expired and no construction problems remain outstanding. This part of the expenditure is therefore incurred when certified.

Expenditure prior to commencement of the qualifying activity

1.63   Expenditure on machinery or plant incurred for the purposes of a qualifying activity by a person about to carry it on is treated as incurred on the day on which the trade actually commences. [*Sec 12.*] For the purposes of determining whether a first-year allowance is available and the rate applicable, it is necessary to have regard to the actual date on which the expenditure is incurred. [*Sec 50.*] Consequently expenditure incurred:

14

(*a*)   before 2 July 1997 in respect of a qualifying activity commenced after 1 July 1997 will not qualify for a first-year allowance;

(*b*)   during the year ended 1 July 1998 in respect of a qualifying activity commenced during that year will qualify (subject to satisfaction of the normal rules);

(*c*)   during the year ended 1 July 1998 in respect of a qualifying activity commenced after that date will qualify (again subject to the normal rules).

1.64   Expenditure incurred prior to incorporation is dealt with in 12.29 below.

Assets created by the claimant

1.65   This is a subject which, more often than not, is dealt with on a common sense basis rather than strictly in accordance with the rules. If the materials are purchased specifically for the construction of the asset and do not, therefore, form part of the trader's own trading stock, the expenditure will be incurred on dates ascertained by application, as far as possible, of the general rules.

1.66   If the materials are appropriated from trading stock there will be the usual adjustment to the profit and loss account to recognise the fact that stock has been appropriated other than to trading purposes. Usually such adjustments follow the principle in *Sharkey v Wernher (1955) 36 TC 275* that such an appropriation is deemed to be a sale at market value. However, in Statement of Practice A32 the Revenue stated that 'The decision is not considered to apply to ... expenditure incurred by a trader on the construction of an asset which is to be used as a fixed asset in the trade'. This therefore leaves the difficulty that the expenditure will not have been incurred as capital expenditure. In practice such expenditure is transferred from stock to fixed assets at the lower of cost or net realisable value and is usually regarded as having been incurred as capital expenditure on the date of transfer. However, when first-year allowances are at stake, a much stricter attitude may be adopted by some Inspectors.

1.67   In all these matters a practical approach is often agreed with the Inspector, if only to arrive at an acceptable basis of dealing with any associated labour costs and overheads charged initially to revenue account.

1.68   For an unincorporated business capital expenditure cannot include any valuation of the owner's time.

Contributions and subsidies

General

1.69   The legislation includes specific provisions to ensure that one person cannot obtain capital allowances on expenditure which is actually borne or

1.69 *Contributions and subsidies*

'met' by another. However, that other person may obtain capital allowances if the contribution was made for the purposes of his trade, or for the purposes of a trade carried on by the tenant of a building in which the contributor has an interest.

Contributions received

1.70 Expenditure is not to be regarded as incurred by any person to the extent that it has been or is to be met directly or indirectly by any other person. Ignored for this purpose are grants made under the provisions of the *Industrial Development Act 1982, Pt II*, the *Industry Act 1972, Pt I*, or their Northern Ireland equivalents. These equivalents are those specified by *SI 2001/810*, i.e.:

(*a*) any grant made under the *Industrial Development (Northern Ireland) Order 1982, Pt III*, being a grant not exceeding 45% of the expenditure, and made under an agreement entered into before 1 April 2003;

(*b*) any grant made by the Local Enterprise Development Unit out of moneys granted under *Art 30* of the *Industrial Development (Northern Ireland) Order 1982*, likewise not exceeding 45% of the expenditure and being a grant made under an agreement entered into prior to 1 April 2003; or

(*c*) where any grant is made at a rate higher than 45% of the expenditure, the first 45% of that grant.

1.71 Also ignored are:

(i) insurance proceeds or other compensation in respect of assets which have been destroyed, demolished or put out of use (the amount, defined by *Secs 61* (plant), *316* (industrial buildings), etc. is effectively the net proceeds or compensation [*Sec 535*]); and

(ii) contributions received from a person other than a public body where that person would not be entitled to either capital allowances or a trading deduction in respect of that expenditure. [*Sec 536.*] A 'public body' is defined as the Crown or any public or local authority in the United Kingdom. [*Sec 537(3).*]

1.72 In *McKinney v Hagans Caravans (Manufacturing) Ltd [1997] STC 1023*, the term 'public authority' (now referred to as a 'public body') was held to include an international fund set up to promote economic and social advance in Northern Ireland. There is no simple test for identifying a public body, but key criteria (not all of which need necessarily be met) include:

(*a*) a constitution which derives from some public source;

(*b*) performance of a public service;

(*c*) public control and accountability;

16

(*d*)   absence of private profit;

(*e*)   public funding.

1.73   It is assumed that, for the purposes of establishing whether the contributor is entitled to allowances, that person is within the charge to tax, whether or not that is in fact the case. [*Sec 536(4).*]

1.74   It is understood that where the contribution is made by an exempt pension fund, no account need be taken of that contribution. The Revenue regards this treatment as concessionary.

1.75   The Revenue has also stated, in a letter to the Football League dated 25 January 1991, that grants from the Football Trust do not reduce qualifying expenditure where they are paid out of the proceeds of Spot the Ball competitions.

Timing and repayment of grants received

1.76   Little importance is attached to the respective timing of the receipt of a grant and the incurring of the expenditure to which it relates. Expenditure may be incurred before the person becomes entitled to a grant or subsidy or before he has applied for one. However, the grant, once received, should be deducted from the expenditure otherwise qualifying for allowances (CA, para 424). This follows from the case of *Cyril Lord Carpets Ltd v Schofield (1966) 42 TC 637* (see Appendix 4).

1.77   If a person subsequently repays a grant (whether compulsorily or voluntarily), he may be able to claim capital allowances on the amount repaid, but only if the circumstances fall within the terms of ESC B49, i.e.:

(*a*)   the grant was made by the Crown, government or any other public body; or

(*b*)   the repaid grant is taxable in the hands of the person who made the grant as a balancing adjustment or a revenue receipt.

Contributions paid

1.78   Subject to certain conditions, capital allowances will be available to a person contributing a capital sum to expenditure incurred on the provision of an asset by another person. [*Sec 537.*] This will apply where the contribution is made:

(*a*)   for the purposes of a trade carried on (or to be carried on) by the contributor [*Sec 538(1)* (plant), *Sec 539(1)* (industrial buildings)]; or

(*b*)   for the purposes of a trade carried on by a tenant of land in which the contributor has an interest. This allows relief for contributions made, *inter alia*, by a lessor of a building towards expenditure of his tenants or of anyone else, provided it is for the purposes of his tenant's trade(s). [*Sec 539(1)(b)(ii)* (industrial buildings).]

1.79 These rules do not apply where the person making the contribution and the person receiving it are connected persons (*Sec 537(2)* and see 19.13–19.19 below).

1.80 If the contribution was made in respect of a trade carried on (or to be carried on) by the contributor, and the trade is transferred, allowances will thereafter be available to the transferee. Where part only of the trade is transferred, an appropriate proportion of the allowances will be transferred. [*Sec 538(4)–(6), Sec 542.*] If the contribution was made in respect of a trade carried on by a tenant, allowances are given to the person who has the 'contributor's interest' in the land at the end of the relevant chargeable period. [*Sec 539(3)–(5).*]

1.81 A person who makes a contribution towards plant and machinery does not have to account for a subsequent disposal of the asset (indeed, he may not even be aware of it). Generally, the contributor will continue to claim allowances regardless of whether the asset is disposed of, or even ceases to exist. Only if the contributor's relevant activity is transferred, does he cease to claim.

A disposal is likely to be a rarity, therefore, where the plant is moveable, or where it is fixed to a building used for the contributor's trade. However, in the case of property investors, any sale of a property will be treated as a transfer of (part of) the relevant activity (i.e., the Schedule A business).

It appears therefore that where a property investor contributes to fixtures, then later sells that property, he should bring in a disposal value in respect of contribution allowances. This is often overlooked, but can be in the contributor's favour. The contributor could, for example, make an election under *Sec 198* (see 4.22) in respect of this disposal value. If this election were for £1, allowances would be retained by the contributor, and a balancing allowance could arise in certain circumstances.

This possibility is generally overlooked. It is often thought that a *Sec 198* election does not apply to contribution allowances, because such an election is only possible where a disposal value is brought into account under item 1 of the table in *Sec 196*, i.e. where there is a disposal under *Sec 188*. *Section 188* applies only if a person has been treated as the owner of a fixture under certain named sections. A contributions allowance is given under *Sec 538*, which is not one of the sections listed in *Sec 188*. Consequently, a *Sec 198* election cannot be made in respect of contribution expenditure.

However, this reasoning is erroneous. *Section 538* does not grant allowances as a right, but merely treats the contributor as if it owned the asset 'for the purposes of Part 2' (i.e. plant allowances), and that even for contributions allowances, the requirements of Part 2, including the fixtures chapter, must be met. In essence, so the argument runs, *Sec 538* enables the contributor to benefit from the fixtures rules, but then the claim itself is made under *Sec 176*, etc. Following this argument to its conclusion, a *Sec 198* election is possible.

Sums payable in respect of depreciation

1.82   No allowances will be given to a person using machinery or plant for the purposes of a trade, if in a particular chargeable period that person receives sums which:

(*a*)   are in respect of, or take account of, the depreciation to the machinery or plant occasioned by its use; and

(*b*)   do not fall to be taken into account as income of that person, or in computing the profits or gains of any trade carried on by him. [*Secs 37, 209.*]

1.83   Where any such subsidies are in respect of part only of any depreciation, the allowances available shall be reduced to such amount as is 'just and reasonable, having regard to the relevant circumstances'. [*Secs 210(1), 212(2).*] What is 'just and reasonable' is a matter for negotiation between the taxpayer and the Revenue.

1.84   Expenditure to which these provisions apply is assumed to have been incurred for the purposes of a separate notional trade, and is therefore excluded from the general plant pool. This notional trade is deemed to be permanently discontinued when the asset begins to be used wholly or partly for purposes other than those of the actual trade. [*Sec 211.*]

1.85   Where an asset has been used, and allowances have been claimed, in a chargeable period prior to that in which it is first subject to these provisions, then it is deemed at that time to have begun to be used wholly for purposes other than those of the actual trade. Therefore, in accordance with *Secs 55* and *61*, a disposal value must be brought into account. Effectively the relevant asset will be 'depooled' at market value. Taxpayers can unwittingly come within these provisions, for example, where a lessor has incurred expenditure on fixtures, but the lease agreement makes the lessee responsible for maintenance or renewal of these fixtures. It may sometimes be preferable, therefore, for the lessor to retain responsibility for maintenance, with perhaps a compensatory adjustment to the amount of rent payable.

1.86   Assets to which this section applies cannot be treated as 'short life assets' (see 13.70 below).

Chapter 2

Construction of New Buildings

Introduction

2.1 The construction of new premises will for most taxpayers be the most expensive project or type of project ever undertaken, and the availability of capital allowances can often significantly reduce the post-tax cost of a project. Almost invariably, expenditure on a capital project will consist of some elements qualifying for a high rate of allowances, and some elements qualifying for a lower rate, or for no allowances at all. The key to maximising allowances is essentially the proper identification or recognition of the former. There can be no question of artificially inflating the expenditure qualifying for allowances: the availability of allowances must stand or fall on the facts of each individual case. All too often, however, the true facts are not brought out, and a valid claim for allowances is foregone.

2.2 For accounting periods ending on or after 1 July 1999, a second problem is that undue delay can make it difficult to provide sufficient supporting documentation to meet the record-keeping requirements of corporate tax self-assessment.

2.3 Some of the expenditure will qualify for tax relief only as a deduction in computing a capital gain or loss on a subsequent sale. Other expenditure will qualify for other types of capital allowances, and it is essential that the claim for such allowances is maximised. When considering eligibility for capital allowances, the major areas of expenditure for most taxpayers will be:

(*a*)   plant and machinery; and

(*b*)   buildings.

2.4 So far as capital allowances for plant and machinery are concerned, the main problem facing the person making a claim is whether or not the particular assets acquired do, in fact, qualify as plant. Once this is accepted, it is generally true that allowances will be given, irrespective of the nature of the particular trade.

2.5 The same is not true of expenditure on buildings. With the exception of buildings in enterprise zones (see 9.1 below) and hotels (see 8.4 below), the system of allowances generally discriminates in favour of industrial and agricultural concerns, and against, for example, the financial, retail and service industries. The precise rules governing which buildings qualify for allowances and which do not are considered in Chapter 7. Depending on the trade carried on, expenditure on a new building could qualify for relief at 4% p.a., or it could fail to qualify at all. Key considerations are as follows:

(i) Is the building in an enterprise zone? (See Chapter 9.)

(ii) Is it a qualifying hotel? (See Chapter 8.)

(iii) Is the use made of the building such that it will qualify as industrial? (See Chapter 7.)

(iv) To what extent can any of the expenditure be said to be in respect of machinery or plant? (See Chapters 13–15.)

Land and landscaping

General

2.6 No capital allowances are available for the costs of acquiring land (*Secs 24* (plant)*, 272* (industrial buildings)) or, in most cases, for expenditure on work done to the land (*Sec 22(1)(b)* (plant)) (but see treatment of land remediation expenditure (Chapter 23) and preparatory works below).

2.7 The cost of landscaping is not generally regarded as construction expenditure for the purposes of buildings allowances. This can appear inequitable, for example, where a new hotel is surrounded by landscaped grounds; the landscaping would undoubtedly be said to perform a function in the hotelier's trade, namely attracting guests by providing pleasant surroundings. Despite this, the Revenue argues that the landscaping does not constitute plant but instead is merely part of the premises, relying on the speech of Lord Lowry in *IRC v Scottish & Newcastle Breweries Ltd (1982) 55 TC 252*. [CA, para 31400].

2.8 Equally impossible is a claim for hotel allowances, as (in common with all forms of industrial buildings allowances) that requires expenditure to have been incurred on *the construction of a building or structure* (CA, para 1039). For this purpose at least, the Revenue does not regard the process of landscaping as 'construction', nor the finished product as a 'building or structure'. In its Press Release introducing *Sch AA1 to CAA 1990* (now *Secs 21–24 of CAA 2001*) in 1993, the Revenue described a structure as 'any substantial man-made asset'. CA, para 22020 expands upon this to say that the word 'structure' embraces artificial works which might not properly be described as buildings; examples of structures are walls, bridges, dams, roads, culverts and tunnels. The meaning of 'structure' has most often been considered by the courts in a rating context, but the following may provide useful 'leads' in difficult cases:

(*a*) *IRC v Smyth [1914] 3 KB 406*;

(*b*) *Cardiff Rating Authority and Cardiff Assessment Committee v Guest Keen Baldwin's Iron and Steel Co Ltd [1949] 1 KB 385*;

(*c*) *BP Refinery (Kent) Ltd v Walker [1957] 2 QB 305*.

2.9 Landscaping in other contexts, for example in the grounds of an office building, is even less likely to qualify for allowances.

Preparatory works

2.10 The cost of work done to land may qualify for allowances where, essentially, it is incidental and necessary to the construction or installation of another asset which will qualify for allowances in its own right. This includes expenditure on:

(*a*) preparing, cutting, tunnelling or levelling land in connection with the construction of an industrial building; and

(*b*) preparing land as a site for the installation of machinery or plant (if no other relief is available) [*Sec 273*].

2.11 The Revenue's view is that expenditure on the drainage or reclamation of land does not qualify for industrial buildings allowances, as it is not expenditure on the construction of a building or structure (CA, para 31400).

2.12 *Sec 273* (see 2.10) only grants industrial buildings allowances, and not plant allowances, even where the installation of plant (para (*b*) above) is concerned.

Incidental expenditure

Planning permission

2.13 The Revenue's view is that the cost of obtaining planning permission is not expenditure on the construction of a building. However, if a builder's price for constructing a building includes the cost of obtaining any necessary consents, there is no disallowance of a part of the total cost (CA, para 31400).

Preliminaries

2.14 A conventional contract for the erection or substantial alteration of a building of any size will usually refer to preliminary expenses. The nature of the expenditure under this heading can vary considerably but will generally include the cost to the contractor of setting up his site organisation and management, e.g. toilets and canteen for his workers, secure compounds for materials, cabins for visiting surveyors and architects, insurance premiums etc. There is little difficulty with these expenses in the case of an industrial buildings allowance claim because they are normally all part of the cost of the building or structure, but any attempt to allocate some of them to machinery or plant is a frequent cause of disagreement with the Inspector. At first sight they are building related but in two respects (and possibly more) significant amounts may refer to machinery or plant.

(*a*) Some of the machinery or plant, common examples being the heating, ventilation and electrical systems and the plumbing and sanitary ware, is installed as part of the actual building process.

(*b*) The main contractor will often have some responsibility for the off-loading, storing and handling of machinery or plant and supervision of its installation.

2.15 The preliminaries relating to such items are claimed on the basis that they are part of the cost of 'providing' the asset, a term which covers more than the actual supply.

2.16 Claimants often seek to get round the problem by apportioning preliminary expenses pro rata to the expenditure on industrial building, machinery or plant or non-allowable items. Sometimes this is accepted but often it is rejected. A considered allocation and/or apportionment is necessary based on the facts.

Fees

2.17 The fees associated with a substantial building project can cover a wide spectrum — lawyers, architects, surveyors etc. Some of these will qualify as incurred on the provision of machinery or plant in their entirety or in substantial part, e.g. electrical and mechanical engineers; some will qualify as expenditure on industrial buildings, e.g. structural engineers; some will not qualify for any allowances, e.g. lawyers. A considered allocation and/or apportionment is necessary based on the facts.

2.18 The Revenue has stated that fees only qualify for capital allowances to the extent that the expenditure is directly related to the acquisition of plant (CA, para 20070). The apportionment to machinery or plant of fees etc. charged on, for example, a building contract therefore needs to be properly planned, with documentation in place to support the claim.

2.19 Where one fee covers both buildings and integral plant, an apportionment is possible, but the onus is on the claimant to prove that a part of the fee does indeed relate to plant. Inspectors are specifically instructed not to accept an apportionment based merely on the cost of plant as a fraction of the total cost (CA, para 20070). Where appropriate, difficulty may be avoided by arranging for fees relating to plant to be separately identified and invoiced.

2.20 Some inspectors have in the past, sought to restrict the qualifying element of fees in accordance with the table below. However, this is understood to have originated in a claim where fees were only one of the disputed items, and where both taxpayer and inspector made concessions. The taxpayer should not therefore think that this table represents either statute or official policy.

Type of cost	*Percentage qualifying as plant*
Legal	Nil
Surveyors	Nil
Project managers	Nil
Mechanical engineers	fee × qualifying plant/total plant
Electrical engineers	fee × qualifying plant/total plant
Service engineers	fee × qualifying plant/total plant
Lift consultants	fee × qualifying plant/total plant
Quantity surveyors	fee × 30% × qualifying plant/total project cost (excluding fees)
Architects	fee × 30% × qualifying plant/total project cost (excluding fees)
Structural engineers	fee × 30% × qualifying plant/total project cost (excluding fees)
Preliminaries	cost × 50% × qualifying plant/total project cost (excluding fees)

Example

2.21   A new office has been erected at a cost of £2,000,000 exclusive of fees and preliminaries. The Inspector has agreed that this cost can be apportioned to:

	£
Building	
(including non-qualifying electrical	
work of £100,000)	1,600,000
Mechanical plant	150,000
Electrical plant	250,000
	2,000,000
Preliminaries	65,000
Fees, etc.	
Architect	100,000
Mechanical engineers	50,000
Electrical engineers	60,000

2.22 Assuming that the office is of normal design and construction with no special features the expenditure qualifying for capital allowances could be derived as follows:

	Machinery and Plant
	£
Mechanical plant	150,000
Electrical plant	250,000
	400,000
Architect	7,500
Mechanical engineers	50,000
Electrical engineers	45,000
Preliminaries	7,500
Total claim for machinery and plant	510,000

The mechanical engineers fees relate to plant which qualifies in its entirety. The electrical engineers fees relate to plant which is 71% qualifying (£250,000 out of £350,000), this has been rounded to £45,000, illustrating that the apportionment of fees is not merely a question of applying a formula.

Although the figures are purely illustrative they demonstrate that the value of a claim can be substantially increased by taking proper account of fees and preliminaries.

2.23 The Revenue's view is that fees can only qualify for allowances if the building to which they relate is actually constructed. If construction is aborted, no allowance is due.

Finance costs

2.24 The cost of financing an acquisition is not capital expenditure (*Ben-Odeco Ltd v Powlson (1978) 52 TC 459*). Interest is not converted into capital simply because it is charged to capital in the payer's accounts but this does not mean that a capital price cannot contain an escalating element calculated in part or in whole as if it were interest. If a price adjustment of this sort is part of the contract with the supplier of the plant, as opposed to a financial institution to which interest would normally be paid there is a better prospect of it qualifying for capital allowances (*Van Arkadie v Sterling Coated Materials Ltd [1983] STC 95*).

25

2.24 *Timing of the claim*

It was confirmed in *Barclays Mercantile Business Finance Ltd v Mawson [2002] EWCA Civ 1853 [2003] STC 66* that where expenditure was incurred on the provision of machinery or plant wholly and exclusively for the purposes of the trade, it was immaterial how the trader acquired the funds to incur the expenditure. Whilst the cost of finance will not itself qualify for allowances, the fact that finance has to be obtained by way of loan does not preclude allowances being claimed on the asset itself.

Builder's Work In Connection

2.25   It is not unknown for Builder's Work In Connection (BWIC) on the installation of plant in a building under construction to be excluded from qualifying expenditure on the ground that *Sec 25* (see 13.24 below) cannot apply because that section refers to alterations to an *existing* building. BWIC on the installation of machinery or plant should be claimable under the general principle that it is part of the cost of provision (i.e. a cost of construction or setting up of the machinery or plant into working order), *Sec 25* being irrelevant.

Preparation of land and other installation costs

2.26   Expenditure on preparing, cutting, tunnelling or levelling of land preparatory to use as a site for the installation of machinery or plant is not itself otherwise eligible for relief as a building or structure, irrespective of the nature of the trade carried on by the claimant. [*Sec 273.*] This provision would appear to allow a shop or office to claim industrial buildings allowances in respect of the cost of preparing land for the permanent siting of, say, rubbish skips or waste compactors. In practice most sundry installation costs can be included in the qualifying expenditure or, if modest, even allowed as revenue expenditure.

Timing of the claim

The traditional claim

2.27   Capital allowances are given in respect of expenditure incurred. This implies therefore that a claim can only be made once the relevant asset has been purchased or built. Certainly the traditional method of making a claim reflects this.

2.28   The practice of many taxpayers is still to consider only capital allowances when the tax computations are being submitted (or when calculating payments on account under corporate tax self-assessment), and to base any claim only on the accounting records of the enterprise concerned. This is all very well where the assets involved are relatively uncontroversial (e.g. industrial machinery or motor cars), but it is no longer appropriate in more complex cases. The use of evidence other than accounting records is considered at 2.45. The problems with timing are considered below.

Typical timescale

2.29   The timescale in a typical scenario, for example the construction of a new, medium-sized industrial building with a potentially high plant content, may be as follows. It is assumed the taxpayer's accounts are made up to a date in month 9 of the project.

Month

1	The project gets underway; plans are drafted and the expenditure is authorised. Local authority planning procedures are initiated.
3	Plans are finalised.
4	Detailed design briefs are drawn up; contractors are appointed. Corporation tax payment on account under self-assessment.
5	Bill of quantities drawn up; work commences.
6–10	Work progresses; the shell is completed and work begins on fitting out. Payments made on basis of surveyor's valuations.
7	Corporation tax payment on account under self-assessment.
9	Taxpayer's accounts year ends.
10	Corporation tax payment on account under self-assessment.
11–13	Fitting-out progresses to completion.
12	Audit takes place.
13	Corporation tax payment on account under self-assessment.
14	Final payments (subject to retentions) are made.
16	Corporation tax payment on account under self-assessment.
19	Corporation tax payment on account under self-assessment.
21	Taxpayer's accounts year ends.
22	Corporation tax payment on account under self-assessment.
24	Audit takes place.
25	Corporation tax payment on account under self-assessment.
27	Tax computations prepared and submitted.
28	Corporation tax payment on account under self-assessment.

2.30   In the above scenario, it is likely that the capital allowances on the new building will be considered initially around month 15 or 16 when the first year's tax computation is prepared. However, because industrial buildings allowances (other than the initial allowances) are not due until the building is brought into use, it is often the case in such circumstances that many taxpayers and their advisers do not fully consider capital allowances until such time as the building is complete. In the above example, full attention might not be given to capital allowances until month 27. There are numerous reasons for considering capital allowances at a much earlier stage. For example to:

(*a*)   ensure ownership of the asset is in the right hands;

(*b*)   consider whether tax-efficient features can be inserted into planning documentation;

(*c*)   consider the effect of '*Section 106*' agreements (see 2.33);

(*d*)   'tweak' the design to improve the tax position;

(*e*)   consider the effect of adoption orders;

(*f*)   form a claim team early on, when all parties are interested (i.e. *inter alia*, their fees are outstanding!);

(*g*)   generally increase the time available to think about difficult areas!;

(*h*)   provide greater accuracy when calculating payments on account under corporate tax self-assessment ('CTSA');

(*i*)   ensure any claim is sufficiently well-supported to avoid exposure to interest and penalties under CTSA.

Note that, although these are advantages in considering capital allowances during construction, it is not essential. Retrospective claims can be made.

Method of ownership

2.31   Certain bodies will have no *direct* interest in capital allowances for the simple reason that they do not pay tax. These include:

(i) pension funds;

(ii) charities;

(iii) local authorities.

2.32   For example, a company pension fund may actually pay for a new building but the company itself will want the allowances. In such cases, it is often possible to arrange the funding in such a way that this is achieved. The pension fund (in this example) could fund the construction before granting a long lease to the company and electing under *Sec 290* (for industrial buildings allowances) for the company to receive the allowances. Note this is not possible in an enterprise zone where *Sec 328* (see 11.26) applies.

2.33   In other cases, several persons may be contributing to a 'pot of expenditure'. If this is the case, care must be taken that the right person incurs the 'right' expenditure, i.e. the taxable person pays for those assets qualifying for allowances. This is also true where contributions are made to a local authority in connection with, for example, agreements under the *Town and Country Planning Act 1990, Sec 106*.

Planning agreements

2.34   Sometimes when a large development is being planned, the taxpayer will have to fulfil certain conditions specified by the local authority before planning permission will be given. Such agreements are often seen as a burden by the taxpayer; however, that burden can be mitigated.

2.35   At the very least, it may be possible to ensure that money spent is incurred in respect of assets qualifying for tax relief rather than on non-qualifying or unspecified assets. For example, suppose a company constructing a new head office is required by the local authority to contribute £75,000 towards the cost of highway improvements. If nothing is done to identify precisely what assets are the object of the contribution, the transaction may attract no tax relief at all. At best, it may be possible to negotiate an apportionment of the expenditure with the Inspector but the success of this is by no means certain.

2.36   The problem should therefore be dealt with prospectively rather than retrospectively. Once the amount of the contribution has been decided, but before the expenditure has been incurred, the suggestion should be made to the local authority that the contribution should be regarded as being wholly or largely in respect of items of plant (for example, traffic lights). The local authority will probably be happy to accept such a proposal and will confirm it in writing. The expenditure may therefore be added to the general pool of expenditure on plant, providing all the other conditions for qualification are satisfied. Of course, it is worth stressing again that the above agreement should be negotiated before any money has been paid!

2.37   Whilst the planning application and planning consent have no statutory impact on the tax treatment, it is often the case that tax-efficient features can be incorporated in the documentation that are of no concern to the planning authorities.

Planning documentation generally

2.38   Imagine, for example, that a new factory is constructed, served by a new road (to be available to the public) as illustrated in Diagram 1.

2.39   If the new road is constructed at the expense of the taxpayer, he will seek to claim allowances. The Inspector, however, may well argue that the entire road is not necessary for the purposes of the trade and that a short road leading from the factory entrance to the existing road would suffice.

2.40   If the problem is considered early enough it may be possible to anticipate potential future events. For example, if the road is at some time likely to become one-way, then recognition of this fact in the planning documents would be strong evidence that the entire road, and not just a short stretch of it, had been constructed for the purposes of the trade. The planning authority will probably have no objection. It will now be clear that the whole road is needed for the purpose of the trade, i.e. for traffic to both enter and exit. Tax relief for the whole of the expenditure should therefore be available as expenditure incurred on an industrial structure.

Adoption orders

2.41   It is common practice with larger developments that the person constructing the building has either to provide or contribute towards roads,

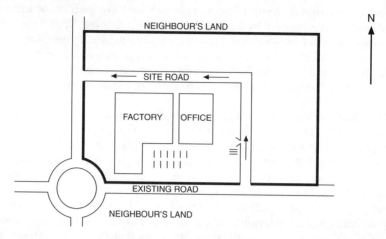

Diagram 1

services or other assets which are then adopted by the local authority under, for example, the *Highways Act 1980, Sec 38*. Some taxpayers will resent the fact that they have to pay for, say, public roads crossing land in which they have an interest. Some will resent even more the fact that these roads or other assets are then taken from them with little or no compensation. However, this can in certain circumstances give rise to a tax advantage. Consider the case of a company constructing a new factory, served by new roads which are subsequently to be adopted for public use.

2.42   The most common form of adoption order is that the local authority assumes responsibility for the top few inches of the road, i.e. the wearing surface and the immediate foundations. The ownership of the underlying land and the rights attached to it remain undisturbed (*Re White's Charities (1898) 1 Ch 659*). If the expenditure on the road qualifies for an industrial buildings allowance (IBA) (by association with the factory), allowances will continue to be given over a period of 25 years. Compliance with the adoption order does not constitute a disposal for IBA purposes, because the ownership of the relevant interest (see 7.1) remains undisturbed, and hence there is no balancing allowance.

2.43   It is assumed, of course, that the taxpayer will continue to satisfy the basic requirement of a claim for writing-down allowance (see 7.16 et seq.) that the road is in use for the purposes of a qualifying activity. It has been suggested that the use after adoption is in the capacity of a member of the public and not as a trader but as far as the author is aware there has not been any attempt to use this distinction (if in fact it exists) to prevent a claim for allowances.

2.44   It may be possible to negotiate another form of adoption order. This is where the local authority takes over not only the surface of the road but the underlying land as well. Under such an agreement, the company would

30

then have disposed of its relevant interest in the land. A balancing allowance should then be given, and (assuming no compensation is payable) tax relief on the whole expenditure is given 'up front' rather than over a period of 25 years. This is only true, however, once the road (or the associated factory) has been brought into use for the purposes of the trade and this should therefore take place before the execution of the adoption order rather than after it.

Note that, whilst a taxpayer will most commonly give up land in accordance with an adoption order, other situations may also require surrender. A compulsory transfer to a landlord, transport authority, etc. may give rise to the same opportunity to generate a balancing allowance.

Documentation

2.45   The items below suggest what information might be required (and why) in order to maximise a claim for capital allowances in connection with a greenfield or brownfield site development. Such a list can never be exhaustive, and each new case will generate new ideas and new sources of inspiration. Similarly, not all of the following will be relevant in every case.

(*a*) *Copy planning approval documents.* These are likely to mention a number of factors relevant to capital allowances, for example, the reasons behind any special features aimed at preventing contaminating neighbouring sites.

(*b*) *Copy agreements under the Town and Country Planning Act 1990, Sec 106 etc.* These agreements are a means by which the planning authority can impose an obligation to carry out or bear the cost of works beyond the cost of the building itself. For example, such agreements often compel the taxpayer to carry out and/or pay for improvements to the highway or sewage network or to provide public amenities. These may, in appropriate circumstances, qualify as industrial buildings or as plant.

(*c*) *Details of any arrangements for any payments under (b) above to be attributed to specific aspects of the works.* Reason: a contribution to capital expenditure incurred by others ranks for capital allowances (subject to conditions) only if the expenditure is on an asset which would normally qualify as plant, an industrial building or structure, a mineral extraction asset or an agricultural building. Attribution to specific items qualifying for allowances is preferable to a lump sum contribution towards general improvements.

(*d*) *Details of moves by an authority towards eventual 'adoption' of any asset.* This will sometimes influence the choice of capital allowance or the negotiating strategy. In particular, adoption can (if properly planned) generate a balancing allowance for IBAs, effectively accelerating allowances.

31

(e) *Details of the various persons involved in construction — not only the main contractor, but also architects, surveyors, project managers, mechanical and electrical engineers etc.* Costings will be required on which to base the capital allowances claim but it is extremely unlikely that the requirements will match all of the 'works packages' into which expenditure is conveniently analysed for construction purposes. There will need to be established, generally through the project manager, a line of communication for this to be obtained.

It will be necessary to discuss construction technicalities with the liaising party who may also be a catalyst for the introduction of any novel items into the claim and may also be able to assist with the exploration of all possible avenues of claim.

(f) *Design briefs.* These facilitate better understanding of the nature and function of the development and generally provide information on which to base claims.

(g) *Establish a line of communication (generally with the project manager) so that any material changes in the design brief can be 'tax audited'.* The design of a large development invariably changes in detail as the work progresses. It is difficult to be specific on what this might affect.

(h) *Site plans, building plans — whatever is available.* The reasons for these are mainly obvious, but also necessary to establish, for example, how many separate buildings exist for IBA and the approach generally.

(i) *Plans and design briefs of any specific item or composite items of plant such as assembly lines which might be supplied/installed by a specialist.* Necessary to maximise opportunities for claims, particularly where a 'plant' claim may be possible on an item which at first sight might appear to be no more than part of a building.

(j) *Plans, design brief etc. of any special aspects of the building, for example a scheme for disposal of effluent.* Again, such detail will assist in identifying where a 'plant' claim may be possible on an item which at first sight might appear to be no more than part of a building.

(k) *Where appropriate, promotional literature.* May, *inter alia*, support arguments based on 'ambience' or 'concepts' in, for example, hotel or leisure industries, or in establishing a qualifying use of the building for IBA purposes.

(l) *Details of energy-efficient or environmentally beneficial plant* qualifying for first year allowances (see 13.14 and 13.15).

(m) *Cost forecast broken down into as many work packages as convenient and showing the likely dates for payment.* This will give an immediate impression of type and magnitude of allowances potentially available, and furthermore, will facilitate agreement of an interim claim for allowances on plant, if as often happens, a development spans a year end.

(*n*) *If development is in phases, the estimated date of completion and commencement of use for each phase.* Necessary for planning claims, and for establishing when IBAs first become due.

(*o*) *Details of the commissioning arrangements.* Commissioning costs are usually mixed. Sometimes can be claimed as revenue; sometimes as capital. Also the commissioning arrangements can have a bearing on commencement date of allowances.

(*p*) *Accounting treatment.* The accounting treatment can have a bearing on commencement date of allowances, but perhaps more importantly can influence whether an item is regarded as building or plant, and, if the latter, whether it is 'long life' plant or, alternatively, provides scope for a short life asset election.

(*q*) *Details of contamination.* Expenditure on cleaning up contaminated land ('remediation') may qualify for tax relief at the rate of 150% (see Chapter 23).

(*r*) *Details of interests in the land.* It is important to establish that the person incurring expenditure has a 'relevant interest' for IBA's (see 7.18) or a qualifying interest for fixtures purposes (see 10.19). There may be more than one person with an interest in the land, and interests may terminate or be created as the project progresses.

Chapter 3

Purchase of a New Building

Introduction

3.1 Chapter 2 considered the position of a taxpayer incurring expenditure on the construction of a new building, and being involved throughout the construction process. Very often this degree of involvement does not take place; it may be that the taxpayer requires new premises, but has few specific trade-related needs, such that the premises can be of a fairly standard design. In such cases, the taxpayer may simply purchase a suitable property that happens to be on the market. In many respects, the capital allowances issues will be the same as for a building constructed to the taxpayer's own needs, although the fact that the building was constructed without the taxpayer's particular trade in mind will inevitably reduce the scope to claim allowances on plant, where it is important that items purporting to be plant do in fact carry on some function related to the trade. As with a purpose-built building, the most relevant type of allowance is likely to be that for industrial buildings — for general definition, etc. see 7.22 et seq.

3.2 The purchase of a second-hand building is dealt with in Chapter 4. If the building is in an enterprise zone, see Chapter 9, and if scientific research allowances may be in point, see Chapter 18.

3.3 Note that expenditure on land does not qualify for allowances. If the price paid for a building includes the cost of the site, the latter must be established (by apportionment if necessary) and excluded from the claim (CA, para 22040, 31305).

Purchase of an unused building

3.4 Whether or not expenditure on a building qualifies for tax relief will depend, generally, on the purpose to which the building is planned to be used. The majority of buildings which do qualify are those of an industrial nature (see Chapter 7).

3.5 Where expenditure is incurred on the construction of a building or structure and the relevant interest is sold prior to being used for any purpose (qualifying or not), there are two consequences for industrial buildings allowances:

(*a*)   the actual construction expenditure is ignored for the purposes of IBAs, and

(*b*)   the purchaser is deemed to have incurred expenditure on the construction of the building or structure equal to the lower of:

    (i)   the capital expenditure incurred on construction of the building, and

    (ii)   the capital sum paid by him. [*Sec 295(1)(2).*]

3.6   The expenditure is deemed to have been incurred on the date the purchase price becomes payable. [*Sec 295(3).*] Where the relevant interest in a building is sold more than once before use, only the last of the purchasers is entitled to allowances under these provisions. [*Sec 295(4).*]

3.7   In the context of deciding whether a building is unused, 'use' means use for any purpose and not just for a purpose qualifying for IBAs. 'Use', however, does not include occupation by a tenant for fitting out by that tenant prior to the commencement of actual production or other use. The fitting-out process is regarded by the Revenue as merely the completion of construction.

Purchase from a developer

3.8   Where a building is purchased unused from a property developer (selling the property in the course of his trade), the actual cost of construction is ignored. In these circumstances, the purchaser is entitled to allowances based on the price paid (including the builder's profit element). [*Sec 296.*] This is logical, given that the builder will be taxed on this profit as income.

3.9   Where there is more than one sale before the building comes into use, the last purchaser is deemed to have incurred qualifying expenditure equal to the lower of:

(*a*)   the price paid by him, and

(*b*)   the price paid by the first purchaser to the builder. [*Sec 296(3).*]

Example

3.10   Murdin Construction Ltd spent £150,000 building a factory unit, with the intention of selling it at a profit. It subsequently sold the building to Norman for £200,000. Norman intended to occupy the building for the purposes of his manufacturing trade, but the loss of a major customer meant that he never used the building. Eventually he sold the building to James for £210,000. James, on bringing the building into use, will be entitled to allowances based on the lower of:

3.10 *Rental guarantees*

(*a*)   the price he paid (£210,000), and

(*b*)   the price first paid to the builder (£200,000).

3.11   If Murdin had not been a builder, James' allowances would be limited to £150,000, being the original construction cost, as this was lower than the price he paid.

Sale of work in progress

3.12   A sale of work in progress on trading account between property developers is not treated as a sale of a building or structure for the purposes of *Sec 295*. Therefore the sale price charged by the final developer will be the 'expenditure incurred on construction of the building' for the purposes of *Sec 295(2)*.

3.13   If a developer holds land in fixed assets, a transfer to current assets (trading stock) might enhance its value and make it more marketable by maximising enterprise zone allowances to an eventual purchaser. It is worth noting that a developer can hold land in two categories: as a developer and as an occupier.

Rental guarantees

3.14   Expenditure does not qualify for IBAs to the extent that the purchase price is inflated by the existence of certain 'arrangements' which are in place at the time the price is fixed, and which have an artificial effect on pricing. [*Sec 357.*] A Revenue Press Release of 29 November 1994 gave rental guarantees as an example of such an arrangement, although where the rents are pitched at an entirely commercial level, the Revenue has indicated that the ensuing uplift in value may not be challenged (CA, para 39620). Other arrangements that the Revenue considers artificial can include:

(*a*)   reverse premiums, if subsequent rents are in excess of an open market value rate;

(*b*)   leasebacks, again if subsequent rents are in excess of an open market value rate;

(*c*)   construction leases, where granted on other than purely commercial terms (CA, para 39620).

3.15   This provision applies to 'determinations' after 28 November 1994.

Plant

3.16   However a building is purchased, it is generally worth considering whether a claim for plant allowances is possible. This is particularly important

36

where no form of buildings allowances is available. As discussed above, it is often the case that businesses which buy ready-completed buildings are those which have few specific trade-related or specialist requirements. In practice, these tend to be businesses operating from offices, warehouses or shops, where as a general rule, industrial buildings allowances are not available.

3.17   In such circumstances, to the extent that the purchase price can be allocated to plant, rather than to the fabric of the building, the purchaser will be able to claim allowances. The circumstances of the vendor will need to be taken into consideration, but particularly where the building is acquired from a property developer, he should have few or no objections. The principles of apportionment of costs are set out at 4.26–4.28.

3.18   Appendix 2 gives a checklist of items which have been accepted as plant, whilst the subject of plant within offices and retail premises is dealt with in Chapters 5 and 6 respectively.

Chapter 4

Purchase of a Second-Hand Building

Introduction

4.1   The taxpayer incurring expenditure on second-hand assets, whether actual buildings or items of plant included within those buildings, will be able to claim allowances under the same general rules as if he were acquiring the assets brand new. There are, however, certain additional rules to be dealt with, and in many cases the amount qualifying for allowances will be restricted.

4.2   An apportionment of the purchase consideration can often effectively reduce the cost of a second-hand building by properly identifying all items qualifying for allowances, which might otherwise be ignored in the wider context of a property acquisition.

4.3   Note that expenditure on land does not qualify for allowances. If the price paid for a building includes the cost of the site, the latter must be established (by apportionment if necessary) and excluded from the claim (CA, para 22040, 31305).

Buildings

General

4.4   As with newly constructed buildings, a building acquired second hand will only qualify for allowances if it falls within one of the prescribed categories, i.e.:

(*a*)   the building is in an enterprise zone (see Chapter 9);

(*b*)   it is a qualifying hotel (see Chapter 8);

(*c*)   the use made of the building is such that it will qualify as industrial (see Chapter 7).

Industrial buildings

4.5   Where an industrial building is acquired second hand, the writing-down allowance is ascertained by taking the *residue of expenditure* at the date of acquisition and writing it off on a straight line basis over the period beginning with the sale and ending with the 25th anniversary of when the building was first used. [*Sec 311.*] Again, where the accounting period is less or more than a year, the writing-down allowance is proportionately decreased or increased. [*Sec 310(2).*] If an industrial building is acquired with one year of its 25-year tax life remaining, the purchase price (or, if lower, original cost) may effectively attract a 100% allowance.

4.6　The residue of expenditure (commonly called the tax written-down value) is generally the original cost, written down by *net* allowances given, including any balancing allowance or charge on the sale itself — see 11.4 et seq.) for details of calculation. Where a building is sold for more than original cost, all allowances given will be clawed back, such that the *residue of expenditure* will be the same as original cost. A second-hand purchaser can never claim allowances on an amount higher than this.

4.7　Where the expenditure was incurred before 6 November 1962, the duration of the writing-down period is 50 years, rather than 25, and writing-down allowances are at a rate of 2% p.a. [*Sch 3, para 66*]. The purchaser of a second-hand building should not assume, therefore, that no allowances are available merely because the building is more than 25 years old.

4.8　It is also sometimes worth reviewing the previous use made of the building being acquired. If a building is in industrial use, but allowances are not claimed, notional allowances (see 7.106) do not have to be written off under *Sec 336* (CA, para 34700). Therefore, if the vendor failed to claim IBAs because he mistakenly thought the use was non-industrial, the notional allowances should be added back to the residue of expenditure, thereby increasing the amount on which the purchaser may claim allowances.

A commercial building (e.g. an office) which qualified for allowances by being constructed in an enterprise zone, is henceforth regarded as an industrial building. Allowances may still, therefore, be available to a subsequent purchaser, even after expiry of the enterprise zone.

Plant

4.9　When a building is purchased second hand, the buyer will be acquiring not only a shell building, but also any plant elements contained therein. This will include not only things that are obviously machinery, but also 'integral plant' such as air-conditioning or heating.

4.10　It is possible for the purchaser to claim capital allowances on such plant. To the extent that such items are fixtures, they are treated as belonging to the purchaser of the building. [*Sec 181.*] This also applies where a purchaser of an interest in land pays a capital sum to discharge the obligations of an equipment lessee to whom the fixtures were previously let. [*Sec 182.*]

4.11　Ideally, such a claim will be based on an apportionment of the total purchase consideration, in accordance with *Sec 562.* Any dispute over the

4.11 *Plant*

apportionment may be resolved by the General or Special Commissioners. [*Sec 563*]. In *Wood (t/a A Wood & Co) v Provan (1968) 44 TC 701* (see Appendix 4), the Commissioners made an apportionment notwithstanding that fact that a separate price for plant was shown in the purchase contract. However, this decision was made before enactment of the provisions for a joint election by purchaser and vendor (see 4.24 below).

4.12 In some circumstances, however, the amount will be restricted to whatever amount is brought into account as disposal proceeds by the vendor. [*Sec 185.*] That said, it must nonetheless be emphasised that the matter is not entirely in the hands of the vendor, and the purchaser is not bound to accept the vendor's apportionment, however unfair that may be.

4.13 It is worth noting that the Revenue cannot deem the *total* proceeds to be an amount other than the actual proceeds, only the apportionment between different assets can be challenged. In order to show that some assets (e.g. plant) have been overvalued, the Revenue must also demonstrate that other assets have been undervalued (CA, para 12100).

4.14 Expenditure on plant generally attracts a higher rate of allowance than expenditure on buildings (see Appendix 1). This may be reversed, however, where an industrial building is acquired towards the end of its tax life (see 4.5). The existence of long life assets (see 13.53) should also not be overlooked.

Restricted claims

4.15 Where the vendor of an interest in land, as defined in *Sec 175*, has claimed allowances in respect of fixtures attached to that land, he is required to bring into account a disposal value.

4.16 Where, on or after 24 July 1996, a person incurs expenditure on fixtures, in respect of which a former owner has been entitled to allowances, then the maximum amount on which allowances may be claimed will be equal to the disposal value required to be brought into account by that former owner (together with any incidental expenditure under *Sec 25* — see 13.24 et seq.).

4.17 If the fixtures are acquired from a taxpayer, the qualifying expenditure will therefore be limited to the disposal value brought into account by the vendor, which in turn will be restricted to original cost (or cost to a person connected with the vendor, if higher – *Sec 64*). If the fixtures are acquired from a non-taxpayer (for example, an exempt fund) allowances may still be restricted to the disposal value brought into account, not by the vendor (for whom there will be no disposal value) but by an earlier claimant. This will only apply, however, if that earlier claimant disposed of the fixtures on or after 24 July 1996. If, since that date, there has been no disposal by a taxpayer, the claim by the new purchaser will not be restricted and will be based on a just apportionment of the total expenditure under *Sec 562*. This restriction does not apply where assets have been severed from the building and sold other than as fixtures. [*Sec 185.*]

4.18   Two key points emerge which the prospective purchaser must not overlook:

(*a*)   the capital allowances on fixtures will be of particular value if they have, since 24 July 1996, been continuously owned by a person who was not entitled to allowances (or indeed, a series of such persons); and

(*b*)   the quantum of any claim may only be established with full knowledge of the history of ownership of the relevant fixtures. The intending claimant should therefore require such details from the vendor as part of the acquisition process. The onus is on the purchaser to prove the capital allowances history of the assets acquired (*West Somerset Railway v Chivers [1995] STC (SCD) 1*).

Different type of allowances previously claimed

4.19   Where the property acquired includes fixtures which have previously been involved in a claim for IBAs or scientific research allowances, the qualifying expenditure is restricted to (in the case of IBAs) the portion of the consideration attributable to the fixtures, on the assumption that the consideration was equal to the residue of expenditure on the relevant interest, or (for scientific research) to the portion of the consideration attributed to the fixtures, limited to original cost. [*Secs 186, 187.*]

Disposal values: anti-avoidance

4.20   Where, with a view to 'avoidance', a vendor brings into account a disposal value which is less than the notional tax written-down value of the relevant plant, that written-down value is substituted for the actual disposal value. Consequently neither a balancing charge nor a balancing allowance will arise. However, this only applies to the vendor — the purchaser's claim will be restricted to the actual (low) consideration. ('Avoidance' is defined as the obtaining or increase of an allowance or deduction, or the avoidance or reduction of a charge.)

4.21   The disposal value may be below tax written-down value for genuine commercial reasons, rather than for reasons of tax avoidance, in which case it may not be challenged by the Revenue. [*Sec 197.*]

Apportionment of consideration: joint election

4.22   In either of the above situations, the parties to a sale may elect to fix the amount to be allocated to fixtures. [*Sec 198.*] The amount so allocated may not exceed the original cost of those fixtures. Obviously, if the total sale price is less than the original cost of the fixtures, then the amount apportioned cannot exceed that. The irrevocable election must be made jointly within two years after the date of the relevant transaction, and must include:

(*a*)   the names and tax references of both parties;

(*b*)   sufficient information to identify both the relevant land and the machinery or plant; and

(*c*)   details of the interest acquired.

(See pro-forma election, Appendix 5.)

4.23   The Inland Revenue has confirmed the acceptability of a single election covering all the fixtures in a single property (but not multiple properties)—Inland Revenue Tax Bulletin 35.

In practice, where an amount has been agreed between vendor and purchaser covering several properties, the Revenue will accept an apportionment between the properties on a reasonable basis, such as book value or floor area.

4.24   It must be remembered that an election under *Sec 198* can only cover plant on which the vendor has claimed allowances. The purchaser may still be able to claim allowances on other items of plant which were not identified as such by the vendor, and are in consequence not covered by the election. It should also be remembered that an election under *Sec 198* relates only to fixtures, and not to movable plant.

Quantifying expenditure on plant

4.25   If the qualifying expenditure is to be calculated on a full apportionment basis, there will be a good deal of work necessary to maximise the claim. The process of establishing the amount qualifying for plant will consist broadly of the following steps:

(*a*)   Land valuation.

(i)   No allowances are due in respect of the purchase of land. The first task, therefore, is to establish the value of the land. Any land valuation will be referred by the Inspector to the District Valuer.

(ii)   The District Valuer will also advise the Inspector, if requested, on the question of apportioning building expenditure between qualifying and non-qualifying.

(*b*)   Building and plant valuation.

(i)   Having determined the value of the land, the taxpayer then needs to split the balance of the purchase consideration between buildings and plant.

(ii)　It is not always necessary to try to estimate those relative values as at the date of the purchase. Bear in mind that the purpose of this exercise is merely to establish the relative proportions of buildings and plant so that those percentages may then be applied to the purchase consideration.

(iii)　The easiest route to take is therefore to value plant and building as at the current time. It is essential to compare like with like. Both elements should therefore be valued according to their current replacement value. It is commonly thought that the plant (and not the building) should be depreciated. This is, however, neither logical nor correct.

(iv)　When inspecting a property for the purpose of identifying plant, the taxpayer and his advisers must be aware of the respective interests, i.e. who has paid for what. For instance, it may be that the freeholder now selling his interest was responsible only for the shell building, and that all fitting out was funded by tenants. In this case the allowances on fittings will remain with the tenants.

Apportionment formulae

4.26　The method of apportioning costs to determine qualifying expenditure is not prescribed by statute. It is therefore a matter for negotiation between the taxpayer, his advisers and the Revenue. Set out below are just two of the possibilities when quantifying, say, the plant content of an office building. The Valuation Office has expressed a preference for the following formula (*Valuation Office Manual*, para 3.31):

$$Q = P \times \frac{A}{B+C}$$

Where　Q = qualifying expenditure
A = the replacement cost of the qualifying assets
B = the replacement cost of the building (including plant content)
C = the land value (i.e. bare site value)
P = purchase consideration

As mentioned above, the Valuation Office formula is not mandatory. A common alternative (using the same notation) is:

$$Q = (P - C) \times \frac{A}{B}$$

The apportionment formula can have a significant impact on the value of a claim.

4.27 Plant

Example

4.27 Snowden Ltd acquired an office building for £40 million in such circumstances that any expenditure qualifying for allowances was to be determined by a just apportionment under *Sec 562*. Its accountants later obtain estimates of the market/replacement values of the various components as follows:

- land   £5 million (C);

- building   £50 million (B);

- plant therein   £20 million (A).

4.28 The two formulae give the following qualifying expenditure. Valuation Office formula:

$$\text{Qualifying expenditure} = £40 \text{ million} \times \frac{20}{50 + 5}$$

$$= £14.5 \text{ million}$$

Alternative formula:

$$\text{Qualifying expenditure} = (40 - 5) \times \frac{20}{50}$$

$$= £14 \text{ million}$$

In this example, therefore, a mathematical detail can cost (at current tax rates) £155,000 in additional tax. With different figures, however, the result could be reversed, with the alternative formula giving the better result.

The Valuation Office Manuals include a number of helpful instructions affecting the method of apportionment. They confirm (para 3.31) that plant ('A' in the formula) does not need to be written down due to its age, as age and obsolescence will be reflected in the purchase price. The bare site ('C') should be valued on the assumption that (i) the site is cleared of all building and external works, (ii) access and services are available up to the boundary, and (iii) planning permission is available for the existing type of development (*Valuation Office Manual*, para 3.33).

The replacement costs used in the formula ('A' and 'B') should include (i) the cost of external works, (ii) professional fees and (iii) finance charges. The last-mentioned is often ignored in practice, as finance charges do not generally qualify for capital allowances, following *Ben-Odeco Ltd v Powlson (1978) 52 TC 459*. If, due to the use of modern materials and building techniques, the cost of erecting a modern substitute would be less than the cost of an identical replacement building, the cost of the modern substitute should be used (*Valuation Office Manual*, para 3.34). Informally, however, the Valuation Office has sought to disapply this rule where the property is listed, or where the ol materials were prestigious, even at the original time of construction.

Practical considerations

4.29 Where a claim for allowances is to be restricted, the requirements of the vendor and of the purchaser are likely to be in direct opposition.

Example

4.30 A Ltd purchased an office building on 1 July 1984 for £750,000. The following year he spent £200,000 on the addition of an air-conditioning system and claimed capital allowances.

4.31 In 1992, A Ltd agreed to sell the building to B Ltd for a total consideration of £2 million. The one matter outstanding was the amount to be apportioned to the air-conditioning. B Ltd would want as high an amount as possible allocated to the plant to maximise its capital allowances claim. A Ltd, however, wants to bring into its pool a low disposal value if indeed it has to introduce one at all.

4.32 In other cases, it may be that the position of, say, the vendor is slightly different. If, in our example, A Ltd had been steadily making losses then its own capital allowances position is of little concern. There may in fact be scope for A Ltd to permit a very high allocation to plant in exchange for a slightly larger selling price.

4.33 The optimum allocation is thus not always achieved, and should not be taken for granted by either party. If the vendor and the purchaser can reach agreement, the inclusion of an allocation of expenditure in the documentation, though not binding on the Revenue, should avoid any later dispute between the parties themselves. Inclusion of the agreed allocation in an election under *Sec 198* (see 4.22) will be binding on the Revenue.

4.34 If the vendor wishes to continue to claim capital allowances, this can be achieved by including in the sale contract (or a *Sec 198* election) the lowest sustainable valuation of the plant. As plant is generally pooled for capital allowances purposes, the effect is that allowances will continue to accrue to the vendor almost indefinitely.

4.35 Of course, it must always be borne in mind that the tax tail should not be allowed to wag the commercial dog. It is undoubtedly simpler (at least in the first instance) to ignore capital allowances altogether. In practical terms, there is some justification for ignoring the capital allowances position only where the amounts involved are known to be insignificant.

4.36 However, both parties should beware of ignoring capital allowances simply for an easy life; such a move may cost more in terms of both time and money in the long run. At an early stage, a 'desk top review' should be undertaken in order to establish entitlement and to be sure that the likely savings from capital allowances exceed the cost of putting the claim together. The purchaser should then notify the vendor of what he requires as regards capital allowances (and vice-versa). If necessary, this should be by means of drafting appropriate clauses for inclusion in the purchase contract. The reasons for taking such action at this stage are threefold:

(i) the vendor will be put on notice that he has certain obligations to fulfil and information to provide;

(ii) if appropriate, the relevant clauses may be 'traded' against others onerous to the purchaser; and

(iii) if such thoughts are only raised when the contract is on the verge of completion, such technical details may be sacrificed in order to 'clinch the deal'.

4.37   The vendor may of course have requirements of his own regarding capital allowances. He may, for example, be seeking a relatively low apportionment of the consideration to plant so as to mitigate any balancing charge. The final agreement is a matter for negotiation.

Documentation

4.38   Using the typical scenario of the purchase of a second-hand office building, inclusive of an unquantified plant content, this section considers what documentation should be put in place.

4.39   The requirements of the purchaser and the vendor are often mirror images of the same problem. For clarity, the requirements below have been considered from the point of view of the purchaser. Not all the items mentioned will be appropriate in every case. It is often better, however, to begin with many demands, which can if appropriate be 'traded' in the course of the purchase negotiations.

- Ideally, a full inventory should be taken of all potential plant included within the building and being sold. There are specialist firms who undertake such work, not always for capital allowances purposes. This is, of course, an extra cost, but the inventory compiler's independence will be an advantage in the purchase negotiations and perhaps in later dealings with the Revenue. If it is not possible to have a detailed inventory, the contract should at least set out the part of the purchase price attributable to the total plant element.

- The purchaser should seek to obtain confirmation from the vendor that the value attributed to each item is less than the 'ceiling' imposed by *Sec 185* (see 4.19 et seq.), which in most cases will be the original acquisition cost to the vendor.

- The vendor should also state which of the items listed on the inventory have been accepted as plant by the Revenue, and whether any have been treated as long-life assets (see 13.54). Whether the assets continue to be treated as plant will depend on the purchaser's use of them.

- In the context of the fixtures legislation, the qualifying expenditure of the purchaser may be restricted by the disposal value brought into account by the vendor. The purchaser should seek, therefore, to at least be kept informed of the vendor's negotiations with the Revenue in respect of the relevant plant. If the figures are material, the purchaser may even wish to review correspondence with the Revenue in draft.

- The purchaser should seek to incorporate in the purchase documentation a statement that the vendor will make available all relevant information to the purchaser, and will provide him with all reasonable assistance for the preparation of his capital allowances claim. The purchaser may also require an undertaking from the vendor that he will sign any appropriate elections, for example in connection with the transfer of allowances under *Sec 290* (see 10.6 et seq.).

- The parties may also wish to incorporate in the contract a statement that an election under *Sec 198* will be entered into, at the request of either party (see 4.24).

- In some cases, the purchaser may try to obtain an indemnity from the vendor regarding the right to capital allowances. That is to say, a failure to obtain allowances would result in the purchaser being reimbursed by the vendor. This is commonly the situation where a landlord constructs a building to his tenants' requirements and the rent payable varies with the success or otherwise of the landlord's capital allowances claim.

4.40   Where an industrial building is being purchased, the following will also be relevant.

- Evidence of the date on which the building was first brought into use, and/or on which additional expenditure on the building was incurred. For expenditure incurred after 5 November 1962, allowances are given over a period of 25 years, prior to that date, over a period of 50 years.

- Confirmation of the amount on which the vendor has successfully been claiming allowances and details of the residue of expenditure after the sale (see 4.5 et seq.). This will impact on the purchaser's qualifying expenditure in that in most cases his claim will be based on the lower of the amount he pays, and the amount paid by the vendor.

- Details of use of the building by lessees or licensees and confirmation that the lease agreements oblige the tenants to use the building only for purposes qualifying for IBAs.

Chapter 5

Offices — Special Features

General

5.1   Offices do not generally qualify for industrial buildings allowances (IBAs), although there are exceptions, notably where the office, rather than merely being the seat of administration, is closely linked to a manufacturing or other qualifying process. This question has been considered by the courts.

5.2   The most important case remains *IRC v Lambhill Ironworks Ltd (1950) 31 TC 393* (see Appendix 4). In that case it was stated:

'An office must be something which clearly has not got anything of an industrial character or is not directly ancillary to the industrial operations conducted or carried on in the rest of the works.'

5.3   In the *Lambhill* case, IBAs were given in respect of a drawing office used by a structural engineering company. The drawing office was clearly very closely related to the 'industrial' activities carried on by the taxpayer, rather than being, for example, used for management or administration purposes.

5.4   A similar line of reasoning was followed in the Irish case of *O'Conaill v Waterford Glass Ltd (1982) TL(I) 122* (see Appendix 4). Here, a computer building was deemed to be an industrial building, because it, and the computer it housed, existed solely or primarily to perform a function related to industrial activities carried on in other buildings on the same site. A similar English case, *Abbot Laboratories Ltd v Carmody (1968) 44 TC 569*, is discussed at 7.85 in the context of what constitutes a separate building.

5.5   A more recent consideration of the term 'office' was in *Girobank plc v Clarke [1998] STC 182*. An office was here defined as 'the place where the central management emanates and where the manager and his staff do their work' (following a Canadian case, *Carter v Standard Ltd (1915) 30 DLR 492*).

5.6   Examples of offices which will not qualify for allowances are accommodation for:

(*a*)   directors and senior executives;

(*b*)   planning and administration;

(*c*)   personnel;

(*d*)   wages staff;

(*e*)   purchasing, sales and marketing departments (CA, para 32312).

5.7   An office may, in appropriate circumstances, qualify for IBAs in an enterprise zone (see Chapter 9) or for scientific research allowances (see Chapter 18). Despite these exceptions, it remains true that the vast majority of offices will not qualify for any form of buildings allowances, and as a result, it is essential to identify items qualifying as plant.

Plant

5.8   A modern office building will generally contain numerous items which may qualify as plant. A more complete list of items potentially qualifying is given in Appendix 2, but the principal items in an office environment will include:

- air-conditioning including ducting and vents;
- blinds and curtains;
- boilers;
- burglar alarms;
- bus bars;
- close circuit television;
- cameras;
- canteen fittings and equipment;
- car park illumination and barrier equipment;
- carpets and other loose floor coverings;
- computers and associated specialised flooring and ceilings;
- communications equipment;
- conduit for security alarm systems;
- cold water systems for drinking and air-conditioning;
- counters and fittings;
- document lifts;
- electrically operated doors — electrical and mechanical components;
- electrical systems designed to suit a particular trade;
- emergency lighting;
- fans and heaters;
- fire alarms;

5.8 *Plant*

- fire protection systems and sprinklers;

- fitted desks;

- gas heating;

- generators;

- hand dryers;

- heating installations, fittings, pipes and radiators;

- hoses and hose reels;

- hot water services and related plumbing;

- intercom installations;

- kitchen equipment;

- lightning protection systems;

- loose furniture;

- movable partitions (where required by trade);

- passenger lifts;

- paging systems;

- racking, cupboards and shelving (removable);

- sanitary installations;

- signage;

- smoke detectors and heat detectors;

- soft furnishings;

- sprinkler systems;

- suspended ceilings forming an integral part of an air-conditioning system;

- switchboards;

- tea and coffee dispensers and vending machines;

- telex and fax systems;

- wash basins and associated plumbing;

- wet and dry risers;

- window cleaning cradles (including tracks and anchorages).

5.9   Not all of these will qualify as plant in every situation, and the general principles of what constitutes plant (see Chapter 13) must be borne in mind. The specific issues concerning some of the more common items are dealt with in Chapter 15.

Example — computer centres

5.10   It is largely true that the scope for a major plant claim will increase with the extent to which the office concerned is modern and 'hi-tech'. An extreme example would be a dedicated computer centre. Computer suites will have many special features, above and beyond the computer equipment itself. These specialised features may include:

(*a*)   raised floors;

(*b*)   air-conditioning;

(*c*)   halon gas or similar fire extinguishing systems;

(*d*)   anti-static floors, walls and ceilings;

(*e*)   humidity controls;

(*f*)   earthing mats and Faraday cages.

5.11   The treatment of such items will depend on the general principles of what constitutes plant, in particular, whether the items perform some trade-related function (see 14.11 et seq.).

5.12   A computer centre can make great demands upon its accommodation. The project design brief will usually explain how the various features of the accommodation are required to perform with and in support of the computer and its associated equipment and, therefore, is generally one of the most comprehensive items of evidence available to support the capital allowance claim. It may show (if appropriate) how the structure itself has been designed to function as part of the ventilation, cooling and humidity control, security and anti-terrorist systems and also to support the relatively massive standard, UPS ('uninterrupted power supply'), back-up and other specialised electrical systems. It will usually be possible to demonstrate that the electrical system is such that it will qualify as a single entity eligible for plant allowances, within the guidelines set out in the Inland Revenue Manual on Capital Allowances, i.e.:

(i)   the electrical system is designed and built as a whole, and is a fully integrated entity;

(ii)   it is designed and adapted to meet the requirements of the trade, rather than being a general purpose or standard system designed to meet the needs of a range of occupants;

(iii)   the end-user items of the installation functions as apparatus in the trader's business; and

(iv)   the electrical system is essential for the functioning of the business (CA, para 21180).

5.13   In such a context, it might be that the expenditure allocated to items of plant would exceed 50% of the cost of the whole building. The Revenue guidelines above do not apply only to very hi-tech buildings: it is understood they stem from an unpublished Special Commissioner's decision regarding a supermarket.

Chapter 6

Retail Property — Special Features

General

6.1   Retail shops, unless they are in an enterprise zone (see Chapter 9) will not generally qualify for any form of industrial buildings allowances (IBAs). [*Sec 277(1).*]

6.2   A retail shop includes any premises of a similar character where retail trade or business (including repair work) is carried on. [*Sec 277(1)(b).*] The question of whether a particular building is to be regarded as a retail shop has been considered regularly by the courts, though not generally for capital allowances purposes. In general terms, a 'retail shop' is characterised not by the design of the building, but by the nature of the trade which is carried on there. In broad terms, a retail shop has been said to consist of a place where facilities are offered and to which the general public can resort for the satisfaction of their wants and needs (*Turpin v Assessment Committee for Middlesborough [1931] AC 446*). The Inland Revenue has confirmed that trade customers are not the public, and so a building which serves only trade customers is not a retail shop (CA, para 32311).

6.3   A retail shop can encompass much more besides the traditional image of a glass-fronted high street store. The reference in *Sec 277(1)(b)* to 'repair work' would extend the definition to include garages; however, vehicle repair premises are covered by a long-standing agreement with the Revenue (see 7.71 et seq.).

6.4   Following an early case, *Finn v Kerslake [1931] All ER Rep 242*, a commonly used example of what does or does not constitute a retail shop (or ancillary premises) is a bakery. A bakery will certainly qualify for IBAs under *Sec 274*, i.e. used for the purposes of a trade consisting of the manufacture of goods or materials or the subjection of goods or materials to a process. This will remain so even if it primarily supplies retail outlets owned by the same concern. However, if the bakery forms part of a shop (as is now prevalent in large supermarkets), or if it supplies only one shop, it is likely that the bakery will be considered to be in use for purposes ancillary to the purposes of a retail shop. It is understood that the Revenue will take this approach if at least 90% of the bakery's output is sold in the shop.

6.5   A retail shop is often easily identifiable. A more difficult issue is often whether a building is *ancillary to the purposes of a retail shop* — expenditure on such a building is also prohibited from qualifying for IBAs by *Sec 277(1)*.

To a great extent, it is a matter of degree whether a building is used for such purposes. To return to our bakery example, where a bakery supplies to:

(*a*)   an attached retail shop,

(*b*)   other retail shops owned by the bakery, and

(*c*)   retail shops owned by others,

it will be necessary to take into account factors such as the proportion of output going to the attached shop, the mix of wholesale and retail sales, and so on.

6.6   Roundsmen are treated as retail outlets if a retail shop exists, but otherwise they are not. Retail sales do not, of themselves, constitute a retail shop, and by extension, if no retail shop exists, there can be no purposes ancillary to it.

6.7   The question of whether a building was used for a purpose ancillary to the purposes of a retail shop was one of the matters discussed in *Kilmarnock Equitable Co-operative Society v CIR (1966) 42 TC 675* and in *Sarsfield v Dixons Group plc [1998] STC 938*. In the latter case, it was stated:

'A building is used for a purpose which is ancillary to the purposes of a retail shop if its user is confined to furthering the purposes of the retail shop, i.e. subservient and subordinate to retail selling.'

6.8   In the case of *Dixons Group*, a transport undertaking carried on by one group member consisted of receiving, storing and delivering goods to be sold in retail shops operated by other companies in the group. The transport undertaking was of a substantial size in terms of investment, number of employees and turnover, and made a taxable profit. Despite this, it was held to remain 'subservient and subordinate, and therefore ancillary' to the purposes of the retail shops.

6.9   In practical terms, the availability of allowances is likely to revolve around the degree to which the 'qualifying' activity can be shown to be independent of other 'excluded' activities with which it interacts.

Plant

6.10   It remains true, however, that the vast majority of retail premises will not qualify for any form of buildings allowances, and as a result it is essential to identify items qualifying as plant. Listed below are the main items one would expect to find in a retail shop which, in appropriate circumstances, would qualify as plant for the purposes of capital allowances.

• False ceilings:	— allowed only where the false ceiling is an integral part of an air-conditioning system (e.g. forming one side of a duct);
	— surface mounted lighting track;
	— flo-track and similar grilles.

- Decorative screeds: — only if informative, e.g. giving directions or advertising services.

- Floor finishes: — carpet and reusable carpet tiles;

  — coverings/finishes serving a particular function, e.g. non-slip, heavy duty.

- Internal partitions: demountable, where the movement of the partitions is required for the purposes of the trade. (NB the reasons why the demountable partitioning is needed for the trade should be formulated in advance.)

- Doors: — mechanical or electrical components (e.g. for revolving or sliding doors);

  — internal doors forming 'airlock' to preserve internal temperature, regulate flow of customers;

  — automatic doors: electrical and mechanical parts, pressure pads.

- Security: — automatic door closers and similar fittings. Mesh link and roller shutters where required in addition to ordinary doors for the purposes of the trade;

  — kiosk/gondola shutters;

  — security shutters in addition to ordinary doors, where they form an active part of a security alarm system;

  — burglar bars, if part of alarm system;

  — security mirrors, e.g. two-way or convex type.

- Windows: — hygiaphones acting as security windows;

  — security windows around cash desks, etc.

- Walls and ceiling finishes: — allowable only where it can be demonstrated that they perform some function specific to the trade.

- Fire safety expenditure: — fire-fighting apparatus, e.g., sprinklers, hydrants, reservoirs, extinguishers;

  — structural items, e.g., fire shutters, fire and smoke curtains, fire escapes, fire doors, fire corridors. (Further information may be necessary with respect to precise requirements of fire authority.)

- Plumbing: — cold water piping serving toilets, etc. (not mains supply);

  — hot water piping from source of heat to appliance;

  — tiling and splash backs.

- Vehicle access, etc.: — dock levellers, platforms;

  — speed restrictors ('sleeping policemen');

  — car park lighting;

  — automatic barriers (e.g. card-controlled);

  — signs;

  — security cameras;

  — bollards;

  — trolley parks (metalwork only);

  — floodlighting;

  — skips (including cost of levelling prepared land).

- Outbuildings: — fuel stores, fuel tanks.

- Protective structures: — brick, concrete, metal or wooden structures built around plant for the protection of the plant itself or of employees/members of the public, e.g. around liquefied petroleum gas (LPG) stores.

- Cost of alteration to existing buildings: — alterations to an existing building incidental to the installation of plant and machinery, e.g. metal framework for space heaters, strengthening floors for the installation of racking, alterations to the building so that plant can be installed.

- Miscellaneous: — security cages.

- Heating systems, etc.: — items of machinery, e.g., air handling plant, boilers, radiators, space heaters;

  — builder's work in connection with the above;

  — services of gas, electricity and water to the plant which are exclusive to that item of plant (e.g. water piping back to the point where the pipe serving only a particular item of plant branches off from the distribution system).

6.10 *Plant*

- Sanitary:
  — toilets;

  — toilet accommodation (e.g. cubicles);

  — sinks/washbasins;

  — urinals;

  — hand dryers;

  towel and soap holders;

  — mirrors;

  — showers;

  — additional fittings for the disabled;

  — drinking fountains;

  — macerators, etc.;

  — supply or waste pipes solely serving the above;

  — hot water piping;

  — potable water system.

- Fire protection:
  — smoke detectors;

  — heat detectors;

  — fire and smoke alarms;

  — sprinklers;

  — breakglasses;

  — emergency lighting;

  — fixtures to emergency exits;

  — fire corridors;

  — electricity/water supplies to alarms, etc.;

  — roof lights forming part of smoke control system;

  — smoke extraction systems.

- Electrical:
  — electrical system serving particular items of plant (e.g. point of sale (POS) equipment/heating);

  — telemecanique or similar trunking system;

  — display lighting;

  — high bay lighting system;

— sockets and cabling used exclusively by items of plant, e.g., computers, POS equipment;

— temperature and light level sensors;

— distribution boards;

— generators;

— switchgear;

— security cameras;

— videoscan equipment;

— video recording equipment.

- Fixtures and fittings: — external signs;

— aisle/product signs;

— display units;

— shelving;

— display lighting and lighting track;

— entrance barriers;

— lockers (e.g. for staff);

— gondolas;

— litter bins.

- Communications, etc: — paging system/intercom;

— piped music/PA system.

- Shop fronts: — external signs;

— lettering (removable);

— window display — floors and backs.

- Lifts: — lift cars;

— lift machinery and indicators;

— pits to house lift machinery (NB shafts not allowable after 30 November 1993);

— electrical supply.

The Revenue guidelines allow that an entire electrical system may be regarded as plant if certain conditions are met (*CA, para 1552* – see 5.12 and 15.13). These guidelines were first formulated following a claim successfully made by a supermarket chain.

Conversion into flats

6.11   A 100% first-year allowance is available where parts of business premises are converted into flats (*FA 2001, Sec 67, Sch 19*). This is most commonly met where flats are sited above shops.

This is one of a number of provisions aimed at urban regeneration. Other measures include reduced rate of VAT, an exemption from stamp duty and enhanced relief for cleaning up contaminated land.

Capital allowances, including a 100% first-year allowance, will be available for expenditure on converting or renovating certain flats above business premises.

Where qualifying expenditure is incurred, a first-year allowance of 100% is given. If all or part of this is disclaimed, writing-down allowances of 25% per annum are available.

Expenditure which qualifies is that which is incurred on the renovation of a flat or the conversion into a flat of part of a qualifying building. A qualifying building is one which was built before 1 January 1980, where the ground floor is authorised for business use, and the upper floors (not more than four storeys) were originally intended to be used as dwellings.

There are detailed rules as to what constitutes a qualifying flat. It must:

(*a*)   be in a qualifying building;

(*b*)   be suitable for letting as a dwelling;

(*c*)   held for the purpose of short-term letting;

(*d*)   have four rooms or less (excluding bathrooms, kitchens and some hallways).

It must *not*:

*   be a high value flat (or part of a scheme involving high value flats);

*   be let to a person connected with the person incurring the expenditure.

Whether or not a flat is a high value flat is determined by reference to a table of notional rents included in *Sec 393(5)*.

Balancing adjustments (allowances or charges) may arise on disposal, etc. However, no balancing adjustment is made if the disposal, etc. occurs more than seven years after the time when the flat was first suitable for letting as a dwelling.

A balancing allowance is denied where the proceeds of the balancing event are less than they would have been as the result of a tax avoidance scheme (*Sec 570A*). The provisions of *Sec 570A* apply for flat conversion allowances as they do for industrial buildings allowances (see 11.21).

Chapter 7

Industrial Property — Special Features

Introduction

7.1   Chapters 2, 3 and 4 highlighted the fact that expenditure on most types of building will not qualify for allowances. The main exception to this rule is where the building concerned is an *industrial* one. However, the question of whether or not a building qualifies is not governed by whether it has a broadly industrial character, but whether the use to which it is put is one of the qualifying activities specified by the legislation. A claim for industrial buildings allowances (IBAs) should always be considered, even where it is not immediately obvious.

7.2   A separate system of allowances applies to agricultural buildings. In many ways, agricultural buildings allowances are similar to IBAs, and are given in respect of expenditure on farmhouses, farm buildings, cottages, fences and other works. In appropriate circumstances, taxpayers may find that a claim for either type of allowance (but not both) may be possible. Agricultural buildings allowances, however, tend to be of relatively little relevance to the majority of businesses or property investors, and are not dealt with further in this book. For a thorough review, see *Tolleys Capital Allowances*.

Qualifying expenditure

General

7.3   Industrial buildings allowances are given where a person incurs capital expenditure on an industrial building or structure, as defined in the legislation. The definition is considered below under 7.22 et seq. [*Sec 271.*]

The site

7.4   No allowances are due in respect of expenditure on the acquisition of any land, or of rights in or over land. [*Sec 272(1).*] Where land is acquired and a new building constructed, the separate cost elements are usually easy to identify. However, on a subsequent sale and purchase, any consideration will be for both the building and the site upon which it stands. In this case, the consideration will need to be justly apportioned, so as to isolate that part qualifying for allowances. [*Sec 356(1)*].

7.5 *Qualifying expenditure*

7.5 Expenditure incurred on preparing the land so as to render it suitable for supporting a building will qualify as part of the cost of the building, eligible for allowances. Allowances will also be due on the cost of preparing, cutting, tunnelling or levelling land for the purposes of preparing the land as a site for the installation of machinery or plant where no allowance could otherwise be made. [*Sec 273.*] Of course, it would normally be preferable if such expenditure could be claimed to be incurred on the provision of the machinery or plant (see 13.8 et seq.), thus qualifying for a higher rate of allowances.

Building alterations and repairs

7.6 Where a trader incurs capital expenditure on alterations to an existing building incidental to the installation of machinery or plant, that expenditure itself qualifies for allowances as if it were part of the machinery or plant. [*Sec 25.*] Other alterations to a qualifying building and repairs which are not allowed as trading deductions qualify for IBAs. [*Sec 272(2).*] In general terms, allowances are given on an improvement to a building as if the improvement were a separate building.

Demolition costs

7.7 Where a building is to be demolished, and a balancing adjustment arises in accordance with *Sec 314* if the person incurring the costs of demolition owns a relevant interest, the net cost of demolition is added to the residue of expenditure incurred on construction of the property. [*Sec 340.*]

7.8 Where no balancing adjustment could arise (for example if the demolished building was a non-qualifying one), the demolition cost might form part of the cost of preparing the site for a replacement building, if any.

Roads on industrial estates

7.9 Expenditure in respect of a road on an industrial estate is treated as qualifying for allowances if the building and structures on the estate are used wholly or mainly for a qualifying purpose within *Sec 274*. [*Sec 284(1).*] If a road is included in the lease of a building, it will qualify for IBAs only if that building so qualifies (CA, para 32340). This applies equally to private roads on a trading estate in an enterprise zone, where the buildings are commercial buildings within the extended meaning of 'industrial'. [*Sec 284(2).*]

7.10 The Revenue's view is that if a road is to be taken over by a local authority, it does not qualify for IBAs because the person incurring the expenditure does not have a relevant interest (see 7.18 et seq.). It is suggested that this can be overcome by proper timing of construction, use and adoption (see 2.41–2.44).

Allowances available

New buildings

7.11   A writing-down allowance of 4% of qualifying expenditure is made where certain conditions (see 7.16) are fulfilled. [*Sec 310(1)*.] Where the accounting period is less or more than a year, the writing-down allowance is proportionately decreased or increased. [*Sec 310(2)*.]

7.12   Allowances may be disclaimed in a particular year, effectively extending the tax life of the building (see Chapter 20).

Second-hand buildings

7.13   Where an industrial building is acquired second-hand, the writing-down allowance is ascertained by taking the *residue of qualifying expenditure* at the date of acquisition and writing it off on a straight line basis over the period beginning with the sale and ending with the 25th anniversary of when the building was first used. [*Sec 311*.] As with 'first-hand' buildings, allowances may be disclaimed in a particular year, thereby effectively extending the tax life of the building (see Chapter 20). Where the accounting period is less or more than a year, the writing-down allowance is proportionately decreased or increased. [*Sec 311*.]

7.14   The residue of expenditure (commonly called the tax written-down value) is generally the original cost, written down by *net* allowances given, including any balancing allowance or charge on the sale itself — see 11.4–11.17 for details of calculation. Where a building is sold for more than original cost, all allowances given will be clawed back, such that the *residue of expenditure* will be the same as original cost. A second-hand purchaser can never claim allowances on an amount higher than this.

7.15   Where the expenditure was incurred before 6 November 1962, the duration of the writing-down period is 50 years, rather than 25, and writing-down allowances are at a rate of 2% p.a. [*Sch 3, para 66*]. The purchaser of a second-hand building should not assume, therefore, that no allowances are available merely because the building is more than 25 years old.

Conditions for allowances

7.16   Writing-down allowances may be claimed where three conditions are fulfilled:

(*a*)   qualifying expenditure has been incurred on a building;

(*b*)   the claimant is, *at the end of a chargeable period*, entitled to the *relevant interest* (see 7.18 et seq.) in relation to that expenditure; and

(c)   the building or structure is at that time an *industrial* building. [*Secs 271(3), 309.*]

Time conditions must be met

7.17   It is worth emphasising that the conditions only need to be met at the end of the chargeable period. Even if a building only qualifies for IBAs on the last day of an accounting period, that suffices for full allowances to be given. In extreme cases, a difference of one day in bringing a building into use (see 7.22 et seq.) can result in either an acceleration or a delay of allowances by a whole year.

Relevant interest

7.18   A claim for IBAs in respect of any expenditure can be made only by the holder of the 'relevant interest' relating to that expenditure. When the relevant interest changes hands so does the entitlement to relief. However, it should not be thought that all transactions in a property result in a change to the relevant interest or its ownership. In particular the grant of a lease out of the relevant interest does not generally cause allowances to cease, providing the building continues to be in qualifying use (but see 11.26 et seq. regarding the realisation of a capital value).

7.19   When a person incurs expenditure on a building, his relevant interest will in essence be whatever interest he has in that building, at the time that the expenditure is incurred. [*Sec 286(1).*] The relevant interest can therefore take a variety of forms, i.e. freehold, long leasehold, short leasehold, or even a licence. Not every form of licence, however, will qualify. In *JC Decaux (UK) Ltd v Francis [1996] STC (SCD) 281*, the taxpayer had the right to access land for the purpose of cleaning, maintaining and repairing plant installed on it. It was held that this was a mere contractual right which could not be raised to the status of an interest in land. A tenancy at will will qualify because it is a form of lease (CA, para 33040). Likewise, an equitable interest or an agreement to obtain the freehold or a lease can be the relevant interest (CA, para 33040). Where the same person holds more than one interest in a property, and one is reversionary upon the others, that will be the relevant interest. [*Sec 286(3).*]

Example

7.20   Timms Ltd bought a freehold plot of land in 1996 and in the same year constructed a factory thereon. The following year, Timms granted a long lease to a pension fund in return for a significant premium. The pension fund then granted a shorter lease back to Timms.

7.21   In 1998, Timms added an extension to the factory. The relevant interest for this extension was the freehold, which was reversionary on all others (both that held by Timms and that held by the pension fund).

The meaning of industrial

General

7.22   There is no requirement that an industrial building or structure should rise above ground level; therefore, roads, car parks and yards may be eligible for allowances. The type of assets which may qualify can often in practice be deduced from *Secs 21* and *22*, which define buildings and structures for the purpose of denying plant allowances.

7.23   An 'industrial building or structure' is defined by *Secs 271(1)(b), 274, 275* as a building or structure being in use for the purposes of one of a number of trades or activities (see Tables A and B of *Sec 274* below). In a sense it is therefore incorrect to speak of a 'qualifying building' as it is in fact the *use* to which a building is put that is either qualifying or not. It is possible to conceive of two buildings identical in construction, one of which is used as a warehouse and qualifies for allowances, whilst the other is used as a retail shop (perhaps a carpet or furniture store) and attracts no allowances.

Table A

Trades which are "Qualifying Trades"

1. *Manufacturing*   A trade consisting of manufacturing goods or materials.

2. *Processing*   A trade consisting of subjecting goods or materials to a process. This includes (subject to *Sec 276(3)*) maintaining or repairing goods or materials.

3. *Storage*   A trade consisting of storing goods or materials —
   (*a*) which are to be used in the manufacture of other goods or materials,
   (*b*) which are to be subjected, in the course of a trade, to a process,
   (*c*) which, having been manufactured or produced or subjected, in the course of a trade, to a process, have not yet been delivered to any purchaser, or
   (*d*) on their arrival in the United Kingdom from a place outside the United Kingdom.

4. *Agricultural contracting*   A trade consisting of —
   (*a*) ploughing or cultivating land occupied by another,
   (*b*) carrying out any other agricultural operation on land occupied by another, or
   (*c*) threshing another's crops
   For this purpose "crops" includes vegetable produce.

5. *Working foreign plantations* — A trade consisting of working land outside the United Kingdom used for—
   (*a*) growing and harvesting crops,
   (*b*) husbandry, or
   (*c*) forestry.
   For this purpose "crops" includes vegetable produce and "harvesting crops" includes the collection of vegetable produce (however effected).

6. *Fishing* — A trade consisting of catching or taking fish or shell-fish.

7. *Mineral extraction* — A trade consisting of working a source of mineral deposits.
   "Mineral deposits" includes any natural deposits capable of being lifted or extracted from the earth, and for this purpose geothermal energy is to be treated as a natural deposit.
   "Source of mineral deposits" includes a mine, an oil well and a source of geothermal energy.

Table B

Undertakings which are "Qualifying Trades" if carried on by way of trade

1. *Electricity* — An undertaking for the generation, transformation, conversion, transmission or distribution of electrical energy.

2. *Water* — An undertaking for the supply of water for public consumption.

3. *Hydraulic power* — An undertaking for the supply of hydraulic power.

4. *Sewerage* — An undertaking for the provision of sewerage services within the meaning of the *Water Industry Act 1991*.

5. *Transport* — A transport undertaking.

6. *Highway undertakings* — A highway undertaking, that is, so much of any undertaking relating to the design, building, financing and operation of roads as is carried on—
   (*a*) for the purposes of, or
   (*b*) in connection with,
   the exploitation of highway concessions.

7. *Tunnels* — A tunnel undertaking.

8. *Bridges* — A bridge undertaking.

9. *Inland navigation* — An inland navigation undertaking.

10. *Docks* — A dock undertaking.
    A dock includes—

(*a*) any harbour, and
(*b*) any wharf, pier, jetty or other works in or at which vessels can ship or unship merchandise or passengers,
other than a pier or jetty primarily used for recreation.'

The precise activity carried on in the individual building should not be looked at in isolation. Rather, one should consider the overall activity in respect of which the building is used (*Blunson v West Midlands Gas Board (1951) 33 TC 315*).

7.24   In the context of deciding whether a building is used or unused, 'use' means use for any purpose and not just for a purpose qualifying for IBAs. 'Use', however, does not include occupation by a tenant for fitting out by that tenant prior to the commencement of actual production or other use. The fitting-out process is regarded by the Revenue as merely the completion of construction.

Part of a trade

7.25   It is worth observing, however, that allowances may still be available where only part of a trade qualifies. *Sec 276(2)* reads:

'If a building is in use for a partly qualifying trade, allowances are only available if that building is in use for the qualifying part of the trade.'

7.26   The qualifying activity does not have to be the major part of the trade carried on. In *Kilmarnock Equitable Co-operative Society v IRC (1966) 42 TC 675*, it was held that it was necessary only to distinguish 'a definitely identifiable part of their individual operations … a quite separate activity'. In *Girobank plc v Clarke [1998] STC 182*, the High Court held that the sorting of documents by a bank was sufficiently identifiable to be regarded as a part of a trade, however, the claim failed on other grounds.

7.27   The relative size of each separate part of the trade or undertaking should be irrelevant. However, it was held in *Bestway Holdings Ltd v Luff [1998] STC 357* that in order to be regarded as a part of a trade for this purpose, the activities in question must be a 'significant, separate and identifiable part of the trade'. This is confirmed by *Inland Revenue Tax Bulletin* (Issue 40).

7.28   The question of part of a trade qualifying is considered further in the context of storage at 7.94 below.

Other qualifying undertakings

7.29   Tables A and B extend IBAs to a number of activities which qualify for allowances if carried on by way of trade. Some of these activities are highly specialised, and are not considered in detail here. These are:

(*a*)   water, sewerage, electricity and hydraulic power undertakings;

(*b*)   tunnel, bridge and highway and inland navigation undertakings;

(*c*)   mineral extraction;

(*d*)   catching or taking of fish or shellfish;

(*e*)   agricultural contracting and the working of foreign plantations.

7.30   The activities most commonly met in practice will be transport and dock undertakings.

Transport undertakings

7.31   Falling under this heading will be any undertaking providing commercial transport, whether of passengers or of goods. This would therefore include a haulage company, a bus company or an airline. Also included are private rail companies and taxi firms. However, a trade which consists of hiring out 'self-drive' vehicles will not qualify.

7.32   The provision of transport as part of wider trade may also qualify — see *Buckingham v Securitas Properties Ltd (1979) 53 TC 292*, where allowances were given in respect of the vehicle service bay of a security service company.

7.33   In practice, allowances will be given in respect of such premises as waiting rooms, garages or freight sheds, but not in respect of general administrative buildings or retail outlets. The question of whether a transport undertaking was ancillary to the purposes of a retail shop was considered in *Sarsfield v Dixons Group plc [1997] STC 283* — see 6.7.

7.34   It is important to bear in mind the rule that where the cost of non-qualifying parts of a building is not more than one quarter of the total, the whole may be regarded as qualifying for allowances. [*Sec 283(2)*] (see 7.80 et seq.). For example, retail units at an airport terminal may well represent only a small part of the total expenditure and would therefore be allowed.

Dock undertakings and inland navigation

7.35   A 'dock' includes any harbour, wharf, pier or jetty or other works in or at which vessels can ship or unship merchandise or passengers. [*Sec 274, Table B, item 10.*] Excluded, however, are any piers or jetties used primarily for recreation. However as the exclusion only extends to piers and jetties there may yet be scope for negotiation. Examples of expenditure qualifying under this heading will be:

(*a*)   walls and floors of docks, basins, locks and gates thereto;

(*b*)   piers, breakwaters, jetties and mooring facilities, whether fixed or floating;

(*c*)   roads and other hard surfaces;

(*d*)   buildings and structures within the dock area, together with others elsewhere specifically used for the purposes of the dock undertaking.

Manufacturing and processing

General

7.36   Manufacturing and processing share many common features, and the two activities are considered together in the following paragraphs.

Manufacture

7.37   The meaning of 'manufacture' has not been considered by the courts in the context of IBAs. Decided cases from other areas of the law suggest, however, that the term may be construed widely, and that manufacture does not necessarily mean the creation of an end product from raw materials. The construction of a product from component parts (or a step in such production) would be regarded as manufacture (*Prestcold (Central) Ltd v Minister of Labour [1969] 1 All ER 69*).

Goods or materials

7.38   In most cases, 'goods or materials' will be recognised for what they are. In three cases, certain items have been excluded from the definition.

(*a*)   In *Bourne v Norwich Crematorium Ltd (1967) 44 TC 164* it was held that human remains were not 'goods or materials' and that cremation was not, therefore, the subjection of goods or materials to a process.

(*b*)   Similarly, in *Buckingham v Securitas Properties Ltd (1979) 53 TC 292* it was held that coins and bank notes were not 'goods or materials'.

(*c*)   More recently, the Court of Appeal, reversing the decision of the High Court, held that information-bearing documents were not 'goods or materials' in *Girobank plc v Clarke [1998] STC 182*.

7.39   The interpretation of the word 'goods' in the *Securitas* case as only meaning 'merchandise or wares' was supported by Nourse LJ in *Girobank,* who derived comfort both from the commercial context of [*Sec 274*] and also from Parliament's choice of the words 'goods or materials' rather than 'goods or chattels'. Nourse LJ also thought, at least so far as the items dealt with by Girobank were concerned, that if they were not goods, then they could not be materials. However, no further explanation was given. Clearly, whether or not items qualify will depend on the context. Coins and bank notes (whether British or foreign) would be 'goods or materials' for the purpose of a trade consisting of their manufacture.

Increasingly, data is stored, transferred and analysed in electronic form, without ever being printed in hard copy. Although the point hasn't been tested by the Courts, it is extremely unlikely that such data could be regarded as 'goods or materials'.

Subjection to a process

7.40   In *Kilmarnock Equitable Cooperative Society Ltd v IRC (1966) 42 TC 675* it was said that the subjection of goods or materials to a process may be something other than manufacture, and still qualify for allowances. The Lord President said:

'An industrial building may connote something other than a place where goods or materials are manufactured: it may include ... a place where goods or materials are subjected to a process which falls short of the manufacturing of a new article.'

7.41   In this particular case, the screening and bagging of coal was held to qualify as such a process. To put this in a wider context, a building used for the sorting of goods, breaking bulk, packing and so on may therefore qualify for IBAs.

7.42   A process should certainly not be thought of as something restricted to heavy industry. Examples of other processes qualifying for relief include:

(*a*)   cleaning and bagging of coal;

(*b*)   breeding rodents for experimental purposes;

(*c*)   developing and printing photographs;

(*d*)   cutting steel tubes to customers' requirements;

(*e*)   cutting and binding carpets to customers' requirements;

(*f*)   sorting of rags, scrap metal, etc.;

(*g*)   preparation of pre-packed cooked meals;

(*h*)   cleaning, sorting and pre-packing fruit and vegetables;

(*i*)   ripening fruit (after picking, not while still growing);

(*j*)   egg packing;

(*k*)   tea or coffee blending;

(*l*)   wine bottling;

(*m*)   whisky blending;

(*n*)   car servicing (unless part of a retail shop — see 7.71);

(*o*)   fitting tyres and exhausts (unless part of a retail shop — see 7.71);

(*p*)   packaging and breaking bulk, assuming uniformity of treatment;

(*q*)   shrink wrapping;

(*r*)   seed cleaning.

7.43   The above list is indicative of the type and range of activities that have qualified: there will be many others.

7.44   In *Bestway Holdings Ltd v Luff [1998] STC 357*, the term 'process' was not extended to activities which were merely preliminary to sale, and which in isolation were 'limited, mundane and of no substantial significance'. In contrast, obiter dicta in *Buckingham v Securitas Properties Ltd (1979) 53 TC 292*, suggested that the cleaning of antique coins in preparation for sale would be regarded as a process.

There are conflicting authorities on the necessity for a process to change the goods in some way. On balance, the absence of any physical change should not prevent an activity from being a 'process'. This may enable IBA's to be claimed, for example, on buildings used for quality control.

Repairing

7.45   The reference to the subjection of goods or materials to a process includes the maintaining or repairing of goods or materials. [*Sec 274, Table A, item 2.*] However, where those goods or materials are used in the repairer's trade, one has to examine whether that trade itself qualifies for IBAs. The expression 'used in a trade' probably connotes that the assets are held as fixed assets, rather than trading stock.

Storage of goods or materials

General

7.46   Four particular types of storage qualify under *Sec 274, Table A, item 3*. These are:

(*a*)   the storage of goods or materials which are to be used in the manufacture of other goods or materials;

7.46 *Storage of goods or materials*

(*b*) the storage of goods or materials which are to be subjected, in the course of a trade, to any process;

(*c*) the storage of goods or materials which, having been manufactured or produced or subjected, in the course of trade, to any process, have not yet been delivered to any purchaser; and

(*d*) the storage of goods or materials on their arrival in the United Kingdom from a place outside the United Kingdom.

7.47 In each case, to qualify for allowances, the storage activity must constitute a trade. For many years, the Revenue held the view that qualifying storage could not be merely an incidental part of another trade (e.g. wholesaling or retailing). Either storage had to constitute the only trade (i.e. the storage of goods on behalf of the owners of the goods for a fee), or it should be a separable part of the trade (capable perhaps of being contracted out on a commercial basis). In the 1951 case *Dale v Johnson Brothers (1951) 32 TC 487*, which the claimant lost because it held the goods as purchaser, Sheil J stated: 'it will not do that the trade is storage plus something else or something else plus storage. It must simply be a keeping or custody.'

7.48 This view appeared to be in contradiction of *Sec 276* (see 7.25 et seq.). In *Bestway Holdings Ltd v Luff [1998] STC 357*, it was held that storage in this context referred to a form of warehousing, and not merely the storage that any wholesaler wants for his goods. The court rejected the taxpayer's claim that storage should be taken to mean 'keeping in reserve for future use or disposal'. Lightman J found that the key factor was the purpose for which the goods are stored — storage must be an end in itself, and not merely incidental to some other purpose, such as sale. This is confirmed by *Inland Revenue Tax Bulletin* (Issue 40). However, a warehouse or store may qualify under another heading, for example because it is used for the purposes of a manufacturing trade, even if the storage is not an end in itself.

7.49 In *Saxone, Lilley & Skinner (Holdings) Ltd v IRC (1967) 44 TC 122*, it was considered appropriate to look at the use to which the building was put, rather than at the general trade carried on by the claimant. The most important case on this subject, however, is *Crusabridge Investments Ltd v Casings International Ltd (1979) 54 TC 246*, where it was held that the claimant need not carry on a trade of storage nor even a trade qualifying under another heading, provided that some part of the trade consisted of a qualifying storage activity, and the building in question was used for that part of the trade. The same case confirmed that, if a claim is in respect of storage of goods which are to be subjected to any process, the storage and the processing need not be carried on by the same person.

Example

7.50 Askham operates as a manufacturer and wholesaler of electrical goods. He occupies two warehouses. Warehouse A is used for the storage of electrical components which are to be used in the manufacture, by Askham, of televisions and radios. Warehouse B is used to store compact disc players, which Askham does not have the technology to manufacture himself. The machines are therefore held in Warehouse B only until sold to customers.

7.51 Warehouse A will qualify as an industrial building by virtue of its use to store goods or materials (i.e. components) to be used in the manufacture of other goods or materials (i.e. electrical products). Warehouse B, on the other hand, will not qualify. It is used for the storage of finished goods, but these goods have been delivered to a purchaser, i.e. Askham. The fact that the whole trade is not a qualifying one does not preclude allowances for Warehouse A. In contrast, Warehouse B does not attract allowances because it is not itself used for the qualifying part of the trade.

7.52 Askham would be well advised to reconsider his warehousing policy. He might find it feasible to store both his manufactured and bought-in goods indiscriminately through both warehouses. He might then be able to take advantage of the decision in *Saxone, Lilley & Skinner*, discussed at 7.95 and Appendix 4.

Imported goods storage

7.53 In order to qualify, a warehouse for imported goods need not necessarily be in the immediate vicinity of a port or airport (or indeed the Channel Tunnel). The acid test is whether the goods are being stored for the first time in the United Kingdom, and are still in transit and have not, therefore, reached their final destination. This was put forward in *Copol Clothing Co Ltd v Hindmarch (1983) 57 TC 575*, and is confirmed by Revenue Instructions (CA, para 32224).

7.54 Note that the place of storage need not be a warehouse in the conventional sense — the 'goods' may have arrived by pipeline and be stored in tanks.

Delivery

7.55 It can be seen that the concept of delivery can be important in deciding whether certain stores and warehouses qualify for allowances. Delivery may be something less than actual physical delivery. One important factor will be the passing of title and it may be that delivery merely implies the 'making available' to a purchaser of the goods or materials. In *Dale v Johnson Bros (1951) 32 TC 487*, goods were delivered to a selling agent and title passed. It was held that the agent did fall within the term 'any purchaser' in *Sec 274, Table A, item 3(c)*, and IBAs were therefore not available.

Staff welfare facilities

7.56 The term 'industrial building or structure' includes any building or structure provided by the person carrying on a qualifying trade or undertaking for the welfare of workers employed in that trade or undertaking and in use for that purpose. [*Sec 275.*] Note, however, that a landlord cannot claim relief for expenditure in respect of his tenants or their employees. Examples of qualifying buildings include:

(*a*)   car parks;

(*b*)   canteens or rest rooms;

(*c*)   social clubs;

(*d*)   creches or day nurseries;

(*e*)   medical facilities;

(*f*)   garages;

(*g*)   sports facilities;

(*h*)   hostels.

(CA, para 32320.)

7.57   Where the person providing the welfare facilities is carrying on a trade which qualifies in part for IBAs, then only the welfare facilities used wholly or partly by employees in that part of the trade will qualify for allowances (CA, para 32320).

7.58   So, if a business with a manufacturing operation and a retail shop provides separate canteens for the employees in each, only the one used by the factory workers will attract allowances. It would be best in such circumstances to allow all employees to visit either canteen. Provided there were no separate areas set aside for either factory or shop workers, the canteens should qualify in full, by virtue of the *Saxone, Lilley* case (see 7.95).

7.59   A building which is sometimes used by outsiders (that is, non-employees) will nonetheless qualify for allowances if it was provided for the welfare of workers (CA, para 32320). The Revenue suggests that a shop provided by an employer for his workers cannot attract IBAs, because *Sec 277* denies allowances to retail shops (CA, para 32320). However, the long-standing definition of a shop is 'a place where facilities are offered and to which the general public can resort for the satisfaction of their wants and needs' (*Turpin v Assessment Committee for Middlesbrough [1931] AC 446*). A shop which is open only to employees of a particular business cannot be said to be open to the general public. The Inland Revenue also claims that office staff and management are not 'workers' and that welfare facilities provided for them cannot therefore qualify (CA, para 32320). However, this point does not seem to be taken in practice.

Sports pavilions

7.60   Allowances will be given where a building is occupied by a person carrying on a trade and used as a sports pavilion for the welfare of employees.

72

[*Secs 271(1), 280.*] At first sight, sports pavilions appear to be another example of welfare facilities (see above) but the important difference is that sports pavilions will attract allowances regardless of the nature of the trade, unlike welfare facilities where the trade must be one qualifying for IBAs. However, the allowance is not extended to those carrying on a profession or vocation.

7.61   The important factor is not the original design or intended purpose of the building but the use to which it is put. The Revenue's view is that a 'sports pavilion' should:

(*a*)   be by a playing field, pitch or track; and

(*b*)   exist primarily for the convenience of the players (rather than the spectators) for changing, bathing, waiting for their turn to compete etc.

7.62   Social clubs, therefore, would not normally qualify. However, if the club is close to, say, a tennis court or bowling green and provides any of the facilities referred to in (*b*) above, a claim might be possible in respect of expenditure apportioned to the qualifying parts.

7.63   Note that it is at least doubtful whether the term 'sports pavilion' includes buildings where the sport actually takes place, for example, squash courts or pool or snooker rooms.

7.64   Normally, occupation by the trader is a pre-requisite for claiming IBAs. However, it is understood that where a trader contributes towards a sports pavilion owned by another person, allowances will be given. Where the 'other person' is a public or local authority, the allowance will be given to the trader where use is reasonably commensurate with the level of the contribution.

Non-qualifying buildings

General

7.65   A number of types of building are excluded from qualifying for industrial buildings allowances. [*Sec 277*]. These include buildings and structures in use as, or as part of, any of the following:

(*a*)   a dwelling-house;

(*b*)   a retail shop;

(*c*)   a showroom;

(*d*)   a hotel (subject to special rules for 'qualifying hotels' (see 8.4));

(*e*)   an office.

7.66   A building is also ineligible for allowances if it is used for any purpose ancillary to the purposes of a dwelling-house, retail shop, showroom, hotel or office.

7.67 Non-qualifying buildings

7.67 This is examined further below, in connection with retail shops.

Dwelling-houses

7.68 As stated above, expenditure on dwelling-houses does not qualify for IBAs. This remains true when the dwelling-house is situated in an enterprise zone, in contrast to expenditure on hotels, offices etc.

7.69 'Dwelling-house' is not defined for IBA purposes. In the case of *Riley v Read (1879) 1 TC 217*, the meaning of 'to dwell' was described, albeit in another context, as 'to live in a house; that is, to live there day and night; to sleep there during the night, and to occupy it for the purposes of life during the day'.

7.70 In the context of long life machinery and plant, the Revenue has stated that a dwelling-house includes a person's second or holiday home, but does not include accommodation used for holiday letting or as a university hall of residence, or a hospital, nursing home or prison. (*Inland Revenue Tax Bulletin 30*). Nor is a block of flats a dwelling-house, although the individual flats may be (CA, para 11520).

Retail shops

7.71 A retail shop includes any premises of a similar character where retail trade or business (including repair work) is carried on. [*Sec 277(1)*.] The question of whether a particular building is to be regarded as a retail shop (or as ancillary to a retail shop) is considered in 6.1.

7.72 The reference above to 'repair work' would extend the definition to include garages. A vehicle repair workshop is considered to fall within *Sec 274, Table A, item 1* or *2*, but is normally excluded from an allowance by *Sec 277(1)*, as being in use as, or for purposes ancillary to, a retail shop. However, in an agreement with the Motor Trade Association, the Revenue has indicated that it will accept a workshop as an industrial building where:

(*a*)   it is completely isolated from the rest of the motor dealer's premises;

(*b*)   it does not include the reception area for motor cars; and

(*c*)   access to it by the public is discouraged.

7.73 Allowances will not be refused because the workshop is not physically separated from showrooms, offices etc. Unless the whole building is occupied for a non-qualifying purpose, e.g. showrooms, allowances may be given where the workshop occupies a distinguishable part of the building which is not used to any substantial extent for purposes other than vehicle repair.

7.74 Where the workshop is used partly but not mainly for a non-qualifying purpose, e.g. the storage of parts or accessories sold in the retail part of the business or partly but not mainly for a purpose ancillary to the purposes of a retail shop (e.g. the preliminary inspection and preparation of cars for sale in the showroom) a proportionate part of the allowance may be given. Where, however, a non-qualifying use is less than one-quarter of the total use, no restriction is made. [*Sec 283(2).*]

Showrooms

7.75   Showrooms are generally excluded from being regarded as industrial buildings, irrespective of whether they are used for retail or wholesale purposes. There appears to be no authority as to what constitutes a showroom, and dictionary definitions may not always be helpful. In *Bestway (Holdings) Ltd v Luff [1997] STC (SCD) 87*, the Commissioners stated: 'In the last resort the decision as to what is and what is not a showroom must be one of impression.' The same might also apply for other types of premises where legal authority is lacking, for example, a mill or office. In many cases, such as in the motor trade, it is impossible to distinguish between a showroom and a retail shop.

7.76   Whether or not a room is a 'showroom' may be a matter of degree. The display of a manufacturer's wares in a reception area does not change the nature of that room into a showroom.

7.77   In many cases, the problem will be avoided because expenditure on the 'showroom' part of such a building will be not more than 25% of the total, and would therefore fall to be allowed by virtue of *Sec 283(2)* — see 7.80 et seq. below.

Hotels

7.78   Hotels in general are outside the definition of an industrial building, but expenditure incurred on a 'qualifying hotel' after 11 April 1978 will qualify for relief under *Sec 271(1)(b)(ii)* (see 8.4).

Offices

7.79   Offices do not generally qualify for IBAs, although there are exceptions, notably where the office, rather than merely being the seat of administration, is closely linked to a manufacturing or other qualifying process. A drawing office or sorting office would often qualify for IBAs in this way. Of course, it is open to debate whether either is really an 'office' in the first place. A more complete consideration of this question is set out in 5.1.

De minimis exception

7.80   Where part of a building qualifies for IBAs and part does not, allowances will be given on the whole cost of the building providing the expenditure incurred in respect of the non-qualifying part is not more than 25% of the total expenditure on the building. [*Sec 283(2)*.] Before 16 March 1983, the appropriate percentage was 10%.

7.81   It is important to remember that cost is the deciding factor: some claimants fall into the trap of looking instead at floor space. A calculation based on floor space may sometimes be an acceptable substitute for one based on cost, but it should not be assumed that the two calculations would always give the same result due, for example, to office and other areas being fitted out to a different specification. Where expenditure on the non-qualifying part of a building exceeds 25% of the total, allowances will be given only on the expenditure incurred in respect of the qualifying part. [*Secs 283(2), 571(1)*.]

Example

7.82   Bailey, who carries on a manufacturing trade, constructed two new buildings in the year ended 31 December 1998. Details were as follows:

	Building A	*Building B*
Total cost (£m)	5.0	8.0
Office cost (£m)	1.0	2.5
Total area (sq ft)	15,000	20,000
Office area (sq ft)	5,000	5,000

Allowances given will be based on expenditure of:

(*a*)   building A: £5 million (non-qualifying expenditure is not more than 25% of the total);

(*b*)   building B: £5.5 million (non-office part only).

Separate building or extension?

7.83   In general terms, it is possible to obtain allowances on, say, an office by adding it on to an existing (qualifying) building, rather than constructing a new, separate building just a few feet away. This depends, however, on the expenditure on the office not being more than 25% of the total cost of the shop and the existing building. This will usually only be the case if the existing building is itself relatively large or is not very old. Even a small extension is, at current prices, likely to cost in excess of 25% of the total, if the original building was constructed many years ago.

7.84   There is no real definition of what constitutes a separate building either in statute or case law. The question of what is a 'unified structure' was considered in *Lancashire Electric Power Co v Wilkinson (1947) 28 TC 427.*

7.85   The most regularly quoted case is *Abbott Laboratories Ltd v Carmody (1968) 44 TC 569*. Here the taxpayer had constructed four buildings on a 53-acre site, which were treated as a single unit for the purposes of rates and, up to 1962–63, for Schedule A income tax. One block, used solely for administration and not in itself qualifying for IBAs, was connected to another block by a covered passage. In view of this, the company claimed that the two blocks should be treated as one building for IBA purposes. This contention was not accepted by the courts, which ruled that no allowances could therefore be given for expenditure on the administration block by taking advantage of the *de minimis* rule. It was held that on the particular facts of the case, the administration block was not sufficiently physically integrated with the other structural units. This would not necessarily apply in every case.

7.86   Other cases, however, conflict with this decision. In an Irish case, *O'Conaill v Waterford Glass Ltd (1982) TL(I) 122* expenditure on a separate building housing a computer was held to qualify for allowances, as the computer installation existed to serve the other parts of an industrial complex. Under the Irish equivalent of the *de minimis* rule, the whole complex was treated as one building.

7.87   Following the *Abbott Laboratories* case, it is often assumed that buildings connected by covered walkways are always regarded as separate buildings. This is not necessarily so, but the precise circumstances of the case must be looked at. In *Cadbury Bros Ltd v Sinclair (1933) 18 TC 157*, it was held that a block containing dining facilities and changing rooms, connected by bridges and walkways to a factory, was rightly treated as a single part of an entire complex. However, the reader should be aware that this case considerably pre-dates the introduction of IBAs as we know them. Key features for a successful claim on this basis may include:

(*a*)   a common power supply, water supply or heating system;

(*b*)   the fact that one part cannot be demolished without seriously damaging the other parts;

(*c*)   the impossibility (legally or practically) of selling one part without the others.

7.88   It should be noted that even if a number of buildings are accepted as forming single composite premises, the Revenue's view is that each building must individually satisfy the 25% *de minimis* rule (see 7.80 et seq.) in order to qualify for allowances (CA, para 32750). A block used wholly for administration would fail to attract IBAs, even if its size and cost were minimal compared to the whole site. In such circumstances, allowances might be obtained by moving some qualifying activities to the administration block, with some administrative functions moved to 'qualifying' buildings (provided that did not infringe the *de minimis* rule).

Successive extensions

7.89   When extensions or alterations cause the non-qualifying expenditure on a building to exceed 25% of the total for the first time, no adjustment is required to be made in respect of allowances given in earlier periods. A new *de minimis* calculation must be made following each incurral of expenditure.

Example

7.90 Smith Ltd, which made up its accounts to 31 December each year, operated from a single building, which it built and extended as follows:

	Factory £	Office £	Total £
Construction 1 April 1985	80,000	20,000	100,000
Extension 30 June 1988	—	10,000	10,000
	80,000	30,000	110,000
Extension 4 July 1994	25,000	5,000	30,000
	105,000	35,000	140,000

The effect is:

Accounting periods	Non-qualifying percentage	
1985–87	20%	The whole of the expenditure qualifies for IBAs
1988–93	27%	Only the expenditure on the factory qualifies
From 1994	25%	The whole of the expenditure will qualify as the non-industrial part is 'not more than' one-quarter of the whole

Impact of mixed claims

7.91 Due to the generally higher rate of allowance available, it is normally advisable to claim as much expenditure as possible as plant, rather than as an industrial building. However, if the plant claim is particularly successful, there may be an adverse impact on the *de minimis* calculation.

Example

7.92 Barnes incurs £100,000 on an industrial building, of which £24,000 relates to an office. IBAs will be available on the whole of the expenditure, as the non-qualifying part is less than 25%. Allowances will therefore be at a rate of £4,000 p.a.

7.93   It then occurs to Barnes that expenditure totalling £8,000 (at present treated as industrial) could validly be said to be in respect of items of plant, and he notifies the Revenue of this. However, the net cost of the building is now £92,000, and the non-qualifying part now exceeds 25%. The expenditure must therefore be apportioned, and although overall allowances will be higher in early years, £24,000 of the expenditure will never be relieved at all.

Duality of purpose

7.94   It is possible, of course, for a building as a whole to be in use for a number of purposes, one (or more) of which qualifies for IBAs, whilst the others do not.

7.95   Following the case of *Saxone, Lilley & Skinner (Holdings) Ltd v IRC (1967) 44 TC 122*, it is now established that in such circumstances, allowances will be available on the whole building provided the extent of the qualifying use is not negligible. To paraphrase Lord Reid in that case, the legislation refers only to 'use for the purposes of a trade' — it does not say 'wholly or mainly in use for the purposes of a trade'. Qualifying use is regarded by the Revenue as being negligible if it is less than 10% of the total use (CA, para 32315). This only applies where the part of a building used for a non-qualifying purpose is not separately identifiable. Thus, in the *Saxone, Lilley* case, a warehouse was used to store shoes, one-third of which came within *Sec 274, Table A, item 3(c)*: the storage of goods or materials 'which, having been manufactured or produced ... have not yet been delivered to any purchaser'. The remaining two-thirds of the shoes stored had been bought from third parties and were being stored prior to delivery to retail shops. The predominant use of the warehouse, therefore, did not qualify for allowances. However, because 'qualifying' goods were stored throughout the whole building, the whole building was in use for a qualifying purpose. Any taxpayer who occupies a building for purposes which do not all qualify for allowances will need to ensure, if he can, that the qualifying and non-qualifying areas are not physically segregated.

Example

7.96   Wells carries on a trade falling into two parts. Buildings used for activity A will qualify for IBAs; those used for activity B will not. Wells incurs expenditure on two buildings used as follows:

Building	1	2
Cost	£4 m	£4 m
Percentage Qualifying use	30%	40%

Building 1 contains a separate area dedicated to the non-qualifying use, unlike building 2 where both activities are carried out alongside each other. Allowances will be given as follows.

7.97 *Non-qualifying buildings*

7.97 Building 1 clearly divides into two parts — one qualifies, the other does not. In such circumstances, it will be necessary to apportion the expenditure incurred between the two parts. If the apportioned cost of the non-qualifying part exceeds 25% no allowances in respect of it will be given (see 7.85 et seq. regarding the *de minimis* rule under *Sec 283(2)*). Let us assume (for the purposes of this example only) that the expenditure incurred in respect of the non-qualifying part of the building is in proportion to the intended use (i.e. 30%). Allowances would then only be given for the remaining 70%, i.e. £2.8 million.

7.98 Building 2 does not have any parts used only for non-qualifying purposes. Instead, the whole building can be said to be used for a qualifying purpose, albeit alongside a non-qualifying purpose. As a result, allowances will be given on the whole of the expenditure, i.e. £4 million.

7.99 It should be noted that, as a result of these rules, the greater allowances have been given in respect of the building with the greater non-qualifying use. Such possibilities should be considered when planning a building to be used for more than one purpose. In the example above, we referred to the qualifying percentage. This is normally thought of in terms of, say, floor space, but could equally be calculated on a time or usage basis.

Practical steps to strengthen the claim for allowances

7.100 Where businesses operate at least partly from industrial premises which supply retail shops, certain steps may be taken to strengthen the claim for allowances.

(*a*) *Physical separation.* If possible, the 'industrial' and the 'retail' activities should be carried on from different premises, with no physical link between them. If the cost of the retail premises is less than 25% of the cost of the retail and industrial premises combined, it would be better to group the two in a single building (see 7.80). As was stated in the agreement with the Motor Trade Association referred to at 7.72 above, the public should not have access to any building or part of a building deemed to be industrial.

(*b*) *Legal separation.* It will be of some assistance to the claimant if the 'industrial' and the 'retail' operations are carried out by separate legal entities, e.g. two different companies, albeit in the same group.

7.101 It must be stressed, however, that such steps in themselves do not guarantee the granting of allowances. In addition, such reorganisations of buildings or companies involve issues (and costs) beyond the scope of this book. Capital allowances should never be considered in isolation.

Non-industrial use

General

7.102   A building will only qualify for IBAs in an accounting period if it is in use for one of the prescribed purposes at the end of that accounting period. [*Sec 309(1)(c)*.] For a building which would generally be considered an industrial building, there are three circumstances when the building will not be in qualifying use:

(*a*)   where a building has been completed, but is yet to be used for any purpose;

(*b*)   where a building is, at the end of an accounting period, in use for a non-qualifying purpose; or

(*c*)   where a building is in temporary disuse.

7.103   Each of these sets of circumstances has a different impact on the capital allowances computation.

Buildings yet to be used for any purpose

7.104   The 25-year life of an industrial building will only begin to elapse (and writing-down allowances will only be available) when the building is brought into use. Note that for *agricultural* buildings, this is not the case. Thus, if the construction and fitting out of an industrial building takes more than one year, allowances (other than initial allowances) cannot be claimed in the first year. This will be seen as a disadvantage by most taxpayers, however in most cases the delay is only a temporary one. This provision is necessary to ensure that allowances are not given to taxpayers who have no real intention of using the building for a qualifying purpose.

7.105   A positive aspect, however, is that there is no requirement to account for 'notional' writing-down allowances, as there is in the case of buildings in use for other than a qualifying purpose (see 7.106).

Building used for a non-qualifying purpose

7.106   If a building is, at the end of an accounting period, in use for a purpose which does not attract IBAs, then it is necessary to deduct from the written-down value notional writing-down allowances. [*Sec 336.*] These notional allowances reduce the residue of expenditure that may be carried forward, and hence reduce the total allowances that may be claimed in future. However, the notional allowances themselves may not be treated in such a way as to give relief from tax.

7.107 *Non-industrial use*

Example

7.107 East Ltd. began to construct a building in its year ended 31 December 1991. The building was completed by September 1992, but was only brought into use as a warehouse (qualifying for IBAs) in March 1993. Expenditure on the building was as follows:

	£
Year ended 31.12.91	500
Year ended 31.12.92	1,500

From June 1997 to September 1998, East used the building as a retail shop, before reverting to its original use. Allowances are available as follows:

Year ended 31 December 1991	£
Expenditure	500
Allowances (nil as not yet brought into use)	—
Carried forward	500

Year ended 31 December 1992	
Brought forward	500
Expenditure	1,500
	2,000
Allowances (nil, as still not brought into use)	—
	2,000

Year ended 31 December 1993	
Brought forward	2,000
Allowances (4% — now in use for the first time)	(80)
Carried forward	1,920

Year ended 31 December 1994–96	
Brought forward	1,920
Allowances (3 × 4% of £2 million)	(240)
Carried forward	1,680

Year ended 31 December 1997

Brought forward	1,680
Allowances (NB: this allowance is notional only and may not be offset against profits)	(80)
	1,600

Year ended 31 December 1998

Brought forward	1,600
Allowance	(80)
	1,520

7.108   It is worth pointing out that 'real' allowances are available to reduce profits, despite the fact that for most of the year the building was not in use for a qualifying purpose. The use of a building at the end of the relevant period is the only criterion which decides the availability of allowances. The existence of a period of non-qualifying use will, however, affect the calculation of a balancing allowance or charge (see 11.15 et seq.). If a building is first used for a non-qualifying purpose before subsequently being brought into use for a qualifying purpose, the qualifying expenditure must be reduced by notional allowances in respect of that earlier period of non-qualifying use.

Building let partly to a non-qualifying licensee

7.109   Where a building or structure is used by more than one licensee of the same person, it will not be regarded as 'industrial' for the purposes of allowances unless each of the licensees uses the building (or that part of it to which the licence relates) for a qualifying trade. [*Sec 278.*] This would appear in the first instance to deny allowances for expenditure on a building where even one licensee uses it for a non-qualifying purpose. However, it appears the precise treatment will depend on the circumstances (CA, para 32350). Either there will be completely mixed use of the building, with no part of it used exclusively for non-qualifying trades, or each licensee will use an identifiable part of the building. If the former applies, *Sec 278* will deny any relief. In some ways, this is *Saxone, Lilley* (see 7.95) in reverse. If the latter applies, it is necessary to look at the separate identifiable parts of the building. Allowances will be given in respect of (apportioned) expenditure on those parts of the building used for a qualifying trade. If the non-qualifying parts are not more than 25% of the whole, allowances will be given on the whole of the expenditure by virtue of *Sec 283(2)*.

Temporary disuse

7.110   An industrial building does not cease to be regarded as such simply by reason of temporary disuse (i.e. not being used for any purpose whatsoever). [*Sec 285.*] During a period of temporary disuse, therefore, writing-down allowances continue to be given as normal. Note, however, that this is only the case where the period of disuse is preceded by a period of qualifying use.

7.111   Temporary disuse differs from non-qualifying use in that, where the disuse is only temporary, the allowances given are not merely notional, and can be set against profits in the normal way.

7.112   If, during a period of temporary disuse, there occurs any of the events set out in *Sec 315* then a balancing charge or allowance will be made in the normal manner. A balancing charge will be taxed under Schedule D Case VI (income tax) or under Schedule A (corporation tax).

Chapter 8

Hotels — Special Features

Introduction

8.1   As a rule, hotels offer a much greater scope for capital allowances claims than most other types of building. This is due largely to three reasons.

(*a*)   Hotels are often rich in plant of a type integral to the building. This is discussed in more detail in Chapter 15, but typical examples will be:

    (i)   lifts;

    (ii)   air-conditioning;

    (iii)   heating;

    (iv)   sanitary equipment;

    (v)   signs;

    (vi)   fire detection equipment.

(*b*)   Hotels will often include other assets which are not generally found in other buildings, and which will be regarded as plant in their own right, without applying any special principles. For example:

    (i)   swimming pools;

    (ii)   gymnasium equipment;

    (iii)   laundry equipment.

(*c*)   Hotels can claim plant allowances on a whole variety of assets aimed at creating an ambience (for example, works of art, bric-a-brac). Such a claim would not be possible in, for example, an office. See 8.2 below.

(*d*)   Hotels of a certain type can qualify for industrial buildings allowances. See 8.3 below.

Ambience

8.2   Nothing in the statute expressly permits assets to be regarded as plant for capital allowances purposes simply because they contribute to creating a certain ambience or atmosphere. Rather, the eligibility of such assets is an extension of general principles, as set out in the case of *CIR v Scottish & Newcastle Breweries Ltd (1982) 55 TC 252*, where the taxpayer, carrying on the trade of a hotelier, incurred significant expenditure on lighting and decor (such as murals and sculptures) in its licensed premises. These items were successfully claimed as plant. The Special Commissioners found that the company's trade was not just the provision of food and accommodation, but also the creation of atmosphere or ambience, conducive to attracting custom. The importance of attracting custom had already been shown to be relevant for plant allowances purposes in the case of a swimming pool in *Cooke v Beach Station Caravans Ltd [1974] STC 402*, which was found to perform the active function of attracting visitors to a caravan park. The Special Commissioners' view in *Scottish & Newcastle Breweries* was ultimately upheld in the House of Lords. In consequence of this decision, decorative items in hotels, restaurants and public houses may qualify as plant. The same items would not, of course, be plant if purchased by anyone carrying on a trade of which the provision of hospitality (and therefore ambience) was not a fundamental part. This was effectively stressed by Lord Wilberforce in the *Scottish & Newcastle* case:

> 'In the end each case must be resolved, in my opinion, by considering carefully the nature of the particular trade being carried on, and the relation of the expenditure to the promotion of the trade.'

8.3   Anyone acquiring or refurbishing a hotel should therefore consider to what extent individual assets contribute (whether actively or passively) to the ambience or atmosphere, whether that is one of luxury, homeliness or liveliness.

Buildings allowances

8.4   With effect from 12 April 1978 expenditure on a *qualifying hotel* has qualified on the same basis (with slight modification) as an industrial building. [*Sec 271(1)(b)(ii)*.] A qualifying hotel is a hotel which complies with the following requirements:

(*a*)   The accommodation is in a building of a permanent nature (which is likely to exclude caravan sites, etc.). It is irrelevant that the hotel might consist of more than one building as long as all of the buildings are used for the same trade and are (broadly) at the same location, enabling them to be regarded by the guests as all part of the one hotel.

(*b*)   It is open for at least four months during April to October (see below).

(*c*)   During that time:

   (i)   it has at least ten letting bedrooms;

   (ii)   the sleeping accommodation offered at the hotel consists wholly or mainly of letting bedrooms (see below); and

   (iii)   the services provided (see below) for guests normally include the provision of breakfast and an evening meal, the making of beds and the cleaning of rooms. [*Sec 279.*]

The season

8.5 The 'season' is the period from April to October, inclusive, which would exclude a hotel open only for winter seasons (or, remembering that IBAs may be given to buildings sited overseas, to hotels open in the summer months of the southern hemisphere). Such a hotel could qualify for allowances if it remained open in the season, but operated on a reduced basis (e.g. no entertainment, pool or hairdresser). The value of the allowances must be measured against the additional costs of staff, heating, etc. The Revenue has stated that in practice 120 days would be regarded as equivalent to four months (CCAB TR 308). It should be noted that out of season there are no restrictions on the use of the accommodation.

Letting bedrooms

8.6 A 'letting bedroom' is a private bedroom available for letting to the public generally and not normally in the same occupation for more than one month. [*Sec 279(9)*.] A hotel with a large residential guest list could, therefore, be in difficulty with this rule. 'Public' means just that and will exclude clubs, hostels and similar premises open only to members or specified groups of people. As accommodation in a qualifying hotel must consist wholly or mainly of letting bedrooms, a large establishment which otherwise would not qualify cannot do so merely by setting aside ten or more bedrooms for use by the general public. The possibility of 'hiving off' the hotel function should therefore be considered in appropriate cases.

Provision of services

8.7 The Revenue has stated that the mere availability of services would not satisfy the test in *Sec 279(1)(c)(iii)*: there had to be reasonable use (CCAB TR 308). However, in Statement of Practice SP 9/87, of which the following is an extract, the Revenue adopted a revised interpretation of the meals requirement:

'Hitherto, the Revenue view of the meals requirement has been that, while it would not expect that all guests should actually consume such meals, mere availability of breakfast and an evening meal was not sufficient.

The Revenue have now decided that they will regard the test as satisfied where the offering of breakfast and dinner is normal in the hotel's carrying on of its business. The Revenue will not regard it as satisfied where the service of meals is exceptional, eg if either breakfast or an evening meal is available only on request.'

Expenditure incurred before 12 April 1978

8.8 Expenditure incurred before 12 April 1978 cannot qualify for hotel allowances. *Secs 295(3)* and *296(4)* (which refer to expenditure being deemed to have been incurred on a date later than that on which it was actually incurred) do not apply, when ascertaining entitlement to allowances, to deem expenditure on hotels to have been incurred after 11 April 1978 if, in fact, it was incurred on or before that date. [*Sch 3, para 58.*]

Conversion costs

8.9   The cost of converting an existing building into a hotel can qualify in the same manner as construction expenditure. This applies equally where a non-qualifying hotel is converted into a qualifying one, for example by beginning to open during the 'season'.

8.10   Furthermore, where a hotel is extended so that for the first time it has ten or more bedrooms, allowances will be available on earlier expenditure, provided it was incurred after 11 April 1978. In such circumstances, the qualifying expenditure will be written-down by allowances representing the previous period of non-qualifying use.

Meaning of 'hotel'

8.11   There is no statutory definition of a hotel for the purpose of capital allowances so it is necessary to have regard to what is commonly regarded as such. Usually the answer lies in the consideration of a 'bundle' of facts. It is clear that a hotel is something more than a collection of rooms which are let without any other type of service whatsoever. Many roadside restaurants have a separate residential block in which a furnished room can be booked without the right (or the requirement) to enjoy any services other than basic accommodation. Such arrangements would not generally amount to the provision of hotel services, but allowances have, in practice, been granted.

8.12   A hotel is normally evidenced by the provision of hospitality which in turn is normally evidenced by the availability, at no extra charge, of room service in the form of bed-making and other 'creature comforts' and the availability of facilities such as 'public' rooms and lounges available to all residents. The decision in *CIR v Scottish & Newcastle Breweries Ltd (1982) 55 TC 252* (see above) indicates that a hotel normally provides a degree of ambience in its decor. The Revenue accepts that an establishment is a hotel if it meets the requirements of the *Sec 1(3)* of the *Hotel Proprietors Act 1956*, i.e. it is:

'held out by the proprietor as offering food and drink and, if so required, sleeping accommodation, without special contract, to any traveller presenting himself who appears able and willing to pay a reasonable sum for the services and facilities provided and who is in a fit state to be received.'

8.13   Many hotels are now part of a complex providing a wide range of conference and/or recreational activities. It is often difficult to decide whether the hotel is part of the latter or the latter is part of the hotel. If possible, it is best to ensure that the hotel operates as the 'umbrella' organisation managing in some way the provision of the leisure facilities with special terms for its residents.

Creation of a leasehold

8.14　An election under *Sec 290*, transferring allowances to a lessee, may be made in respect of a hotel (see 10.6 et seq.).

Staff welfare

8.15　Buildings provided for the welfare of workers can be included in a claim irrespective of whether they are on the same site or separate buildings. [*Sec 279(7)*.] The Revenue has confirmed that this provision covers hostels which employees occupied but was not intended to give relief for flats and houses provided for the individual employees.

8.16　However, where the running of a hotel is carried on by an individual, either alone or in partnership, any living accommodation normally occupied by him or his family when the hotel is open during the season is excluded. [*Sec 279(8)*.] Where accommodation was excluded by this provision there will be no restriction of allowances provided the 25% rule (see 7.80 et seq.) is satisfied (CCAB TR 308).

Actual use

8.17　A qualifying hotel must be in use for the purposes of a trade carried on by the claimant or a lessee throughout a period of 12 months. Such a period will normally be the 12 months ending with the last day of a chargeable period or its basis period [*Sec 279(3)*] but if the hotel was first used on a date after the beginning of that period, the period throughout which such use must extend will be the 12 months beginning on that date. [*Sec 279(4)*.] If during the period of 12 months just mentioned, a hotel had fewer than ten letting bedrooms until a date which was too late for it to qualify by reference to those 12 months, it may instead qualify by reference to the 12 months beginning on that date. [*Sec 279(5)*.]

Example

8.18　The Restawhile Hotel Ltd commenced to trade on 1 January 1994. Its accounting date is 31 December. The hotel has complied with the definition of a qualifying hotel in all respects except that prior to 30 June 1997 it had only eight letting bedrooms. The status of the hotel is as follows:

8.18   *Building allowances*

(*a*)   Accounting periods to 31 December 1997, 1998 and 1999 — non-qualifying for all years.

(*b*)   Accounting period to 31 December 2000 — qualifying hotel by virtue of *Sec 279(5)* because it has complied with the definition in *Sec 279(1)* for 12 months beginning on 30 June 2000.

(*c*)   Accounting period to 31 December 2001 — qualifying hotel by virtue of *Sec 279(3)* because it has complied with the definition for the whole of its accounting period.

If the hotel had ceased to qualify in March 2001, it would not meet the requirements of *Sec 279(5)* for a full 12 months of qualifying use. No allowances would therefore be available.

Allowances and charges

8.19   The writing-down allowance is 4%, as for industrial buildings. [*Sec 310.*] It continues during any period of temporary disuse until two years after the end of the chargeable period or basis period in which the temporary disuse commenced. [*Sec 317(4).*] The writing-down allowance then ceases.

8.20   A balancing adjustment arises on the occurrence of any of the events specified for industrial buildings in *Sec 315* (see 11.4). It is irrelevant whether, at that time, the building is a qualifying hotel. If the event is the sale of the relevant interest (see 7.18 et seq.) the writing-down allowance is re-computed as for an industrial building (see 4.5 et seq.). If none of the events specified in *Sec 315* occurs and a period of two years elapses during which the building is not a qualifying hotel, the relevant interest therein must be deemed to have been sold at the end of that period at its market value and a balancing allowance or charge calculated accordingly. [*Sec 317(2).*] The deemed sale may occur up to (almost) five years after the building ceased to be a qualifying hotel given that the temporary disuse provisions may operate for the first (almost) three years.

This 'two-year rule' does not apply to hotels in enterprise zones. [*Sec 317(5).*]

Chapter 9

Enterprise Zones

Introduction

9.1   There are a small number of specially designated areas where, in addition to other privileges, an initial allowance of 100% is available for new building. The designation of enterprise zones is generally reserved for what are considered areas of special need (see Appendix 3).

Allowances available

9.2   A building in an enterprise zone will, provided the appropriate conditions are met, attract a 100% initial allowance [*Sec 306*] against qualifying enterprise zone expenditure. [*Secs 298, 299, 300.*] No allowances are available, however, for the cost of the land itself. If the building is never completed, and construction is permanently abandoned, the initial allowance is withdrawn. [*Sec 307.*] If, on the other hand, construction work is halted temporarily, for example during a recession in trade, the allowance will not be withdrawn.

9.3   A taxpayer may choose to limit his claim to a specified amount, or indeed not claim the allowance at all. [*Sec 306(2).*] Where less than the whole initial allowance is claimed, the balance of expenditure is available as a writing-down allowance of 25% p.a. on a straight line basis. [*Sec 310(1)(a).*] Such writing-down allowances only commence when the building is brought into use. Use is not a pre-requisite for the initial allowance to be given.

9.4   Writing-down allowances may be disclaimed in any particular year [*Sec 309(2)*], in which case they are available in later years, still at the rate of 25%.

9.5   Despite the accelerated rate of allowances compared to buildings elsewhere, buildings in enterprise zones nonetheless have a 25-year tax life and a claw-back of allowances may be possible if the building is sold within that time. See Chapter 11 for the treatment of the sale of property. It should also be noted that a subsequent purchaser (within the 25 years) will be entitled to allowances, on the same basis as with any other 'industrial' building — see 4.5.

9.6   Because enterprise zone property is often seen primarily as an investment-based tax shelter, it is perhaps more likely than is normally the case, that a person claiming allowances will be incurring expenditure on a building that he does not intend to occupy for his own trade. If the intention is to let the building to tenants, the allowances will be given as an expense of that rental business. [*Sec 353.*] In order to make enterprise zone allowances available to smaller investors, the concept of an Enterprise Zone Property Unit Trust (EZPUT) was created. If investment is made via such a vehicle, it nonetheless remains the individual investors who are entitled to the allowances (CA, para 39700).

Time limit on expenditure

9.7   To qualify for the special allowances, expenditure must be incurred:

(*a*)   within ten years of the enterprise zone first being designated as such, or

(*b*)   under a contract entered into within the ten-year period, provided the expenditure is actually incurred not more than 20 years after such designation. [*Sec 298.*]

9.8   In cases falling within (*b*) above, Inspectors are instructed to consider the validity of the contract and whether the building ultimately constructed is that which was originally contracted for. If changes have been made, the Revenue will be concerned to see that they are indeed merely variations of the original contract, rather than constituting an entirely new contract (CA, para 37150).

Extent of enterprise zones

9.9   Enterprise zones generally cover only a relatively small area, for example, individual industrial estates. The initial allowance does not extend to the rest of the town or area. Details of current enterprise zones are given at Appendix 3.

9.10   It must be stressed that the boundaries of enterprise zones are not flexible — it is possible to miss out on the initial allowance simply by building on one side of the road rather than the other, and if a building straddles the boundary, then the expenditure must be apportioned into qualifying and non-qualifying parts (CA, para 37390). The *de minimis* rule (see 7.80 et seq.) is not relevant.

9.11   A building already situated in what is subsequently designated as an enterprise zone will not qualify for the initial allowance, because qualifying expenditure may only be incurred during the ten-year life of the zone. Additions to such a building carried out during the life of the zone may also fail to attract the initial allowance, because the extent of the enterprise zone may well have been designated in such a way as to exclude existing buildings.

The onus is on the would-be claimant to make sure his building falls within the zone.

Qualifying buildings

General

9.12   Enterprise zone allowances are a form of industrial buildings allowances, and are given in respect of buildings and structures that would otherwise qualify for IBAs under *Sec 274* (see 7.22 et seq.). However, the range of buildings qualifying in an enterprise zone extends beyond this. *Sec 271(1)(b)(iv)* extends allowances to commercial buildings and structures.

Commercial buildings

9.13   A commercial building is defined by *Sec 281* as a building which is used for the purpose of a trade, profession or vocation or, whether or not for such a purpose, as an office or offices.

9.14   Unusually, an office may qualify despite not being used for a trade. Expenditure on a building which is occupied by, for example, a charity will therefore qualify for allowances.

9.15   One type of building that will seldom, if ever, qualify for enterprise zone allowances is the 'dwelling-house', that is to say, houses, flats and other properties used for residential purposes. The one exception to this is where the dwelling-house is classified as industrial by being part of a larger qualifying building and representing not more than 25% of the total cost thereof. [*Sec 283(2)*.] This provision often removes the need, for example, to calculate and disallow that part of the expenditure relating to a care-taker's lodging.

Hotels

9.16   To qualify for 'normal' IBAs, a hotel must fulfil certain conditions, for example having a minimum of ten letting bedrooms [*Sec 279*] — see 8.6. However smaller hotels or establishments operating in a slightly different way (e.g. motels) will qualify for allowances in enterprise zones. This is because they may nonetheless qualify under the heading of commercial buildings.

9.17   It is important however not to fall into the trap of assuming that all types of building providing lodging can be brought under the broad umbrella of hotels. The Revenue has, for example, resisted claims for allowances on time-share apartments on the grounds that they constituted a dwelling-house (see 7.68 et seq.).

Change of use

9.18   The person incurring the expenditure does not have to occupy the building himself, but may grant a lease or licence without suffering any withdrawal of allowances [*Sec 305*], unless he realises a *capital value* [*Sec 328*] (see 11.26 et seq.).

9.19   Any change of use of a building which has previously qualified for enterprise zone allowances will be ignored with the one exception of commencement of use as a dwelling-house.

9.20   Should a building begin to be used as a dwelling-house, writing-down allowances, if any, will be suspended but there will be no balancing adjustment. This effectively means that where the 100% initial allowance has been claimed, any change of use to that of a dwelling-house is without any immediate effect for capital allowances purposes. This rule is in any case not invoked if the dwelling represents no more than 25% of the whole building.

Plant

9.21   One area of interest will be the treatment of plant which becomes an integral part of an enterprise building, and could arguably qualify either for plant allowances or buildings allowances. The normal priorities of the investor are reversed, of course, by the existence of a 100% initial allowance for expenditure on buildings. Outside enterprise zones, the priority is normally to have as much of the total expenditure as possible classified as plant, in order to obtain the writing-down allowances of 25% p.a., as opposed to 4% on industrial buildings (and nothing at all on commercial buildings). Where an initial enterprise zone allowance is available, the incentive is to classify all debatable expenditure as building. Fortunately, there should be no major disputes on this point, because although *Sec 7* excludes the possibility of claiming more than one type of allowance on the same expenditure, it does not specify any order of precedence. Consequently, where a taxpayer is entitled to the 100% initial allowance, he may choose to treat as qualifying expenditure any amounts spent on the provision of machinery or plant which is an integral part of the building.

9.22   The question arises of whether plant is actually attached to a building. Consider, for example, storage racking in an enterprise zone property. If the racking is free-standing and would be removed upon vacation of the building, it would not qualify for the 100% allowance. If, however, the racking were fixed to the building and would remain in the building through a succession of tenants, the enterprise zone allowances should be available.

9.23   Expenditure on the thermal insulation of a building in an enterprise zone will be treated as expenditure on the building. *Sec 28*, which would normally treat such expenditure as being on the provision of machinery or plant, does not apply.

Purchase of a completed building

9.24   In most enterprise developments, it is not the case that the individual or company looking to claim allowances will themselves be incurring expenditure on the construction of a building. It is more likely that they will be purchasing a completed building from a developer. The 'history' of an enterprise zone development is likely to be similar to the following scenario.

(*a*)   The freehold interest in the site is owned by an enterprise zone authority.

(*b*)   The authority enters into a building agreement with a developer.

(*c*)   Under the terms of such an agreement, the developer is obliged to construct a building, and in return, is entitled to call for the transfer of an interest in the land upon completion of the development.

(*d*)   The interest transferred may be the interest held by the authority or a long lease granted out of it, and the developer may have the right to have that interest granted to a named third party, rather than to itself.

(*e*)   The developer will incur these costs on trading account, and will not itself be eligible for capital allowances.

(*f*)   At this stage, if not before, the developer will seek investors to whom he can sell the building in order to make his profit.

(*g*)   In order to make the investment more attractive, the developer may also be prepared to give some form of rental guarantee.

The importance and meaning of use

9.25   The treatment of an acquisition will depend on whether or not the building has been 'used', and whether the purchase takes place within two years of first use. In the context of deciding whether a building is unused, 'use' means use for any purpose and not just for a purpose qualifying for IBAs. 'Use', however, does not include occupation by a tenant for fitting out by that tenant prior to the commencement of actual production or other use. The fitting-out process is regarded by the Revenue as merely the completion of construction.

Purchase of an unused building before expiry of the zone

9.26   The most straightforward situation will be where an investor purchases an unused building directly from a developer before the expiry of the enterprise zone. In such circumstances, *Sec 296(2)* requires the construction expenditure actually incurred (by the developer) to be ignored, and instead the investor is deemed to have incurred expenditure on construction on the date on which the purchase price becomes payable.

9.27   Where the building is purchased directly from a developer, the amount paid by the investor will be the amount qualifying for allowances. Where, however, the building is purchased not from the developer, but from an intermediary, the expenditure qualifying for allowances will be the lower of the amount paid by the investor, and the amount paid to the developer on the sale of his interest. [*Sec 296(3)*.] The effect of this is to give allowances based on original cost plus developer's profit, but not on the profit of any intermediary.

9.28   Where the vendor of the building is not a developer, but, for example, a trader who intended the building for his own use but has changed his mind, then that vendor's profit is excluded from expenditure qualifying for allowances. The new investor will only be able to claim allowances on the lower of the amount he pays for the interest, and the actual expenditure incurred in the original construction of the building. [*Sec 295(2)*.] A building purchased directly from a developer may therefore be worth more in terms of allowances than an identical building purchased from someone else because qualifying expenditure in respect of the former will be augmented by the developer's profit. The purchaser will therefore need to be certain that the vendor is a genuine developer. This fact should not just be assumed, and a warranty of this fact may well be required.

9.29   Where only part of a building has been brought into use, there are two possibilities:

(*a*)   the whole building will be regarded as having been brought into use, or

(*b*)   only the relevant part of the building will be regarded as having been used, in consequence of which any expenditure will be apportioned between the 'used' part and the 'unused' part, and each part of the expenditure dealt with separately.

9.30   The question of which is the correct treatment will depend on the circumstances. The former treatment is likely to be appropriate where, for example, the person constructing the building is the sole user but chooses not to occupy the whole. Where, however, a building is divided into distinct units and only some of those units are let, it may be possible to adopt the alternative treatment.

Purchase of unused building after expiry of zone

9.31   Where an enterprise zone building is sold before being brought into use (but after the expiry of the zone), then the actual expenditure is in the first instance ignored for the purposes of calculating allowances, and instead the purchaser is entitled to allowances based on a deemed amount of expenditure. This deemed amount will be the lesser of the price paid by him or the actual expenditure on construction. [*Sec 295*.] Furthermore, where construction operations continued after the expiry of the zone, the deemed amount qualifying for allowances will be restricted to reflect the proportion of work undertaken before that expiry. [*Sec 302*.]

Example

9.32   Lovell incurred expenditure on the construction of an office building in an enterprise zone which was first designated as such on 24 April 1984. The expenditure is analysed as follows:

	£	
Land	200,000	20 December 1993
Building	500,000	20 December 1993
Extension	100,000	15 May 1994

The 100% initial allowance was claimed but before use commenced, the building was sold to Marian and Terry on 4 July 1994 for £650,000, of which £200,000 related to the land. The effect of the sale on allowances is as follows:

(*a*)   Lovell: the 100% allowance given will be claimed back.

(*b*)   Marian and Terry: the expenditure qualifying for allowances is:

$$\text{Qualifying expenditure} \times \frac{\text{The part of the construction expenditure incurred within the time limit}}{\text{Total expenditure on construction}}$$

i.e.

$$450,000 \times \frac{500,000}{600,000} = £375,000$$

9.33   Marian and Terry will be able to claim an initial allowance of £375,000 in the chargeable period in which they purchased the building. Where the building is sold more than once before being brought into use, the provisions of *Sec 302* only have effect as regards the last of those sales. In all cases the rules contained in this section are subject to *Sec 298*, that is, that expenditure must be incurred within 20 years of the enterprise zone first being designated as such.

Purchase within two years of first use

9.34   For expenditure incurred on or after 16 December 1991, the 100% initial allowance is also available to the purchaser of a *used* building, provided that the building was first used not more than two years before the purchase. [*Sec 303.*]

9.35   As with the purchase of an unused building after the expiry of the zone, the amount of expenditure qualifying for initial allowances will be calculated by reference to that proportion of the construction work undertaken during the ten-year life of the zone. The provisions of *Sec 303* apply only to the first sale of the relevant interest after the building has been brought into use, and operate regardless of whether the interest was sold before the building was first used. [*Sec 303(1)(d).*]

9.36   It should be noted that if the sale of the relevant interest takes place more than two years after the building was first used, the purchaser will be entitled to neither the initial allowance nor the enhanced 25% writing-down allowance. Instead, the writing-down allowance will be calculated so as to write off the residue of expenditure over the balance of the building's 25-year life.

9.37   Clearly, any potential purchaser of a used building will need to know exactly when that building was brought into use, and may well require a warranty to be given in this regard by the vendor (see 9.39). On the other hand, the vendor himself may be holding out the availability of enterprise zone allowances as an inducement to potential purchasers, and so he too will need to establish the date of first use.

9.38   One inherent problem is that 'use' has not yet been satisfactorily defined. The Revenue has indicated that it does not regard a building as having come into use simply because it is occupied by a tenant who is fitting it out.

Warranties

9.39   The purchaser of an enterprise zone building will need to seek certain warranties from the vendor, in order to establish that the allowances available will be as expected. These warranties include the following:

•   Confirmation that the whole site is or was in an enterprise zone, so that expenditure will not need to be apportioned into a qualifying and non-qualifying part.

•   Confirmation that the whole of the developer's expenditure was incurred prior to the expiry of the zone, again to prevent any need for apportionment of expenditure into qualifying and non-qualifying elements.

•   Confirmation that the vendor is a genuine property developer and has been accepted by the Revenue as such, or alternatively details of the circumstances of acquisition by the vendor.

•   Confirmation that the building has not been brought into use, or that it has been used for less than two years (in which case precise dates should be given).

•   Agreement by the vendor to provide the purchaser with all information necessary for the submission of a claim for allowances.

•   Details of any other interests in the property.

Chapter 10

Property Investors — Specific Issues

Introduction

10.1   For most types of capital allowance, it is not a requirement that the assets should be used, or the premises occupied, by the person incurring the expenditure. The effect of this is that allowances are available, in appropriate circumstances, to property investors, as well as to owner-occupiers.

10.2   An exception to this rule is the case of scientific research allowances, where there is a specific requirement that the expenditure is related to the trade of the person incurring the expenditure. Where a property investor (very often a group property company holding properties occupied and used by its trading associates) incurs expenditure on an asset to be used for scientific research by its tenant, that requirement is unlikely to be met.

Buildings

10.3   Buildings held by a property investor will, if they are to qualify for allowances, have to meet the same conditions as those held by owner-occupiers. In essence, this means allowances will only be available for:

(*a*)   industrial buildings (see Chapter 7);

(*b*)   qualifying hotels (see Chapter 8); and

(*c*)   commercial buildings in enterprise zones (see Chapter 9).

10.4   The broad requirement is merely that the building is in use for a qualifying purpose at the end of a chargeable period, whether by the owner or by a tenant, licensee, etc. The landlord therefore needs to ascertain, when considering a potential tenant, whether that tenant's trade will enable the building to qualify for allowances. All else being equal, it will be advantageous to select a tenant who is carrying on a qualifying trade, rather than one who is not.

10.5   Similarly, it is worth stressing that in order to qualify for a full year's allowances, the property need only be in qualifying use on the last day of that year. Depending on the circumstances, it may be worth offering an additional incentive to ensure that a tenancy begins shortly before the end of one year, rather than at the start of the next. The landlord should be mindful, however, that a building needs to actually be *in use* (see 7.22 et seq.). It is not sufficient that a tenant has moved into the building and is fitting it out for his own needs.

Transferring allowances to lessee

10.6   Where a long lease is granted out of the relevant interest in an industrial building, the allowances generally remain with the holder of the relevant interest. However, the lessor and lessee may elect jointly to transfer the right to allowances to the lessee, where the new lease is for a period which exceeds 50 years. [*Sec 290(1)*.] The long lease is then regarded as the relevant interest, and any capital sum paid by the lessee in consideration of the grant of the lease is regarded as consideration for purchase of that relevant interest. [*Sec 290(2)*.] The capital sum must be apportioned between land and buildings, so that the former can be excluded from the claim for allowances (CA, para 12300).

See proforma election, Appendix 5.

10.7   The election must be made within two years after the date on which the lease takes effect. [*Sec 291(4)*.] Inspectors were formerly instructed to refuse a late election unless, within the two years, there has been a clear indication of an intention to elect, or all parties concerned have submitted computations on the basis that such an election has been or will be made. This concession now appears to have been removed, making a formal election essential (CA, para 33100). An election is not possible where:

(*a*)   the lessor and the lessee are connected [*Sec 291(1)*] (see 19.13–19.19); or

(*b*)   it appears that the sole or main benefit which may be expected to accrue to the lessor from the grant of the lease and the making of an election is the obtaining of a balancing allowance [*Sec 291(2)*] (see 11.4 et seq.).

10.8   Condition (*a*) above will not prevent an election being made where the lessor is a body discharging statutory functions and the lessee a company of which it has control. [*Sec 291(1)*.]

10.9   No such election is possible where construction is yet to commence [*Sec 290(1)(a)*].

Plant

General

10.10   Expenditure on plant will qualify for allowances if it is incurred for the purposes of a qualifying activity (see 13.18). This includes property letting.

10.11   Where a lessor incurs expenditure on fire safety, relief is given by ESC B16.

10.12   Expenditure incurred by a property investor on fixtures in a let building does not qualify for first-year allowances (see 13.10).

Fixtures

The basic problem and its solution

10.13   Prior to 11 July 1984, where a person (normally a lessee) incurred expenditure on an item of machinery or plant (e.g. a lift or heating system) which formed part of a building he did not own, no allowances were strictly available. This anomaly, brought to public attention by *Stokes v Costain Property Investments Ltd (1984) 57 TC 688*, resulted from the application of general property law and its interaction with specific capital allowances legislation. In brief, such fixtures, being inseparable from the building, became the property of the owner of the building. Capital allowances were not therefore available to the person incurring the expenditure because the building, and hence the fixtures, did not belong to him as required by *Sec 11(4)(a)*. Nor could the landlord claim allowances, for although he owned the building, and hence, under general land law principles, owned the fixtures, he had not incurred the expenditure. Concern regarding this perceived injustice eventually led to the specific rules on fixtures which now make up *CAA 2001, Pt 2, Chap 14.*

FA 2001 removed the requirement for the person incurring expenditure to have an interest in land, where that person is an energy services provider. [*FA 2001, Sec 66, Sch 18 —* see 17.25.]

The nature of fixtures

10.14   A fixture is defined by *Sec 173(1)* as:

(*a*)   'plant or machinery that is so installed or otherwise fixed in or to a building or other description of land as to become, in law, part of that building or other land', and

(*b*)   'includes any boiler or water-filled radiator installed in a building as part of a space or water heating system'.

This is most commonly applied to lifts, heating systems, air-conditioning, telephone systems and wiring although the net can be stretched wider. Where any question arises as to whether any machinery or plant has become, in law, part of a building or other land and that question is material with respect to the liability to tax (for whatever period) of two or more persons, that question is determined, for the purposes of the tax of all those persons, by the Special Commissioners. [*Sec 204(1)–(3).*]

10.15   The case of *J C Decaux (UK) Ltd v Francis [1996] STC (SCD) 281* considered the distinction between chattels and fixtures. Key factors were held to be the degree of annexation to the land and, most importantly, the object of that annexation. This approach is reflected in Revenue guidance. In *Decaux*, the essential question was whether the items (automated public conveniences, bus shelters etc.) were fixed for the better enjoyment of the items themselves, or whether they were installed as an amenity or feature of the land to which the public had recourse.

10.16 The question of what constitutes a fixture is more usually a question of land law, rather than revenue law, and full consideration of this subject is therefore beyond the scope of this work. However, a useful summary of the relevant law (since 1872) is to be found in *Botham v TSB Bank plc (1976) 73 P & CR D1, CA; Holland v Hodgson (1872) LR 7 CP 328* and *Berkley v Poulett (1976) 241 Estates Gazette 911, CA*.

10.17 Following the *Decaux* case above, *FA 1997, Sch 16* directed that where affixation to the land is merely incidental, allowances are available on leased fixtures irrespective of whether the lessee is carrying on a trade. For this to apply, the following conditions must be met:

(*a*) the plant is fixed to land (and not to a building);

(*b*) the equipment lessee has an interest in that land (see 10.19) at the time he takes possession of the plant;

(*c*) the plant may be severed from the land (and will belong to the lessor) at the end of the lease;

(*d*) the plant is of type which may be re-used following such severance;

(*e*) the lease is accounted for as an operating lease.

[*Sec 179.*]

10.18 In *Melluish v BMI (No 3) Ltd [1995] STC 964*, it was held, following the non-tax case *Hobson v Gorringe [1897] 1 Ch 182*, that the intention of the parties as to the ownership of fixtures was only material so far as such intention could be presumed from the degree and object of the affixation. The contractual terms between the parties could not affect the question of whether, in law, a chattel had become a fixture and therefore belonged to the owner of the land.

10.19 Various provisions require the person incurring expenditure to have an 'interest in land'. This is defined as:

(*a*) the fee simple estate or an agreement to acquire such estate (generally the freehold);

(*b*) a lease or (except in the context of leasing plant and machinery) an agreement to acquire a lease (defined in *Sec 174*);

(*c*) Scottish equivalents of the above;

(*d*) an easement or servitude or an agreement to acquire such an interest; or

(*e*) a licence to occupy land provided it is an exclusive licence (CA 26100).

[*Sec 175.*]

10.20 The Revenue has confirmed that where a tenant is permitted to occupy land without a formal lease or licence, that nonetheless qualifies as an interest in land for this purpose.

10.21 The reference in (*b*) to leasing machinery or plant must relate to plant leased as a trade, separate from any building to which it is fixed. It cannot apply to fixtures in a let property, as to do so would be for *Sec 175* to contradict itself.

Expenditure on 'new' fixtures

10.22 *Sec 176* applies where the holder of an *existing* interest in land (see *J C Decaux (UK) Ltd v Francis* below) incurs expenditure on 'new' fixtures. Such fixtures are treated as belonging to the person incurring the expenditure.

10.23 In the case of *J C Decaux (UK) Ltd v Francis [1996] STC (SCD) 281*, it was confirmed that the interest must be in place when the expenditure is incurred, it is not sufficient that it comes into being upon, and as a result of, the incurring of the expenditure. However, a formal agreement to create such an interest may itself enable allowances to be under (*a*) or (*b*) in 10.19.

Expenditure on fixtures incurred by equipment lessor

10.24 Chapter 17 (17.15 et seq.) deals with the situation where machinery or plant which becomes a fixture is not owned by the tenant of the building, but rather is leased to him by a third party (i.e. not the owner of the building or indeed anyone with an interest in the building).

Acquisition of existing interest in land — 'second-hand' fixtures

10.25 The person who first installs fixtures in a building is catered for by *Sec 176* (see 10.19 et seq.). Where a building is sold second hand for an amount which includes a capital sum in respect of existing fixtures, those fixtures are treated as belonging to the purchaser. [*Sec 181.*] This treatment also applies where a purchaser of an interest in land pays a capital sum to discharge the obligations of an equipment lessee to whom the fixtures were previously let. [*Sec 182.*] However, allowances are denied if another person has an interest in the same land, was treated as owning the fixtures prior to the sale, is entitled to an allowance in respect of those fixtures, and has made such a claim [*Sec 182(2)*].

10.26 The amount qualifying for allowances may be restricted by reference to original cost. [*Sec 185.*] The practical implications of this are considered in 4.15 et seq.

10.27   Plant

Creation of a new interest in land — 'second-hand' fixtures

10.27   *Lessor entitled to allowances.* Sec 181 (above) covers the situation where an existing interest in a building changes hands. *Sec 183* deals with the creation of a new lease where the incoming lessee pays a capital sum for existing fixtures. In such circumstances, the lessor and lessee may elect jointly for the fixtures to be treated as belonging to the lessee provided that the lessor would have been entitled to allowances on the fixtures in the chargeable period (or its basis period) in which the lease was granted. A lessor who cannot fulfil this condition through not being within the charge to tax (e.g. a pension fund) will be regarded as being within the charge to tax for this purpose. [*Sec 183(1)(b)*.] The election must be made within two years of the lease taking effect. However no election may be made if the parties are connected. [*Sec 183(1)(d)*.] Note that it is the lessor's position and not that of the lessee which is important here.

See proforma election, Appendix 5.

10.28   *Lessor not entitled to allowances.* Where the lessor was not entitled to allowances (other than simply through not being within the charge to tax) the fixtures are treated as belonging to the lessee, who will then be entitled to capital allowances, but only if:

(*a*)   at the time the lease is granted no person has previously been entitled to allowances; and

(*b*)   if the fixture has not been used for the purposes of a trade by the lessor or a connected person [*Sec 184.*].

Allowances will be denied where another interest in the land exists, and the person with that interest was treated as owning the fixtures prior to the sale, has made a claim, and remains entitled to claim allowances on those fixtures — a 'prior right'. [*Sec 184(2).*]

10.29   In *West Somerset Railway v Chivers [1995] STC (SCD) 1*, the onus of proving that no person had previously been entitled to allowances was held to fall on the claimant. This is also relevant where *Sec 185* is in point (see 4.17).

Example

10.30   A Plc is a property developer. During 1993 it incurred expenditure of £2 million in erecting an office building including £50,000 in respect of air-conditioning. In 1996 the building was leased at a premium to B. Of the total premium £75,000 was allocated to the air-conditioning.

10.31   B will obtain capital allowances on the £75,000 for although A Plc was not entitled to allowances (its own expenditure was on trading account and not capital), the fixtures have not been used for the purpose of A Plc's trade.

10.32   Where the property acquired includes fixtures which have previously been involved in a claim for IBAs or scientific research allowances, the qualifying expenditure is also restricted [*Secs 186, 187*] — see 4.19.

Deemed disposal of fixtures

10.33   A person claiming capital allowances on fixtures is required to bring a disposal value into account on the occurrence of any of the events listed in *Sec 61* (see 11.4 et seq.). In addition, a fixture is treated as ceasing to belong to a person when that person ceases to have the qualifying interest in the building to which the plant is fixed. [*Sec 188(2)*.]

10.34   In certain circumstances the qualifying interest is deemed to continue even though it has actually ceased. It is assumed in each of the following cases that the interest has continued in the form of the new interest. The relevant circumstances are as follows:

(*a*)   The qualifying interest ceases to exist because it is merged into another interest acquired by the same person. [*Sec 189(2)*.]

(*b*)   The qualifying interest is a lease and, on its termination, a new lease of the relevant land (with or without other land) is granted to the lessee. [*Sec 189(3)*.]

(*c*)   The qualifying interest is a licence and, on its termination, a new licence to occupy the relevant land (with or without other land) is granted to the licensee. [*Sec 189(4)*.]

(*d*)   The qualifying interest is a lease and after expiry of the lease, the lessee remains in possession of the relevant land with the consent of the lessor but without a new lease being granted to him. [*Sec 189(5)*.]

10.35   When, on the termination of a lease (or of a licence) a fixture is treated as ceasing to belong to the lessee (or licensee) then it is treated as beginning to belong to the lessor. [*Sec 193*.]

10.36   If a 'fixture' ceases to be a fixture by virtue of being permanently severed from the relevant land, it is treated as ceasing to belong to the person to whom the 'fixtures' legislation deems it to belong. This is not the case where the severed fixture does actually continue to belong to that person. [*Sec 191*.]

Disposal value of fixtures

10.37   *Continuation of qualifying interest.* If the qualifying interest is sold and the fixture is not permanently severed from the land, the disposal value is taken to be the amount treated as expenditure incurred by the purchaser. This will, in most cases, be the actual proceeds. If the amount is less than the open market value, then that value is substituted for the actual proceeds unless the purchaser's expenditure on the fixture will qualify for capital allowances as plant or for scientific research allowances. [*Sec 196.*]

10.38 *Expiry of qualifying interest.* If the fixture ceases to belong to the former owner because of the expiry of the qualifying interest, then, except insofar as the former owner receives any capital sum, the disposal value will be nil. Any actual proceeds or compensation received will, of course, be taken into account. [*Sec 196, Table, item 4.*]

Example

10.39 Rhubarb Ltd is the lessee of an office building and during the tenancy it installs a small lift for distributing internal post. The total cost of the lift and installation is £20,000. The following year, Rhubarb Ltd goes into receivership and the residue of the lease is assigned to Custard Ltd for £30,000 of which £10,000 is agreed to refer to the fixture. After a further two years, Custard Ltd is liquidated and the residue of the lease is abandoned.

10.40 The lift ('the fixture') is deemed to belong to Rhubarb Ltd and normal capital allowances are available. On the assignment of the lease by the receiver, Rhubarb Ltd has to bring into account a disposal value. This is the agreed consideration of £10,000, even if it is below market value, because Custard Ltd is entitled to allowances. Custard Ltd is entitled to normal capital allowances on expenditure of £10,000. When the company ceases to trade a disposal value has to be brought into account by virtue of *Sec 61, Table, item 6.* This value would in practice be nil.

10.41 Immediately after the abandonment of the lease, the fixture is deemed to belong to the lessor. No capital allowances are available, however, because it has not itself incurred any capital expenditure.

Restriction of qualifying expenditure

10.42 Where, on or after 24 July 1996, a person incurs expenditure on fixtures, in respect of which a former owner has been entitled to allowances, then the maximum amount on which allowances may be claimed will be equal to the disposal value required to be brought into account by that former owner, together with any incidental expenditure incurred by the new owner under *Sec 25.* [*Sec 185.*]

Chapter 11

Sale of Property

Introduction

General

11.1   The primary tax implication on the sale of fixed assets is often the realisation of a capital gain or loss. The interaction of capital allowances with capital gains tax is dealt with in Chapter 21. However, where the property being sold has in the past qualified for capital allowances, there may be a claw-back of the allowances previously given, or, dependent on the circumstances, an additional balancing allowance.

Ascertainment of proceeds

11.2   The proceeds of a sale will in many cases be obvious. Any part of the sale price which ultimately proves to be irrecoverable, however, is disregarded. If the vendor disposes of his right to receive any part of the proceeds, those proceeds are not taken into account, but any consideration received for disposing of his rights will be. If consideration for the sale consists of shares in the purchasing company, the proceeds will be the value of the shares issued (CA, para 11540).

11.3   Where a site (with a building on it) is sold for redevelopment, it may be that the building is worthless, and the whole of the proceeds relate to the site. This will depend on the facts of each individual case.

Industrial buildings

Balancing adjustments

11.4   When an industrial building is sold, then depending on the level of proceeds, compared to its tax written-down value (or 'residue of expenditure'), there may be either a further 'balancing allowance' to write the cost down to zero, or a claw-back of allowances already given (a 'balancing charge'). It should be noted that where the building concerned has qualified for *agricultural*, rather than *industrial*, buildings allowances, a balancing adjustment is only made following a joint election by vendor and purchaser

11.4 *Industrial buildings*

— otherwise writing-down allowances are given, apportioned on a time basis in the year ownership changes.

11.5 In addition to an outright sale, a balancing allowance or charge also arises when one of the following events occurs in respect of the *relevant interest* (see 7.18 et seq.):

(*a*) that interest, being an interest dependent on a foreign concession, comes to an end on the coming to an end of that concession;

(*b*) that interest, being a leasehold interest, comes to an end otherwise than on the person entitled thereto acquiring the interest which is reversionary thereon;

(*c*) the building or structure is demolished or destroyed (see 11.11 et seq.) or, without being demolished or destroyed, ceases altogether to be used;

(*d*) any capital value is realised under *Sec 328* (see 11.26 et seq.); or

(*e*) an additional VAT rebate (see 21.5 et seq.) in respect of any of the capital expenditure is made under *Sec 350* to the person entitled to the relevant interest.

[*Sec 315.*]

11.6 This is subject to the proviso that no balancing adjustment (either allowance or charge) shall be made where the relevant event occurs more than 25 years after the date of the original expenditure (50 years for expenditure incurred before 6 November 1962). [*Sec 314(4).*]

11.7 This rule also applies to buildings in enterprise zones. Thus it is the case that, although expenditure on such buildings will generally be written off over a maximum of four years (there is a 25% writing-down allowance as an alternative to the 100% initial allowance), the building is still deemed to have a 25-year tax life and a claw-back of allowances may be possible if the building is sold within that time.

11.8 The proceeds to be brought into account are set out in *Sec 316* — they generally consist of the net sale proceeds, insurance, salvage or compensation moneys. Where these are less than the residue of expenditure, a balancing allowance is made equal to the shortfall. [*Sec 318(2)(3).*] If the amount of those moneys or proceeds exceeds the residue of expenditure, a balancing charge is made equal to the excess. [*Sec 318(4)(5).*] A balancing charge, however, cannot exceed the total allowances given. For this purpose, only 'real' allowances are taken into account — a 'notional' allowance (see 7.106) can never give rise to or increase a balancing charge. [*Sec 320.*]

Note that, in contrast to allowances on plant, the discontinuance of a trade (without an actual sale, etc.) is not a balancing event requiring a disposal value to be brought into account.

Example

11.9   Church Ltd (making up accounts to 31 December each year) incurred expenditure of £200,000 in constructing a factory which was first brought into use on 1 April 1970. Writing-down allowances were given at the rate of 4%, i.e. £8,000 p.a. On 1 April 1991, the building is sold to Chapel Ltd for £100,000. The residue is calculated thus:

	£
Cost	200,000
Allowances	
(20 × £8,000)	(160,000)
	40,000
Proceeds	(100,000)
Balancing charge	60,000

The residue of expenditure before sale (£40,000) is increased by the amount of the balancing charge. The residue of expenditure at the time of sale is therefore £100,000. Chapel Ltd will be entitled to writing-down allowances of:

$$\frac{\text{Residue at the time of sale}}{\text{Years from sale to end of 25 years}} = \frac{100,000}{5}$$

$$= \text{£20,000 p.a.}$$

The writing-down allowance for any period may not exceed the residue of qualifying expenditure. The sum of all writing-down allowances (together with any initial allowance) cannot therefore exceed the amount of the original qualifying expenditure. [*Sec 312.*]

Use and disuse

11.10   Temporary disuse (see 7.110 et seq.) is treated as industrial use, and does not, therefore, give rise to a balancing adjustment. [*Sec 285.*] The Revenue considers that a building has 'ceased altogether to be used' where (*inter alia*):

(*a*)   it has become derelict;

(*b*)   it has become unfit for further use;

(*c*)   it is to be demolished because it is in the path of new roads;

(*d*)   it is in a site which is to be redeveloped.

(CA, para 35050).

11.11   *Industrial buildings*

Demolition

11.11   The Revenue gave guidance on the meaning of 'demolition', and on related issues, in a letter to the London Docklands Development Corporation on 23 May 1996. The Revenue requested that the letter be made available to all parties concerned with buildings damaged by the terrorist bombing on the Isle of Dogs, the majority of which had qualified for IBAs under *Sec 305* (enterprise zones). Although written in that specific context, the content of the letter is of more general application.

11.12   The letter states that, for the purposes of *Sec 315*, a building will not be treated as demolished or destroyed to the extent that the cost of reinstating it is treated for tax purposes as an allowable deduction as expenditure on repairs. Whether work amounts to a repair or to an improvement is a question of fact or degree. One needs to consider whether the building as a whole has been materially improved or altered. Intriguingly, the Revenue accepts that where the original steel frame of the building remains standing and is re-used, expenditure would remain allowable as a deduction. Further, where the steel frame or other part of the structure requires straightening or realigning, this too will amount to a repair rather than an improvement or alteration.

11.13   For more general guidance on the meaning of 'demolition', see the non-tax case of *Drake v Foottit (1881) 7 QBD 201.*

11.14   The Revenue acknowledges that where a building is demolished shortly *after* a sale, it may well be that the building was worthless, and the entire proceeds relate to the land alone.

Buildings which have not only been 'industrial'

11.15   Special rules apply where the building or structure has to some extent been used other than as an industrial building or structure, or for scientific research. [*Sec 319.*] In such circumstances, any balancing allowance or charge is adjusted by reference to:

(*a*)   'the relevant period of ownership', which is the period beginning with the date the building was first used for any purpose, and ending with the date of the event giving rise to the balancing allowance or charge (NB if in that period the building has been sold, the relevant period begins only on the day following the most recent sale) [*Sec 321*];

(*b*)   'the starting expenditure', which is the capital expenditure incurred on construction of the building or structure, unless the person receiving or suffering the balancing allowance or charge is not the person who incurred that expenditure (e.g. a subsequent purchaser), in which case the 'capital expenditure' is the residue of expenditure at the beginning of the relevant period [*Sec 322*]; and

(*c*)   'the adjusted net cost', which is the difference between the capital expenditure and the amount of any proceeds, reduced by applying the fraction (I/R) where

I = parts of relevant period for which building was used as an industrial building, and

R = total relevant period (in days).

[Sec 323.]

11.16 Where the sale proceeds are more than the starting expenditure, a balancing charge is made equal to the net allowances made. *[Sec 319(4)(5).]* Where the sale proceeds etc. are less than the starting expenditure then, if the adjusted net cost of the building or structure:

(i) exceeds the allowances given, a balancing allowance shall be made of an amount equal to the excess; or

(ii) is less than the allowances given, a balancing charge shall be made of an amount equal to the shortfall. *[Sec 319(3).]*

11.17 However a balancing charge or allowance will not be made where a building is sold between connected persons, and treated by *Sec 569* (see 19.4 et seq.) as having been sold for a sum equal to the residue of expenditure immediately prior to the sale. *[Sec 569(5).]*

Example

11.18 Potts Ltd (accounting date 31 December) incurred expenditure of £130,000 on the construction of a factory which was first brought into use on 1 April 1988. Apart from being used for non-industrial purposes for 15 months from 1 July 1992, it was used as a factory up until 30 April 1998, when it was sold for £125,000. The impact on capital allowances is as follows:

	£
Cost	130,000
Writing-down allowances	(20,800)
1988–91 (4×4%×£130,000)	
	109,200
Notional allowances (see 7.39)	
1992 (4%×£130,000)	(5,200)
	104,000
Writing-down allowances	
1993–97 (5×4%×£130,000)	(26,000)
	78,000
Balancing charge	42,420
1998 — see below	
Residue after sale	
	120,420

	£
Capital expenditure	130,000
Net sales proceeds	(125,000)
Net cost	5,000

Relevant period (1 April 1988–30 April 1998) = 121 months
Period of qualifying use = 106 months

	£
Adjusted net cost $\left(\dfrac{5,000 \times 106}{121} \right)$	4,380
Allowances given (not notional)	46,800
Balancing charge	42,420

Anti-avoidance: restriction of balancing allowance

11.19 Where the relevant interest in an industrial building is sold to a connected person, *Sec 568* requires open market value to be substituted for the actual proceeds received (if any). In the absence of anti-avoidance legislation, this would be open to abuse, in that if the market value could be artificially depressed, the value of any balancing allowance would be proportionately increased. For example, one way of depressing the market value would be to grant a lease in the building to a connected person on such terms that the value of the landlord's relevant interest decreased. If this interest was then transferred to another connected person, a balancing allowance would be triggered. *Sec 325* counters such schemes where:

(*a*) the relevant interest in a building or structure is sold subject to a subordinate interest;

(*b*) a balancing allowance would (but for these rules) be made; and

(*c*) any of the three persons involved are connected, or it appears that the sole or main benefit arising (from the sale or from the grant of the subordinate interest) would be the obtaining of an allowance.

[*Sec 325(1)–(3).*]

11.20 In such circumstances, the net proceeds to the vendor:

(i) are increased by the amount of any premium receivable by him for the grant of the subordinate interest; and

(ii) where no rent, or no commercial rent, is payable in respect of the subordinate interest, are taken to be what the proceeds would have been if a commercial rent had been payable and the relevant interest had been sold in the open market (increased by the amount in (i) above).

[Sec 325(4).]

The net proceeds are not increased, however, beyond such amount as eliminates the entire balancing allowance — this provision cannot create a balancing charge. *[Sec 325(5).]*

11.21 Despite the provisions of *Sec 325* (see 11.20), some taxpayers still sought to generate balancing allowances on related party transactions using tax avoidance schemes, which sought to artificially reduce the market value of an asset by making it subject to, for example, a mortgage or restrictive covenant. The asset would then be transferred between connected persons such that the low market value would generate a balancing allowance.

With effect for balancing events occurring on or after 27 November 2002 (unless they are in pursuance of a contract entered into earlier), *Sec 570A* denies a balancing allowance where:

- a claim is made for industrial buildings allowances;

- a balancing event (e.g. a sale) occurs which gives rise to a balancing allowance; and

- the proceeds of that balancing event are lower than they would otherwise be, as the result of a tax avoidance scheme.

It appears that even if a genuine balancing allowance would have arisen on the sale of the property, the use of a tax avoidance scheme will rule out entitlement to that allowance. This form of tax avoidance can therefore leave the taxpayer in a worse position than he would have been if applying the rules normally. The Inland Revenue Explanatory Note suggests that only the ' artificial' part of the balancing allowance will be denied, but that view is not borne out by the legislation as drafted.

So far as the purchaser or transferee is concerned, any claim must be based on the reduced amount of proceeds (i.e., as if the tax avoidance scheme had worked). *[Sec 570A(4)]*.

Leases

11.22 The relevant interest does not cease to be so by reason of the creation of a lease to which that interest is subject. *[Sec 288.]* The grant of a lease does not generally, therefore, give rise to a balancing adjustment. See, however, 11.26 et seq. on realisation of a capital value where a subordinate interest is created in an enterprise zone property.

11.23 In *Woods v R M Mallen (Engineering) Ltd (1969) 45 TC 619*, the holder of a 99-year lease had constructed an industrial building. After a number of years, he granted a sub-lease for the remainder of the term of his own interest, less three days. It was held by the courts that he had not disposed of the relevant interest. The sub-lease was not the same interest as that held by the person granting that sub-lease. The effect was therefore that the holder of the head-lease was able to continue to claim allowances, rather than suffer a balancing adjustment. For many years, the tax avoidance possibilities of this fact were exploited to the full, particularly by investors in enterprise zones.

Example

11.24   Denton acquired a freehold industrial unit in an enterprise zone for £2 million in 1992. At the same time, and for the same price, his twin brother acquired the unit next door. Five years later, Denton sold his unit for £2.5 million. His brother granted a 199-year lease of his unit, again for a premium of £2.5 million. Their capital allowances claims are as follows:

	Denton £	Twin £
1995		
Additions	2,000,000	2,000,000
Allowances	(2,000,000)	(2,000,000)
1997		
B/fwd	nil	nil
Proceeds (restricted to cost)	(2,000,000)	
Balancing charge	2,000,000	
Carried forward		nil

Long leases — joint election to transfer allowances

11.25   As described above, where a long lease is granted out of the relevant interest in an industrial building, the allowances generally remain with the holder of the relevant interest. However, the lessor and lessee may elect jointly (provided they are not connected) to transfer allowances to the lessee on the grant of a lease, for more than 50 years. [*Sec 290.*] This is more fully explored in 10.6 et seq.

Realisation of capital value

11.26   As shown above, it was possible for many years to avoid a balancing charge by granting a lease of a building, rather than selling it outright. This was open to abuse, particularly where the building concerned was in an enterprise zone. Typically, an enterprise zone investor will have received 100% tax relief in year one. In the absence of anti-avoidance legislation, he could dispose of a lesser interest in the property (normally the grant of a long lease) and thus recoup all or most of his original investment, without suffering a claw-back of relief. In some cases, the subsequent creation of the lesser interest was envisaged as part of a scheme to attract the initial investment. These were known as 'guaranteed exit schemes'.

11.27 Rules to prohibit such abuse are in *Sec 328*, which has effect for expenditure incurred under a contract entered into on or after 13 January 1994. When the legislation was first proposed, it was intended to apply wherever a capital value was realised in respect of a current or former industrial building. This intention was modified, however, before the legislation came into force. Instead, except where a guaranteed exit scheme is concerned, the 'capital value' rules will only be applied:

(*a*) where a capital value is realised within, broadly, the first seven years of a building's life [*Sec 330*]; and

(*b*) where the building concerned is in an enterprise zone. [*FA 1994, Sec 120(8)*.]

11.28 Where this applies, the capital value realised will be brought into account, and give rise to a balancing charge or claw-back of allowances [*Sec 328(1)*], but these provisions cannot give rise to a balancing allowance [*Sec 328(2)*].

11.29 A capital value is realised when, in respect of a building in an enterprise zone, on which industrial buildings allowances have been given, there is paid an amount of capital value which is attributable to an interest in land (the 'subordinate interest') to which the *relevant interest* is or will be subject. [*Sec 328(5)*.] For example, where a lease is granted out of a freehold for a premium, the freehold is the relevant interest, which will thereafter be subject to the lease. The lease is an interest in land to which the premium is attributable. Capital value equal to that premium must therefore be brought into account. This applies only if the payment (in this case, the premium) is made not more than seven years after the agreement relating to the capital expenditure was entered into. This might be open to abuse. For example, it might be that a taxpayer could enter into a contract for capital expenditure, but the contract would only become unconditional after three years. Thus, of the seven-year period covered by the capital value rules, three would expire before the expenditure was irrevocably committed. Therefore, where the agreement for capital expenditure is conditional, the seven-year period runs from the time when it becomes unconditional. [*Sec 330(1)(b)*.]

11.30 Capital value is deemed to be attributable to the subordinate interest if it is paid:

(i) in consideration of the grant of that interest;

(ii) in lieu of any rent payable by the person having the subordinate interest (e.g. a leaseholder) or in consideration of the assignment of such rent; or

(iii) in consideration of the surrender of the subordinate interest, or the variation or waiver of any terms on which it was granted.

[Sec 329(1).]

11.31 Capital value means any capital sum, monetary or otherwise. However, it excludes any amounts which are treated as rent or profits by virtue of the *TA 1988, Sec 34*. *[Sec 331(1).]* *Sec 34* deals with cases where a short lease (i.e. one for a term not exceeding 50 years) is granted at a premium, and part of the premium is treated as an income receipt, rather than capital.

11.32 Where no premium is given, or the premium is less than would be the case if the transaction were at arm's length, then the latter 'arm's length' premium will be brought into account, rather than the actual premium paid. However this only applies where no commercial rent is payable. Therefore genuine transactions on normal commercial terms should not be 'caught' by this provision. *[Sec 329(2).]*

11.33 The capital value rules also apply where any of the following events occur:

(*a*) any rent payable is assigned;

(*b*) the subordinate interest is surrendered; or

(*c*) there is a variation or waiver of any of the terms on which the subordinate interest was granted,

and where any consideration given is less than would be the case if the transaction were at arm's length.

[Sec 329(4)(5).]

Capital value — guaranteed exit arrangements

11.34 As referred to above, the capital value rules normally only apply in the first seven years after the expenditure is incurred. This limitation is removed where:

(*a*) the person acquiring the relevant interest did so in accordance with arrangements which provided for the subsequent sale of that interest or the realisation of a capital value; and

(*b*) such a sale or other relevant event is required by the acquisition arrangements, or is made more likely by virtue of such arrangements. *[Sec 330(3)(4).]*

11.35 In such cases, a balancing charge may arise under the capital value rules at any time in the first 25 years after the incurral of the expenditure. The 'capital value' rules will not apply where an election is made under *Sec 290* (see 11.25), thus transferring allowances to, for example, the lessee. Where, within the seven years following the incurring of expenditure, an agreement giving rise to the realisation of a capital value becomes unconditional, then even if the capital value is actually not realised until after the expiry of those seven years, it will be treated as being realised within that period.

Capital value — effect on grantee

11.36 The capital value rules require a disposal value to be brought into account by the person granting the lease etc., but they do not deem any qualifying expenditure to be incurred by the grantee. This is less favourable, of course, than if the relevant interest were actually sold, in which case the purchaser would be entitled to allowances.

Termination of leases

11.37 The table below summarises the treatment when a lease comes to an end.

1	Lease ends; no new lease granted; lessee remains in possession.	Lease is treated as continuing as long as the lessee is in possession. [*Sec 359(2)*.]
2	Lease contains option for grant of new lease; new lease is granted.	New lease is treated as continuation of old lease. [*Sec 359(3)*.]
3	Lessor pays any sum to lessee; sum is in respect of leased building.	Lease treated as surrendered in consideration of the payment. [*Sec 359(4)*.]
4	Lease granted to new lessee; new lessee pays a sum to old lessee.	Leases treated as same lease, assigned to new lessee in consideration of payment. [*Sec 359(5)*.]

Plant

Balancing allowances and charges

11.38 When plant is disposed of, a disposal value may have to be accounted for, giving rise to balancing allowances or charges. The precise treatment will depend on whether the original expenditure on the plant was pooled.

No disposal value need be accounted for, if the plant in questiion had not been the subject of a capital allowances claim. [*Sec 64*]. This was highlighted by the Inland Revenue as a change in law, upon the enactment of *CAA 2001*.

This does not apply where the plant was previously acquired from a connected person who did have to bring in disposal proceeds. [*Sec 64(2)(3)*]. It is not therefore possible to 'trap' allowances in a group by transferring plant intra-group, with the transferee then failing to make a claim.

Pooled assets

11.39   These rules apply on the disposal of assets which have been included in the general pool or the 'inexpensive' car pool (see 16.5). If, in a chargeable period, the total disposal proceeds exceed the qualifying expenditure (i.e. the brought forward written-down value plus additions in the period), there will be a balancing charge equal to the excess. [*Sec 56(6)*.] Such an occurrence is relatively rare, but it is far more common than the occurrence of a balancing allowance. A balancing allowance on plant (other than depooled plant) will generally only arise where the trade is permanently discontinued (or is deemed to be permanently discontinued).

11.40   Note that even the disposal of all the assets in the pool does not generate a balancing allowance, so long as the trade continues.

Depooled assets

11.41   Balancing allowances or charges will arise on the disposal (or deemed disposal) of individual assets not included in a pool, for example 'short life' assets or expensive motor cars. These are discussed in 13.70 and 16.6 et seq.

11.42   The amount brought in as a disposal value will in most cases be the net proceeds to the person disposing of the asset, including any compensation or insurance proceeds. [*Sec 61*.] Market value is substituted for actual proceeds where the plant is sold at below market value, unless:

(*a*)   the buyer will be entitled to capital allowances on the expenditure; or

(*b*)   there is a charge to tax under Schedule E (for example where the asset is given to an employee). [*Sec 61, Table, item 2*.]

11.43   The second condition is held to be fulfilled, even where the employee does not ultimately pay any tax, because the gift of the car falls within the exemption for termination payments given by *TA 1988, Sec 188*.

11.44   The disposal value cannot exceed the capital expenditure originally incurred on provision of the machinery or plant. [*Sec 62*.]

However, where the plant was acquired from a connected person, the limitation is to the highest capital expenditure incurred by any of the connected parties. [*Sec 62(2)(3)*].

Fixtures

11.45   Special rules may apply where fixtures are disposed of with a building. These are considered in Chapter 10.

Chapter 12

Acquisition of a Business

Acquisition of shares

12.1   Where the acquisition of a business is effected by purchasing the shares in the company carrying on that business, there are no implications for capital allowances. Allowances continue to be due to the company as if the share transfer had not taken place. If the company's accounting date is changed in order to match that of its new parent, then to the extent that that results in an accounting period of more or less than 12 months, writing-down allowances will be restricted or increased accordingly.

12.2   In certain circumstances, a change in ownership combined with a major change in the nature of the trade can result in the prohibition of losses being carried forward. This equally applies to losses representing surplus capital allowances as to other losses. [*TA 1988, Sec 768.*]

Acquisition of a trade

General

12.3   Where there is a succession to a trade or other business, the treatment of assets qualifying for capital allowances will depend on whether those assets are machinery and plant or other assets.

Machinery and plant

12.4   Where there is a change in the ownership of a trade, the trade is generally treated as discontinued by reason of *TA 1988, Sec 337(1)* (companies) or *Sec 113* (other persons, where no person is engaged in the trade both before and after the change). In such circumstances, any property which, without being sold, was in use for the trade immediately before and immediately after the change, is treated as if it was sold (at market value) to the person taking over the trade. [*Sec 265.*] The twin effects of this are that the former owner of the trade must bring in a disposal value (i.e. market value), and the successor is entitled to writing-down allowances, but not first-year allowances, on the same amount. It was held in *Parmar (t/a Ace Knitwear) [2002] EWHC 1085 (ch), [2002] STC 846* that the absence of actual consideration for plant did not mean that plant had not been transferred, if that was in fact the case.

12.5 The legislation is explicit that the requirement that the property must be in use is met where it is merely provided and available for use. [*Sec 265(3)*.] These provisions apply to all qualifying activities (see 13.18) other than an employment or office. [*Sec 265(5)*.]

12.6 An occurrence which commonly takes place in connection with a succession to a trade, although it need not, is that a person begins to use for trading purposes an asset which he already owns. Where a person brings into use for a trade an asset which he had purchased himself other than for use in a trade (or which is received by way of gift), the amount to be brought into account as qualifying expenditure is the open market value of that asset restricted to original cost if the asset is brought into trading use on or after 21 March 2000. [*Secs 13, 14*.]

See proforma election, Appendix 5.

Election by connected persons

12.7 Where the parties involved in the succession are connected an election may be made (within two years of the succession), the principal effect of which is that the plant in use at the time is deemed to be transferred at tax written-down value (i.e. at such a price which does not give rise to a balancing allowance or charge). [*Secs 266, 267*.] In addition to being connected (as defined by *TA 1988, Sec 839*) the two parties must fulfil two conditions:

(*a*) each of them must be within the charge to tax in the United Kingdom; and

(*b*) the successor must not be a dual resident company within *TA 1988, Sec 404*. [*Sec 266(1)*.]

Succession to a qualifying activity by inheritance

12.8 Where a person succeeds to a qualifying activity either as a beneficiary under a will or on the intestacy of a deceased person, he may elect that any plant passing to him with the activity is treated as transferred at the lower of:

(*a*) the open market value;

(*b*) unrelieved capital expenditure (i.e. the tax written-down value of the pool). [*Sec 268*.]

12.9 Where the successor later sells or otherwise disposes of the machinery and plant, the disposal value brought into account will be limited to the capital expenditure incurred by the deceased. [*Sec 268(6)*.]

Assets other than plant

12.10 Similar provisions apply to all expenditure qualifying for allowances except machinery and plant (considered above), scientific research and dwelling-houses let on assured tenancies.

12.11 Where under *TA 1988, Sec 113* or *Sec 337* (see above), the transferred activity is treated as ceasing, and any property which, without being sold, was in use for the trade immediately before and immediately after the change, that property is treated as if it was sold (at market value) to the person taking over the activity. [*Sec 559.*] Again, the twin effects of this are that the former owner of the trade must bring in a disposal value (i.e. market value), and the successor is entitled to writing-down allowances, but not initial allowances, on the same amount. Relevant activities include a trade, property business, profession or vocation, but not an employment or office. [*Sec 559(5).*]

12.12 In contrast to the treatment of plant (see above), the legislation does not make clear whether the requirement that the property must be in use is satisfied by merely being provided and available for use. (In connection with this see the case of *Schapira v Kirby (1970) 46 TC 320.*)

Election by connected persons

12.13 Where the parties involved in the succession are connected an election may be made under *Sec 569* (within two years of the succession), the principal effect of which is that the assets are deemed to be transferred at tax written-down value, thereby avoiding a balancing allowance or charge (see 19.4 et seq.).

See proforma election, Appendix 5.

Company reconstructions without a change of ownership

General

12.14 Special rules apply where one company ceases to carry on a trade (or part of a trade) and another company begins to carry on that trade, and:

(*a*) the trade (or a 75% interest in it) belongs to the same persons at some time in the two years following the transfer as it did at some time in the year preceding the transfer; and

(*b*) within the three-year period referred to above, the trade is not carried on otherwise than by a company which is within the charge to tax in respect of it. [*TA 1988, Sec 343.*]

Sec 343 refers only to a trade, and not to other 'qualifying activities' under *Sec 15*. Consequently, for example, a Schedule A business may not be governed by these special rules.

12.15 The provision does not apply if the successor company is a dual resident investing company within *TA 1988, Sec 404.*

12.16 Where these conditions are met, then for the purposes of capital allowances and losses, the trade is not treated as permanently discontinued and then recommenced, as would otherwise be required by *TA 1988, Sec 337* (see above). Instead, *TA 1988, Sec 343(2)* operates so as to treat the successor as effectively standing in the shoes of the former owner for the purposes of capital allowances. No balancing allowances or charges are calculated in connection with the transfer, and writing-down allowances available to the successor will be identical to those which would have been available to the former owner, had he continued to carry on the trade. In effect, therefore, the machinery and plant is transferred at tax written-down value.

12.17 Where only part of a trade is transferred, the expenditure transferred, and hence the allowances, shall be determined on the basis of 'such apportionments … as may be just'. [*Sec 343(9)*.]

12.18 When dealing with company reconstructions, it is important not simply to assume that *Sec 343* will apply. If the '75% rule' is not met, it may be possible to obtain the same result by making an election under *Sec 266* (see 19.6 et seq.). Such election, of course, is optional, unlike the mandatory provisions of *Sec 343.*

12.19 What purports to be a transfer of a trade may not always be so, notably where the trade consists solely of providing services to the transferee. For example, if the trade is one of leasing plant to the transferee, the trade will simply disappear — the transferee company cannot lease plant to itself! However, advantage may normally be taken of *Sec 61* to transfer the plant at a value convenient for tax purposes.

Transfer of trade during an accounting period

12.20 The transfer of a trade can often be made most smoothly on the accounting date of one (if not both) of the companies involved. For commercial reasons, this is not always possible. In such circumstances, the Revenue view is that allowances should be apportioned between the two companies. This is set out in ICAEW Technical Release TR 500:

'Transfer Of Trade Part Way Through Accounting Period: Entitlement To Capital Allowances March 1983

The transfer of a trade may take place during the currency of the accounting period of the companies concerned. In those circumstances, the Inland Revenue take the view that [*TA 1988, Sec 343(2)*] should normally be applied as follows:

(*a*) writing-down allowances are calculated on the "pool" of qualifying expenditure held by the transferee at the end of its accounting period, and those allowances are apportioned on a time basis for the period in which each company carried on the trade;

(b) first year allowances are given to the company which actually incurred the expenditure, no apportionment being necessary;

(c) any balancing adjustments (whether charges or allowances) are made on the company carrying on a trade in the relevant time, without any apportionment.'

12.21 This treatment applies not only to assets already in the pool at the date of transfer, but also to new assets subsequently acquired (in the same chargeable period) by the transferee. In effect, part of the allowances apportioned to the transferor will relate to these new assets, even though the transferor never actually owned them. If the transferee wishes to avoid this, he may do so by bringing the accounting period to an end immediately after the transfer.

Change of trade, or conversion of investment company to a trading company, or vice versa

12.22 When an investment company is converted into a trading company, or vice versa, or where a person discontinues one trade and commences another one, any machinery or plant owned by that person is deemed to have been disposed of and reacquired at market value [*Secs 13, 61, Table, item 7*]. In practice, this requirement is often overlooked and writing-down allowances continue to be claimed as if the conversion had not taken place. In certain circumstances, it may be to the company's advantage to insist on the correct treatment, for example where to do so would give rise to a balancing allowance.

12.23 If capital allowances have previously been added to trading losses or excess management expenses carried forward as the case may be, they will be lost. In such circumstances, it may be appropriate to disclaim allowances for 'open' years of assessment.

Incorporation

12.24 In the majority of cases, the rules and practicalities of capital allowances are of equal application to companies and to unincorporated businesses. However, it would be a mistake to think that because of this, incorporation of a business can automatically take place with no impact on the capital allowances position. There is a particular risk to first year allowances if the timing of incorporation is not properly planned (see 12.30).

12.25 The basic rule is that on incorporation of a business, assets are deemed to be sold and reacquired at their open market value. A person wishing to incorporate his business therefore runs the risk of crystallising a balancing charge where the market value of plant is higher than its tax written-down value. The reverse situation is relatively rare, as is the scope, therefore, for claiming a balancing allowance.

12.26   A potential balancing charge on plant may be avoided by making an election under *Sec 266* (see 12.7 above), the broad effect of which is to transfer the plant at tax written-down value. For certain other assets, an election for 'tax written-down value' under *Sec 569* (see 12.15) may be made where that value is less than open market value, and so can be used to avert a balancing charge arising on incorporation.

12.27   Where an individual incorporates his business but retains ownership of a building which is nonetheless used by the new company for its trade, the Revenue has agreed that *Sec 559* 'does not appear to permit' allowances to remain with the individual (CCAB Memorandum to the Inland Revenue, December 1982 and reply). In practice this point is rarely taken.

Expenditure prior to incorporation

12.28   When the incorporation of a company is delayed it is not uncommon to find 'pre-incorporation expenditure'. Such expenditure is outside the scope of *Sec 12* (pre-trading expenditure) because it could not have been incurred by the company as a person about to carry on the trade or other qualifying activity due to the simple fact that the company was then not in existence. It might be possible to show that the person who did incur the expenditure commenced to use the asset for trading purposes and that the trade was subsequently transferred to the company. *Sec 266* might then offer a route for the claiming of allowances.

12.29   If the asset is acquired by the company without the original purchaser having used it for the purposes of a trade, and therefore without having been required to bring a disposal value into account, the expenditure on which the company may claim allowances will be the smallest of:

(*a*)   the open market value;

(*b*)   the capital expenditure incurred by the seller; and

(*c*)   the capital expenditure incurred by any person who is connected with the seller. [*Sec 218(3)*.]

Effect on first year allowances

12.30   So far as first year allowances are concerned, incorporation presents four different scenarios:

(*a*)   expenditure is incurred only after incorporation;

(*b*)   expenditure is incurred before incorporation, but the trade only begins after incorporation;

(c)   expenditure is incurred and the trade begins, before incorporation takes place in a *later* accounting period;

(d)   expenditure is incurred, the trade begins, and incorporation takes place in the *same* accounting period.

Scenarios (b) and (d) pose a threat to first year allowances.

Scenario (a) gives rise to no unusual issues — the expenditure is incurred by the company, and is not pre-incorporation expenditure.

Scenario (b) is dealt with in 12.29 above. Note, however, that because the company is deemed to have acquired the assets from a connected person, no first year allowances are due. [*CAA 2001 ss 214, 217*]. If the assets are retained by the unincorporated business, that business may have a Schedule A or plant leasing activity which might enable it to claim first year allowances.

Scenario (c) is fairly straightforward. The unincorporated business claims first year allowances in the accounting period in which the expenditure is incurred (or, if later, when the trade begins). In the year of incorporation, it must bring in a disposal value equal to market value. This raises the risk of a balancing charge, especially as the business has taken advantage of first year plant allowances of up to 100%. An election under *Sec 266* should therefore be made to transfer plant and machinery at tax written-down value. This avoids any balancing charge, and the company would then claim writing-down allowances on the same tax written-down value.

Scenario (d) also presents a threat to first year allowances.

If incorporation takes place in the year in which allowances are first claimed, no first year allowances are due to the partnership (*Sec 46(2)*, General Exclusion 1). Instead, a *Sec 266* election would be required, simply to ensure that there was no balancing charge. The company will also not be able to claim first year allowances (*ss 214, 217*).

Unfair though it seems, it is therefore the case that if a business is incorporated in its first year of operation, no first year allowances will be due, either to the unincorporated business or to the company.

Incorporation of an existing business should therefore only take place once the business has been operated for sufficient time for a tax return to have been filed, including the first year allowances.

Plant: System of Allowances

Introduction — the treatment of plant in this work

13.1   For most businesses, machinery and plant will form the majority of any claim for capital allowances. The capital allowances implications of plant are an integral part of almost any transaction involving capital assets, and relevant planning ideas, etc. are discussed in the chapter dealing with that transaction. For example, where a shop is acquired second hand, key chapters will be Chapter 5 and Chapter 6. Chapters 13 to 15 deal with certain matters which affect plant, regardless of the context. These are as follows:

(*a*)   Chapter 13

   (i)   the manner in which allowances are given;

   (ii)   types of allowances, and conditions which must be met;

   (iii) special treatment for long life assets;

   (iv)   special treatment for short life assets;

(*b*)   Chapter 14

   (i)   the meaning of the term 'plant';

   (ii)   the development of case law;

   (iii) the impact of statute;

(*c*)   Chapter 15

   (i)   the treatment of items of plant commonly found in buildings.

13.2   In addition, Appendix 2 lists various assets which have, in appropriate circumstances, been accepted as qualifying as plant.

Manner of giving allowances

Pooling of expenditure

13.3   Since 1971, expenditure on machinery and plant has (with some exceptions) been 'pooled' for capital allowance purposes. This means that all expenditure is accumulated in one total, from which the allowances are deducted. The resultant balance is known as the 'main pool'. Expenditure on various types of asset is excluded from the main pool and accumulated separately in either a 'single asset pool' or a 'class pool'. These assets are:

Single Asset Pools

(*a*)   expensive cars (see 16.6 et seq.);

(*b*)   assets used only partly for the purposes of the trade (see 13.29 et seq.);

(*c*)   assets attracting a partial depreciation subsidy (see 1.81);

(*d*)   assets qualifying for contribution allowances (see 1.78);

(*e*)   short life assets (see 13.71);

(*f*)   ships;

Class Pools

(*a*)   long life assets (see 13.54);

(*b*)   plant used for overseas leasing (see 17.10).

13.4   Relief is given by a combination of first-year allowances (see 13.5 et seq.), writing-down allowances (see 13.8) and balancing allowances or charges (see 11.38).

First-year allowances

13.5   First-year allowances on plant have not generally been available since 31 March 1986. However, they have been re-introduced eight times on a limited basis:

(*a*)   for expenditure incurred (other than on motor cars) in the 12 months ended 31 October 1993, or for any additional liability arising in respect of such expenditure [*Sch 3, para 47*] — a first-year allowance of 40% was available;

(*b*)   for expenditure incurred (other than on certain excluded assets — see below) by a small or medium-sized enterprise (see below), in the 12 months ended 1 July 1998 [*Sch 3, para 48*] — a first-year allowance of 50% (12% for long life assets — see 13.20) is available;

(*c*)   for expenditure incurred (other than on certain excluded assets — see below) by a small or medium-sized enterprise (see below), on or after 1 July 2000 [*Secs 39, 44*] — a first-year allowance of 40% is available. In contrast to (*b*) above, no first-year allowance is due in respect of long life assets;

(*d*)   for expenditure incurred by a small enterprise (see below) on information and communications technology ('ICT') in the period from 1 April 2000 to 31 March 2004 [*FA 2003, Secs 39, 45, 164*] — a first-year allowance of 100% is available;

(*e*)   for expenditure on energy-saving plant and machinery on or after 1 April 2001, an allowance of 100% is available [*Sec 45A*] (see 13.14). This allowance was extended to assets used for leasing with effect for expenditure incurred on or after 17 April 2002 (*FA 2002, Sec 61*).

(*f*)   for expenditure on electric cars and cars with low CO_2 emissions, on or after 17 April 2002 (*FA 2002, Sec 58*) at a rate of 100% (see 16.20).

(*g*)   for expenditure on gas refuelling stations on or after 17 April 2002 (*FA 2002, Sec 60*), at a rate of 100%.

(*h*)   for expenditure incurred on or after 17 April 2002 in a ring-fence trade (oil extraction) (*FA 2002, Sec 62*), at a rate of 100% (24% for long life assets – see 13.54).

(*i*)   for expenditure incurred on or after 1 April 2003, an allowance of 100% is available for environmentally beneficial plant (see 13.15).

13.6   The meaning of 'incurred' for this purpose is, as for other transactions, set out in *Sec 5*. However, *Sec 12*, which deems pre-trading expenditure to have been incurred on the first day of trading, is specifically disapplied. [*Sch 3, paras 47(2), 48(2)*.]

13.7   No first-year allowance is given where the provision of the asset is connected with a change in the nature or conduct of a trade or other qualifying activity carried on by a person other than the person incurring the expenditure, and the obtaining of a first-year allowance would be the main benefit (or one of the main benefits) arising from the change. [*Sec 46(2)*.] Certain other assets are excluded from qualifying for some or all types of first year allowances (see 13.9).

The meaning of 'small' and 'medium-sized'

13.8   A company or business will be regarded as small or medium-sized for a particular year if (having assumed that an unincorporated business was in fact a company), it qualified as small or medium sized in accordance with the *Companies Act 1985, Sec 247* or *Art 255* of the *Companies (Northern Ireland) Order 1986*. These provisions require a company to meet two or more of the following requirements in that year or the previous year (CA, Appendix 5, para 9):

	Small	*Small or medium-sized*
Turnover not more than	£2.8 million	£11.2 million
Assets not more than	£1.4 million	£5.6 million
Number of employees not more than	50	250

[*CA 1985, Sec 247(3)*.]

13.9 First-year allowances

Excluded assets

13.9 First-year allowances are not available for expenditure on:

(*a*) motor cars, sea-going ships or railway assets [*Sec 46*];

(*b*) machinery or plant for leasing [*Sec 46*]; or

(*c*) long life assets. [*Sec 44(2)*.]

The Treasury notes accompanying this legislation when first published make it clear that the leasing exemption extends to expenditure incurred by property investors on fixtures attached to a building which is let. This is now incorporated in the Revenue instructions. [CA, 23110].

However, the leasing exclusion does not apply in the case of energy-efficient plant qualifying for allowances under *FA 2001, Sec 65*, or *FA 2002, Secs 59 and 61*) (see 13.5).

In addition, software does not qualify for the 100% ICT allowance (see 13.5(*d*), 13.10) if it is acquired with a view to granting to another person a right to use or otherwise deal with the software in question (*Sec 45(4)*). This applies to expenditure incurred on or after 26 March 2003. [*FA 2003, Sec 166 (4)*].

Any form of hire is regarded as leasing for the purposes of *Sec 46*, whether or not a formal lease is in place. The *Revenue Manual* (para 23110) accepts that there is a distinction between (i) the hiring of an asset and (ii) the provision of services which require the use of an asset. The key test, which is not particularly helpful in the concept of fixtures, is whether the overall supervision and control of the asset rests with the owner of the asset, or the person who has 'hired' it.

Qualifying ICT expenditure

13.10 Expenditure on information and communications technology means expenditure on the following classes of assets:

- Computers and associated equipment, including cabling and dedicated electrical systems.

- Wireless application protocol telephones and third generation mobile telephones.

- Devices designed to be connected to television sets to access data networks such as the internet.

- Associated software.

[*Sec 45*.]

Northern Ireland

13.11   The scope of first-year allowances is extended for small companies or businesses acquiring plant for use in Northern Ireland. A first-year allowance of 100% is available on expenditure incurred in the period 12 May 1998 to 11 May 2002. [*Sec 40.*] Excluded assets are as above (13.9 et seq.), with the addition of aircraft and hovercraft. [*Sec 41(1).*] Allowances are not available for goods vehicles used by freight hauliers, nor for plant used in the agriculture or fisheries sector. [*Sec 41(1)(2).*]

The first-year allowance will be clawed back where the relevant plant is used outside Northern Ireland within two years of the date the expenditure was incurred (five years if the expenditure exceeded £3.5 million) [*Sec 43*].

International groups

13.12   The position of a company which is part of an international group depends on whether the expenditure was incurred on or after 12 May 1998. The initial position, which applies to expenditure incurred before that date, was outlined by the Financial Secretary to the Treasury in a Finance Bill debate:

> 'When a small or medium-sized company is a subsidiary of an overseas parent, it will be considered in isolation because it would not be worth imposing on business the compliance costs involved in establishing the position of an overseas group for the sake of a one year tax relief.'

13.13   This does not directly address the position where there are a number of UK subsidiaries, all owned directly by an overseas parent, but on a straightforward reading of the Financial Secretary's words, there is no need to aggregate the various UK companies. However, Revenue press releases of 12 May and 24 June 1998 announced a change. From 12 May 1998 for 100% allowances in Northern Ireland (see 13.11), and from 2 July 1998 for other first-year allowances (see 13.5), the international group must itself satisfy the 'small or medium-size' test.

Energy-saving plant and machinery

13.14   *FA 2001* introduced a 100% first-year allowance on energy-saving plant or machinery. The introduction of this allowance is part of a wider package of measures aimed at helping businesses reduce their energy consumption, and so help the United Kingdom reduce emissions of greenhouse gases.

The rules on energy-saving plant or machinery are slotted into the existing legislation on first-year allowances. Consequently, issues such as the manner of giving allowances, and the scope to disclaim all or part of the allowance, are identical to the existing provisions governing first-year allowances. Note, however, that first-year allowances on energy-saving plant or machinery are *not* restricted to small or medium-sized enterprises.

The expenditure must be on plant which is new (i.e. not second-hand), and must be incurred on or after 1 April 2001.

Certain categories of asset are excluded from first-year allowances. These include:

• 	cars, ships and railway assets; and

• 	assets used for leasing, where the expenditure was incurred prior to 17 April 2002 (*Sec 46(2)*, *FA 2002*, *Sec 62*).

In order to qualify, plant must be of a description specified by Treasury order, or must meet the energy-saving criteria specified by Treasury order for plant of that description. The Treasury may also require that a certificate of energy efficiency is in force, issued by the Secretary of State or devolved equivalents in Scotland, Wales and Northern Ireland.

If such a certificate is later revoked, it is treated as never having been issued.

If only some components of an item of plant qualify for first-year allowances under this heading, the amount qualifying is limited to the amount specified by Treasury order — this overrides the 'just' apportionment which would otherwise apply.

Additions to the types of qualifying technologies were set out in Statutory Instrument SI2002/1818 (Simon's Weekly Tax Intelligence, Issue 30, 25 July 2002).

13.15   *FA 2003* introduced a 100% first year allowance for expenditure on environmentally beneficial plant and machinery incurred on or after 1 April 2003. This is available to both large and small businesses (*Sec 45H*).

The plant acquired must be of a description specified by Treasury order, and meet the environmental criteria set out by Treasury order. In essence, 'environmentally beneficial' plant will have been designed to remedy or prevent damage to the physical environment or natural resources (*Sec 45H(3)*). In some cases, allowances are due only if a 'certificate of environmental benefit' is in force, confirming that particular plant (or plant constructed to a particular design) meets the relevant environmental criteria (*Sec 45I*).

The plant acquired must be new and not second-hand, and must not be a long-life asset (i.e., having an estimated useful economic life of greater than 25 years). In addition, it must not fall within the general exclusions of *CAA 2001, Sec 46*, which include cars, ships, railway assets and assets provided for leasing. [*Sec 45H(1)*].

Although the allowances for environmentally beneficial plant and machinery are similar to those for energy-saving plant and machinery (*CAA 2001, Sec 45A*), the latter may be leased, whereas the former may not.

Allowances are available for environmentally friendly components of larger plant, even if the plant as a whole would not qualify. The amounts qualifying are those specified by the relevant Treasury order, and not a just apportionment of the whole cost. [*Sec 45J*].

If a certificate of environmental benefit is revoked, it is regarded as never having been issued, and tax returns must be amended accordingly. A taxpayer who becomes aware that amendment is needed has three months in which to notify the Inland Revenue.

Writing-down allowances

13.16 Writing-down allowances are generally given at a rate of 25% p.a. of the balance of qualifying expenditure in the pool. This balance will consist of the balance brought forward from the previous chargeable period, plus any new expenditure incurred in the year (together referred to as 'available qualifying expenditure', or 'AQE'), less the total disposal receipts ('TDR') brought into account (see 11.41 et seq.). [*Sec 56(1).*] Writing-down allowances and first-year allowances are not given in the same accounting period.

13.17 The rate of 25% is proportionately increased or reduced if the chargeable period is less or more than one year, or *if the qualifying activity has been carried on for part only of the chargeable period.* The words in italics apply for corporation tax purposes from 6 April 1995. One impact of the change is where a company begins a second or subsequent trade part of the way through an accounting period. From 6 April 1995, writing-down allowances for expenditure on plant used in that new trade will be restricted; prior to that date, they were not. [*Sec 56(3)(4).*]

13.18 Writing-down allowances are given where the following conditions are met:

(*a*) a person carrying on a *qualifying activity* (see 13.18) has incurred capital expenditure (see 1.6 et seq., 14.8 et seq.) on the *provision* (see 13.19 et seq.) of machinery or plant *wholly or partly* (see 13.29 et seq.) for the *purposes of the qualifying activity* (see 13.35 et seq.); and

(*b*) in consequence of his incurring that expenditure, the machinery or plant *belongs* or has belonged (see 13.41 et seq.) to him. [*Sec 11.*]

For the most recent consideration of whether expenditure had been 'incurred', see *ABC Ltd v M* (*Inspector of Taxes*) (Spc 300) – see Appendix 4.

13.18 *Writing-down allowances*

It was confirmed in *Barclays Mercantile Business Finance Ltd [2002] EWCA Civ 1853 v Mawson [2003] STC 66,* that provided the expenditure was incurred on the provision of machinery or plant wholly and exclusively for the purposes of the trade, it was irrelevant whether or not the trader's objective was or included the obtaining of capital allowances, and the *Ramsay* principle could not apply.

Qualifying activity

13.19 One of the conditions precedent to a claim for capital allowances in respect of machinery or plant is that the claimant must be carrying on a qualifying activity. [*Sec 15.*] This includes the following (provided the profits or gains, if any, are subject to tax):

(*a*)   a trade;

(*b*)   an ordinary Schedule A business;

(*c*)   a furnished holiday lettings business;

(*d*)   an overseas property business;

(*e*)   a profession or vocation;

(*f*)   a concern listed in *TA 1988, Sec 552* (mines, transport undertakings, etc.);

(*g*)   the management of an investment company;

(*h*)   special leasing of plant or machinery;

(*i*)   an employment or office (provided the expenditure is *necessarily* incurred) [*Sec 36*].

With effect for chargeable periods ending on or after 21 March 2000, any reference to a qualifying activity in relation to allowances on plant relates only to that part of the activity which is taxable in the United Kingdom.

This does not apply to the legislation dealing with overseas leasing, oil profit sharing contracts, sale and leaseback transactions or successions to a trade, as that legislation includes references to a trade which is not intended to be restricted to a trade taxable in the United Kingdom.

[*Sec 15(1).*]

Provision

13.20 'Provision must cover something more than the actual supply' (*IRC v Barclay, Curle & Co Ltd (1969) 45 TC 221*). It is worth highlighting that what qualifies for allowances is not merely expenditure *on* machinery or plant, but expenditure *on the provision of* machinery or plant. By implication, and in practice, this may therefore go beyond the actual purchase price of the asset to include any expenditure on acquiring title, bringing the asset to the location in which it is to be used and setting it up in working order. Common examples would include:

(*a*)   irrecoverable VAT;

(*b*)   VAT adjustments under the capital items scheme (see 21.5 et seq.);

(*c*)   import duties;

(*d*)   engineers and legal fees;

(*e*)   commissions;

(*f*)   delivery costs;

(*g*)   installation costs.

13.21   Commissioning expenses paid to the supplier of the asset normally qualify as part of the qualifying capital expenditure without any difficulty. The treatment of other costs, normally of a revenue nature, incurred by the purchaser (for example labour and fuel) is sometimes complicated by the adoption of special accounting treatment to avoid distortion of profits. Any such additional expenses charged to revenue will generally be allowed as such in the computations of an established trade or if the requirements of *Sec 12* (relief for pre-trading expenditure) are satisfied. The relief of capitalised expenditure is likely to be by way of capital allowances but a revenue deduction can sometimes be negotiated.

13.22   The cost of removal and re-erection of plant qualifies for allowances (CA, para 21190), but the taxpayer should consider first whether it qualifies as a trading deduction.

13.23   A payment by a company to enable it to retain its title to an item of plant has been held to be part of the cost of provision of that plant (*Bolton v International Drilling Co Ltd [1983] STC 70*).

13.24   Fees and financing costs are dealt with in 2.17–2.24, and hire purchase in 17.1.

Building alterations

13.25   The cost of building alterations connected with the installation of machinery or plant will also qualify for allowances, provided certain conditions are met. Such expenditure must be incurred by a trader on alterations to an *existing* building incidental to the installation of machinery or plant for the purposes of that trade. [*Sec 25.*] In this context, 'incidental' means 'in connection with' and not 'small, minor or insignificant'.

13.26   So long as the trader is occupying the building for his trade, it is irrelevant who owns the building. It is similarly irrelevant whether the plant itself is leased by the trader or owned outright.

13.27 Writing-down allowances

13.27 *Sec 25* overrides *Secs 21* and *22* (assets treated as buildings or structures) (see 14.58 et seq.), but does not apply to expenditure by a lessor for the purposes of a lessee's trade.

13.28 If the conditions for allowances under *Sec 25* are not met, allowances may still be available under general principles, as expenditure on the provision of plant. See also the treatment of installation costs, site preparation and BWIC in 2.25–2.26.

Example

13.29 Brown buys a printing machine which has to be fixed to an abnormally strong floor, so he puts down an extra six inches of concrete on the floor of his existing building. This qualifies for allowances by virtue of *Sec 25*. If the problem had been anticipated by incorporation of the extra thickness of flooring into the building at the time of construction the expenditure on that extra thickness would not have qualified as expenditure on machinery or plant.

Wholly or partly

13.30 In order to qualify for allowances, expenditure must be incurred 'wholly or partly' for the purposes of the qualifying activity. [*Sec 11.*] However, the effect of the expenditure must be distinguished from the object of the expenditure at the time it was incurred. If there is an unavoidable or incidental effect or benefit of a non-qualifying nature the expenditure may nevertheless be treated as incurred with the sole object of being wholly for the purposes of the trade.

13.31 Where a person carrying on a qualifying activity incurs capital expenditure on the provision of machinery or plant partly for the purposes of that activity and partly for other purposes, the expenditure is included in a single asset pool, i.e. dealt with outside the general pool, etc. [*Sec 206.*]

Where there is a reduction in trading use on or after 21 March 2000, and the market value of the asset at that time exceeds the tax written-down value by at least £1 million, the notional trade is treated as ceasing, with a requirement to bring in disposal proceeds equal to market value. The effect is to claw back allowances, to the extent that they exceed the real fall in the value of the asset. The separate pool re-commences the following year, based on that same market value. [*Sec 208.*]

13.32 Where machinery or plant is used for the purposes of an office or employment, there is an additional requirement that the plant must be *necessarily* provided. [*Sec 36.*] 'Necessarily' implies that the duties must objectively require the use of machinery and plant, and the employee or office holder must be obliged to incur the expense of providing it.

'The test is not whether the employer imposes the expense but whether the duties do, in the sense that irrespective of what the employer may prescribe, the duties cannot be performed without incurring the particular outlay' (*Brown v Bullock (1961) 40 TC 1,* at page 10, per Donovan LJ).

13.33 For example, a claim by a vicar in respect of a projector to illustrate his sermon failed because the Commissioners found as a fact that another vicar could perform religious ministry without the equipment and that the taxpayer would have been able to do his job without the equipment (*White v Higginbottom [1983] STC 143*). The fact that the job could have been done better with the projector seems to have been irrelevant.

13.34 It seems that the Revenue interprets the 'necessarily' test in respect of offices and employments as being in place of, rather than in addition to, the 'wholly or partly' test applied to other qualifying activities. This is not of great practical importance for the following reasons:

(*a*) the 'necessarily' test is normally more difficult to satisfy than the wholly or partly test; and

(*b*) the 'necessary adaptation' of *Sec 207* (use partly for a qualifying activity and partly for other purposes) requires that a just and reasonable apportionment shall be made when the machinery or plant is used partly in the performance of the duties and partly for other purposes.

13.35 The 'necessarily' test is specifically excluded in respect of expenditure on the provision of a motor vehicle incurred partly for the purposes of an office or employment and partly for other purposes [*Sec 80(2)* (see Chapter 16)].

Purposes of the qualifying activity

13.36 Expenditure will almost certainly have been incurred for the purposes of the qualifying activity if the asset is being used in the earning of the profits of the activity and is not being used for any other purpose. The phrase 'for the purposes of a trade' is discussed in some depth in *Usher's Wiltshire Brewery Ltd v Bruce (1914) 6 TC 399* and the principles may be extended to other qualifying activities.

13.37 In *Union Cold Storage Co Ltd v Jones (1923) 8 TC 725*, Pollock MR said at page 737:

'in following Usher's case you must look at what is the direct concern and direct purpose for which the money is laid out, and I do not think that you can go to the remoter or indirect results for which it may be possibly useful to lay out money.'

13.38 Problems may sometimes be encountered when a company in a group allows use of its plant by other group members. In *Union Cold Storage Co Ltd*, a company which allowed its plant to be used by an associated company was refused capital allowances. Rowlatt J said, at page 736:

> 'I think "used for the purposes of the trade of the appellant company" means that the appellant company are making profits by using and causing wear and tear of the machinery.'

13.39   Machinery and plant used by an employee for private purposes is generally treated as in use for the purposes of the employer's trade because such use will usually be part of the employee's remuneration package and therefore constitutes use of the plant 'in making profits by using and causing wear and tear of the machinery'. However, when the employee is a controlling shareholder he is able to exercise more personal choice, the effect of which upon a claim for capital allowances in respect of a motor car was considered in *G H Chambers (Northiam Farms) Ltd v Watmough (1956) 36 TC 711*. In that case there was ample evidence to show that (in the words of Vaisey J at page 717):

> 'the car would not have been bought by anyone who in considering the question of its purchase was directing his mind, solely and exclusively, to the necessities of the trader or of the trade as such'.

13.40   The car had therefore been purchased partly for purposes other than those of the trade, i.e. personal choice, which was sufficient to invoke the provisions of what is now *Sec 206* (see 13.29 et seq.). However, in *Kempster v McKenzie (1952) 33 TC 193* (in the context of a sole trader, not an employee), the opposite conclusion was reached. Clearly, each case will be decided on its facts. The Revenue may seek to restrict allowances where there is a 'blatant incongruity' between the asset provided and the commercial needs of the business (CA, para 27100).

13.41   Use of machinery or plant for providing business entertainment is treated as use otherwise than for the purposes of the trade. [*TA 1988, Sec 577*]. If such use is only partial, restricted allowances might still be available. In contrast, expenditure on security assets (see 14.52 et seq.) is always treated as incurred for the purposes of the trade, provided the conditions of *Sec 33(1)(2)* are satisfied. [*Sec 33(3)(4)*].

Belonging

13.42   Writing-down allowances on machinery or plant are given where a person incurs expenditure as a result of which that person owns the machinery or plant. [*Sec 11(4)(b)*.] The phrase 'as a result of which' has only once been given any prominence by the courts, in *Bolton v International Drilling Co Ltd [1983] STC 70*. A drilling rig belonged to the company, but was subject to an option to purchase held by a third party. The company paid £500,000 for cancellation of the option. It was held that, although the rig belonged to the company before the incurring of the £500,000, it would have ceased to do so had this amount not been paid, and therefore (after the date of the option) the rig did belong to the company *in consequence of* incurring the expenditure of £500,000.

13.43   The term 'owns' is not defined by statute and one must therefore look to its ordinary meaning. Whether or not a person owns an item of plant is dependent on the relevant facts of each case. In *BMBF (No 24) Ltd v IRC [2002] EWHC 2466 (Cn) [2002] STC 1450*, the 'belonging' requirement was held to be satisfied where the claimant was able to show that it was, in law or in equity, the absolute owner of the equipment. In most instances, 'ownership' is not a problem because either the asset is purchased outright or it is deemed to belong to a person by specific provision of the legislation, for example, assets acquired under a hire-purchase agreement. [*Sec 67.*] Under general property law, fixtures attached to a building become part of it, and in effect belong to the freeholder of the land on which the building stands. The case of *Stokes v Costain Property Investments Ltd (1989) 57 TC 688 A* highlighted the anomaly that a lessee could not therefore claim capital allowances, even if the fixtures had been added at his own expense, because the fixtures did not belong to him. *CAA 2001, Pt 2, Chap 14* generally rectifies this situation, allowing the lessee to claim allowances (see 10.14 et seq).

Deposits

13.44   A common problem is where a taxpayer pays a deposit for an item of machinery or plant in one accounting period, but the plant is not actually completed or delivered until the following accounting period. In most cases, the purchase contract (or the supplier's standard terms of sale) will state that title shall not pass until all amounts have been paid.

13.45   In such circumstances it may be that, although the taxpayer has incurred capital expenditure under an unconditional obligation, he is initially precluded from claiming capital allowances because the plant does not yet belong to him. In many cases, relief is obtained via *Sec 67* (see 17.1) which refers to expenditure incurred by a person who 'shall or may' become the owner of the machinery or plant. If an agreement can be brought within the scope of that section, a deposit will almost certainly qualify for relief when made. The Revenue has confirmed that in such circumstances, allowances are available even if the asset is never ultimately owned.

13.46   Alternatively, one must rely on the facts, and influence them if one can. For example, if the deposit paid is substantial, the supplier may agree to transfer title at an earlier time than would normally be the case.

13.47   In some cases, *constructive ownership* has been accepted by the Revenue, such as where a machine is being constructed to the customer's specification, and is so specialised that it would be of little or no use to anyone else. In these circumstances, failure to proceed with the contract would result in legal action effectively forcing performance of the contract.

13.48 This may be contrasted with, for example, an aborted contract for construction of an aircraft, in which case the partially constructed aircraft could be readily adapted for supply to another customer. The question of abortive expenditure on machinery or plant is dealt with at 13.51 et seq. below.

13.49 Another factor which may influence the Inspector is the state of completion of the machinery and whether it is merely awaiting delivery at the taxpayer's year end.

Reservation of title to goods

13.50 The Revenue has stated that where goods which have been supplied subject to reservation of title have been delivered to the purchaser then the obligation to pay will have become unconditional for the purposes of *Sec 5(1)* (CA, paras 11700, 11800). However, it also stated that *Sec 5(4)* will not apply because that subsection applies only when the goods are the property of the purchaser. In these circumstances it may be arguable that the goods could be attributed to the purchaser as envisaged by *Sec 5(4)(d)*.

Milestone contracts

13.51 The construction work under such a contract, if it is a building or structure, is usually performed on-site which in most cases will either be owned by the purchaser or be the subject of an interest in land to which he is entitled. Consequently *Sec 271(3)* (industrial buildings allowance — see 7.16) will be satisfied. If the contract also includes some expenditure which can be allocated to machinery or plant, as will generally be the case, the Revenue seems generally to accept appropriate apportionment of each instalment without separate examination of the ownership test (see 13.41 et seq.). Given that in most cases the plant, by virtue of its inclusion in a building, will be a fixture on land in which the purchaser has an interest, the question of ownership is likely to be already satisfied.

Abortive expenditure

13.52 The Revenue has confirmed that allowances will be available where expenditure has been incurred towards the manufacture of plant, but the supplier goes into liquidation before completion (CCAB statement 1972). This would only be the case, however, if the semi-constructed plant did in law *belong* to the taxpayer. Otherwise, the position of the prospective purchaser is less secure. The Inland Revenue Tax Bulletin, Issue 2, February 1992, contained the following comment on abortive capital expenditure on machinery or plant:

'The side note to *Sec 60 CAA 1990* (the predecessor of *CAA 2001, Sec 67*) identifies its application to transactions of hire purchase. [Note the heading to *Sec 67* no longer refers to hire-purchase; however the remainder of this Bulletin remains valid.] However, in certain circumstances this legislation may also apply to abortive capital expenditure incurred on machinery or plant.

A trader may incur capital expenditure on machinery or plant which is never actually owned — perhaps because the buyer withdraws from the supply contract or because the supplier defaults, or for some other reason. In such cases the trader will not qualify for writing down allowance on the expenditure incurred under [*Sec 11*] because it will not be possible to satisfy the "belonging" condition in [*Sec 11(4)(b)*].

[*Sec 67*] deals, however, with a trader who incurs capital expenditure on the provision of machinery or plant for the purposes of the trade "under a contract providing that he shall or may become the owner of the machinery or plant on the performance of the contract". If such a contract exists, *Sec 67(2)* treats machinery or plant as belonging to the trader.

In many cases abortive expenditure (e.g. a deposit paid on machinery which is never actually supplied) may well be incurred under a contract which provides that the taxpayer "shall or may become the owner". If so, that expenditure will qualify for writing down allowance by virtue of [*Sec 67(2)*].

[*Sec 67(4)*] will bring the disposal value of the machinery or plant into account at the time when the taxpayer ceases to be entitled to the benefit of the contract without becoming the owner of the machinery or plant. The disposal value will be calculated by reference to the rules in [*Sec 61*].'

13.53   The provisions of *Sec 67* are outlined further in Chapter 17.

Long life assets

13.54   With regard to expenditure on machinery or plant incurred on or after 26 November 1996 [*FA 1997, Sch 14*], certain assets are deemed to be 'long life assets', qualifying for a reduced rate of writing-down allowances (6% p.a.) rather than 25% p.a. as is generally the case. [*Sec 102.*] Expenditure on long life assets may qualify for first-year allowances of 12% if it is incurred in the period 2 July 1996 to 1 July 1997, but attracts no first-year allowances if incurred after that date. [*Sec 44(2).*] Transitional rules apply for expenditure incurred before 1 January 2001 in pursuance of a contract entered into before

26 November 1996. [*Sch 3, para 20.*] Expenditure incurred on or after 17 April 2002 in a ring-fence trade (oil extraction) may qualify for a first year allowance of 24% (*FA 2002, Sec 63*).

Definition

13.55 A long life asset is an item of plant or machinery which, when new, is estimated to have a useful economic life of at least 25 years. [*Sec 91(1).*] In contrast to short life assets (see 13.71), the question of whether or not an asset has a 'long life' is not determined simply by looking at the period of ownership of the person incurring the expenditure. Rather, that person must estimate (at the time it is first brought into use) the full life of the asset over a number of owners, until such time as it ceases to be used as a fixed asset of any business. [*Sec 91(3)(b).*] Clearly, there will often be difficulties in making such an estimate. For example, many assets, whilst they might be regarded as obsolete or superseded by new technology well within 25 years, could nonetheless continue to be used much longer by a less demanding purchaser.

13.56 The definition of 'useful economic life' for this purpose also conflicts with that in SSAP 12 which, again, considers only the period of ownership of the present owner. Also in contrast to SSAP 12, there is no possibility of revising the estimate once it has been made. Unexpected obsolescence does not, therefore, affect the level of writing-down allowances, which, if once given at 6% p.a., will always be given at the same rate. It is possible, therefore, that a purchaser can find himself bound by long life asset treatment agreed by a prior owner. Where the assets concerned are fixtures, it may be possible to mitigate the exposure by use of elections under *Sec 198*, such that the purchase consideration is allocated primarily to non-long life assets. Conversely, once allowances have been given at 25% p.a., that rate will continue to apply, both for the original owner and for subsequent purchasers, regardless of whether the asset proves to have a longer life than was first estimated.

13.57 Key evidence as to asset life will be provided by the depreciation policy applied to relevant assets. Assets depreciated over more than 25 years will clearly be regarded as long life assets. It has been common practice for many businesses to include certain items of plant (e.g. heating systems) within the 'buildings' category in their accounts and depreciate them accordingly. In future, qualifying plant should instead be separately identified and depreciated over a shorter period. Tax savings may thereby be achieved, but only at the expense of accounting profit.

13.58 Following the introduction of the long life asset legislation, it is understood that Inspectors have been instructed to identify and investigate changes in depreciation policy.

Pooling

13.59 All long life assets are included in a single, separate pool for the purpose of calculating capital allowances. [*Sec 101*.] This separate pool is discontinued only when the actual trade ceases: disposal of all long life assets does not in itself, therefore, cause a balancing allowance or charge to arise [*Sec 65(1)*].

Exemptions

13.60 There are, broadly speaking, three types of exemption from the rules dealing with long life assets — one relates to the quantum of the expenditure, the second to certain types of asset, and the third to fixtures in particular types of buildings.

De minimis limit

13.61 The rules will not apply where the taxpayer's expenditure on potential long life assets does not exceed £100,000 in a chargeable period of 12 months. [*Secs 97, 99*.] This limit is varied pro rata where the chargeable period is of more or less than 12 months. [*Sec 99(3)*.] Where the taxpayer is a company having associated companies, the £100,000 limit is divided by the number of associates (including, of course, the taxpayer itself). [*Sec 99(4)*.]

13.62 Each chargeable period is viewed in isolation, with no question of 'averaging' over a period of years. This means that a taxpayer who generally incurs no expenditure on long life assets will still be subject to the restriction on allowances if, in one particular year, his relevant expenditure exceeds £100,000. Consequently, so far as is commercially possible, it is advisable for a taxpayer to 'stagger' such expenditure over two or more years, so as to fall below the *de minimis* level in each year.

Exempted assets

13.63 Long life asset legislation does not apply to expenditure on:

(*a*) cars (including those which are hired out, and are generally not regarded as motor cars for capital allowances purposes by virtue of *Secs 81, 82, 96*);

(*b*) sea-going ships (other than those primarily used for sport or recreation, or in connection with offshore mineral workings) [*Sec 94*];

(*c*) railway assets (where the expenditure is incurred before 1 January 2011) [*Sec 95*].

13.64 *Long life assets*

Fixtures in exempted buildings

13.64 The long life asset rules do not apply to expenditure on fixtures in a building used *wholly or mainly* as:

(*a*) a dwelling-house;

(*b*) a retail shop or showroom;

(*c*) a hotel;

(*d*) an office.

[*Sec 93.*]

13.65 Fixtures in a building used for purposes ancillary to the above are also exempted. [*Sec 93(1).*] The Revenue has confirmed (Tax Bulletin 30) that the 'wholly or mainly' rule in *Sec 93(1)* will be satisfied if at least 75% of the building is used for one of the exempted purposes. It is largely the case, therefore, that fixtures will only be long life assets where they are attached to buildings which would (if new expenditure were incurred on them) qualify as industrial buildings under *Sec 274* — see 7.22. However, there are exceptions — many leisure facilities, for example, are unlikely to qualify for IBAs and yet are not exempted from the rules on long life assets. Some relief may be had if buildings can be brought within the 'retail shop' exemptions, which is extended to include 'any premises of a similar character where retail trade or business (including repair work) is carried on'. [*Sec 93(1)(b).*] This includes pubs and bars, banks, restaurants and cafes but excludes, however, hotels, cinemas and theatres (Inland Revenue Tax Bulletin 30).

Anti-avoidance — disposal value

13.66 If a long life asset is disposed of, and the amount brought into account as the actual disposal value is less than the notional written-down value of the asset, then the actual disposal value is ignored for capital allowance purposes and a deemed disposal value equal to the notional written-down value is substituted. However, this only applies where the disposal is part of a scheme of arrangement which had avoidance as its main subject, or as one of its main objects. [*Sec 104.*] If a low disposal value is commercially tenable, this rule will not apply.

Revenue practice

13.67 The Revenue will apply the following procedure to determine whether expenditure has been incurred on a long life asset (Inland Revenue Tax Bulletin 30).

13.68 The first step is to determine whether the expenditure is on one asset, more than one asset or only part of an asset. The 'long life' test is to be applied to the item of plant which is regarded as an entity for tax purposes. The case of *Brown v Burnley Football & Athletic Co Ltd [1980] STC 424* is helpful in this respect. Case law dealing with repairs and replacements (e.g. *O'Grady v Bullcroft Main Collieries Ltd (1932) 17 TC 93* and *Samuel Jones & Co (Devondale) Ltd v IRC (1951) 32 TC 513* will also be relevant (see 1.13 et seq.).

13.69 Step two, having established whether there is a single asset or not, is to determine the life of any such asset. It is understood that fixtures will not be regarded as long life assets simply because they are attached to a building which is itself likely to have a long life. It is the anticipated lifespan of the fixtures themselves which will determine the treatment. Many fixtures (e.g. light fittings) will not have a long life, as defined. Exceptions to this, however, may be quasi-structural items such as air-conditioning ducts, water or gas pipes, and some parts of electrical systems. Evidence such as design specifications or manufacturers' literature may also be relevant.

13.70 The Inland Revenue approach to long life assets was more recently confirmed in *Tax Bulletin 57*. Although that *Bulletin* dealt specifically with printing equipment, a number of the points made are of more general application.

The *Bulletin* emphasises that each asset must be dealt with on its own facts. It is possible that two identical assets could have different expected economic lives because of the predicted use of the asset in the particular trade in which it is employed.

Where there is no established second-hand market for a particular category of asset, the Inland Revenue will generally follow the depreciation policy for the asset used in the accounts, provided this is reasonable. Where, however, there is an active second-hand market other factors are relevant. These include how long the particular business typically keeps that type of asset before it is replaced, whether the business has a history of selling assets into the second-hand market or scrapping them, and whether there are rapid technological or market changes in the sector.

Short life assets

Introduction

13.71 Short life assets are not assets with short lives; rather, they are assets which are only expected to be actively used in a trade for a short time, after which they will be sold or scrapped. It would be more accurate, therefore, to describe them as 'short ownership assets'. This is a fundamental difference to 'long life' assets. In certain circumstances, electing to treat assets as short life assets can accelerate tax relief, but this should not be taken for granted.

The problem

13.72 The concept of a short life asset was introduced in 1986 with the intention of solving a specific problem resulting from the pooling system normally applying to machinery and plant. Unless the trade ceases, balancing allowances or charges will not generally occur, and therefore an individual item of plant can continue to attract writing-down allowances at an ever-decreasing rate long after the item has been sold or scrapped. After five years, only 76% of the asset's cost will have attracted tax relief, and even after ten years, this will only have increased to 94% (in each case, assuming no first-year allowance is available). This can be grossly unfair when dealing, for example, with a computer which after three or four years can be so obsolete as to be of no further use in the business.

The solution

13.73 The Revenue therefore announced in a press release of 15 January 1986 a new system designed to be 'of particular assistance to businesses whose machinery and plant has a short working life because of heavy use or rapid obsolescence'. It is not sufficient for the active useful life of the asset to be 'short'. The assets must actually be sold, scrapped or otherwise destroyed for the advantages of the special treatment to be felt. Thus it is that prudent retention of assets taken out of active use (e.g. to be used as back-up in an emergency) is not encouraged.

Details of the special treatment

13.74 It is possible to elect that named assets are dealt with outside the pool system: the legislation achieves this by deeming that each asset for which an election is made is included in a single asset pool. [*Sec 86(1)*.] As such, each asset (or group of assets — see 13.79 below) will be dealt with separately for capital allowances purposes, and will qualify for the normal 25% writing-down allowance available on plant. If the asset is sold or scrapped before the fourth anniversary of the end of the chargeable period in which it was acquired, this is regarded as the 'final chargeable period', and the disposal proceeds (if any) will be used to calculate a balancing allowance or charge. [*Sec 65(2)*.] If, however, the asset has not been sold or scrapped by that date, the balance of qualifying expenditure will be transferred into the general plant pool and will continue to attract allowances in the normal way. [*Sec 86(2)*.]

Making an election

13.75 For a company, an election for the above treatment to apply must be made to the Inspector in writing not more than two years after the end of the chargeable period in which the expenditure was incurred. For individuals etc. operating under the system of self-assessment (including non-resident corporate investors), the deadline for notification will be 12 months after the 31 January following the year of assessment in which the period of account ends. [*Sec 85(2)*.] Such an election is irrevocable [*Sec 85(4)*], and must identify the assets involved, the amount of capital expenditure and the date it was incurred. [*Sec 85(1)*.] If parts of the expenditure are incurred at different times, the two-year deadline for making the election is triggered by the date on which the first part is incurred. [*Sec 85(3)(b)*.]

See pro forma election, Appendix 5.

Ineligible assets

13.76 Certain assets are not eligible for treatment as short life assets. These are:

(*a*) ships;

(*b*) cars (as defined by *Sec 81*) (see Chapter 16);

(*c*) machinery or plant used for 'special leasing', i.e. let otherwise than in the course of a qualifying activity (see 17.20 et seq.);

(*d*) machinery or plant used only partly for the purposes of a qualifying activity (see 13.29 et seq.);

(*e*) machinery or plant which is subject to a partial depreciation subsidy (see 1.69);

(*f*) machinery or plant received by way of gift or originally provided for another purpose (see 12.6);

(*g*) leased machinery or plant on which expenditure is incurred after 26 July 1989, except:

    (i) machinery or plant used for short-term leasing and governed by *Secs 122–125*; and

    (ii) vehicles provided wholly or mainly for persons receiving certain disability allowances, listed in *Sec 82*;

(*h*) long life assets;

(*i*) machinery or plant leased to two or more persons jointly in circumstances where *Sec 116* precludes the making of a first-year allowance;

(*j*) machinery or plant leased outside the United Kingdom which only qualifies for a 10% writing-down allowance in accordance with *Sec 109*;

[*Sec 84*.]

13.77   *Short life assets*

Connected persons

13.77   Transfers of short life assets between connected persons are given special treatment. If a trader disposes of a short life asset to a connected person (defined by *TA 1988, Sec 839* — see 19.13–19.19) before the end of the fourth anniversary of the period in which the asset was acquired, that asset will be treated as being a short life asset in the books of the transferee. The relevant 'fourth anniversary' will be determined by the date that the transferor incurred the original expenditure. [*Sec 89(5)*.]

13.78   Furthermore, both parties may elect (within two years) for the transfer to be deemed to have been at tax written-down value, so that no balancing adjustment arises on the transfer. [*Sec 89(2)(6)*.] In the absence of such an election, the normal rules for transfers between connected persons apply (see 19.8 et seq.).

13.79   Where an asset is sold for less than market value, and the transferee will be claiming capital allowances on his expenditure, the normal rule is that actual proceeds should be substituted for market value. This rule does not apply for short life assets. Unless an election under *Sec 89(6)* is made or there is a charge to tax under Schedule E, market value will be included as the disposal value in the books of the transferor. [*Sec 88*.]

Groups of assets

13.80   In certain cases where it may be appropriate to make a short life asset election, there may be real practical difficulties in doing so. Most commonly, it may be that separate identification of the assets is impossible or impractical in the circumstances of the case. It would be completely unrealistic, for example, to expect the taxpayer with a stock of several thousand returnable containers to be able to keep track of each one. Details of the Revenue's approach to such cases is given in Statement of Practice SP 1/86, set out below.

'Capital Allowances: Machinery And Plant: Short Life Assets
[15 January 1986]

1.   Several representative bodies have raised with the Revenue some practical questions arising out of the new rules for capital allowances on certain short life machinery and plant which come into effect on 1 April 1986. The new rules enable allowances on machinery and plant for which an election is made to be dealt with outside the main capital allowance pool.

2.   In discussions between these bodies and the Revenue several areas were identified where businesses and their accountants might find guidance helpful. This note sets out, in broad terms, how they can be dealt with in ways which will be acceptable to local inspectors. In general, inspectors will want to be satisfied that the accounting and

other records are adequate to support short life asset elections and computations and that the new legislation is not being abused.

3. These guidelines are not, however, a substitute for the statutory rules. Their aim is to complement the legislation so that the new arrangements are introduced and continue to operate as efficiently as possible for businesses themselves, their professional advisers and the Revenue. The intention is to review the guidelines when the arrangements have settled in and, if necessary, revise them in the light of experience.

Election for Short Life Asset Treatment

4. The rules for making elections are set out in FA 1985 s57(2) [*CAA 2001, Sec 85*]. They enable all the machinery and plant acquired in a chargeable period (or its basis period) for which short life asset treatment is wanted, to be included in one election signed by the taxpayer for that period.

5. In general, inspectors will want to ensure that elections and any supporting material, such as a schedule attached to the election or cross references to schedules or analyses supplied with the accounts, provide sufficient information to minimise the possibility of any difference of view at a later date (for example, on a disposal) about what was and what was not covered by an election for any chargeable period etc and that the assets are not in one of the clauses excluded by *FA 1985, Sch 15* [*CAA 2001, Sec 84*].

6. In particular, however, where separate identification of the short life assets acquired in a chargeable period etc is either impossible or possible but impracticable (for example, similar small or relatively inexpensive assets held in very large numbers perhaps in several locations) then the information on the election about the assets, required by FA 1985 s57(2)(b) [*CAA 2001, Sec 85*], may be provided by reference to batches of acquisitions. Where large numbers of similar short life assets are acquired throughout a chargeable period etc it will be acceptable if the costs of those assets for the period are aggregated and shown on the election in one sum.

Capital Allowance Computations

7. The Revenue accept that it may not be practicable for individual capital allowance computations to be maintained for each and every short life asset especially where the assets are held in very large numbers.

8. Where, therefore, the inspector is satisfied that the actual life in the business of a distinct class of assets having broadly similar average lives before they are sold or scrapped is likely to be less than five years (that is, the year of acquisition plus the four following years) computations in the form set out in Example 1 below will be accept-

able. On this basis a balancing allowance will normally become available for the last year of the agreed life of the assets.

9. Where disposal proceeds can be attributed to assets acquired in a particular year they should be brought into the appropriate column(s) of the computation relating to those assets for the year(s) in which the proceeds are received. If attribution in this way is not possible, disposal proceeds may be credited on a FIFO basis; that is all receipts from disposals in any chargeable period etc are to be regarded as related to the earliest period for which a short life asset pool on the lines of these arrangements is in existence.

10. This form of computation is intended primarily for short life assets costing similar amounts which cannot be identified individually. It is possible however that similar arrangements may be helpful where short life assets which have a separate identity are acquired in large numbers such that the business does not in fact keep track of them individually and it would not be reasonable to expect it to do so. Where this is the case, computations based on the above principles and along the lines of Example 2 below will normally be acceptable to inspectors.

11. Given the wide variety of potential short life assets and the widely varying circumstances of individual businesses, other forms of computation may also be acceptable.

Submission of election and computations to inspectors

12. It is suggested that either on the first occasion when an election is made or when any abridged or simplified computations are submitted to inspectors for the first time, an explanation of the way in which the computations will be or have been put together is provided together with a description of the underlying records on which they are based. Inspectors will want to be satisfied that, together, the elections and the computations provide the correct statutory result and that if, for any reason, questions are asked about individual items (for example, on a disposal several years after acquisition), sufficient information will be available to the business or to its accountants to enable complete and satisfactory answers to be given.

Example 1

Assets held in large numbers with a very short life where individual identification is impossible (e.g. returnable containers, linen, tools).

The taxpayer satisfies the inspector that the average actual life (NB not useful life) of tools used in his trade is three years, it is therefore reasonable to presume that those items acquired in year 1 are all disposed of in year 4. He elects for short life asset treatment.

Year of acquisition	1996	1997	1998	1999	Total allowances each year
Cost of tools	1,000	1,200	800	1,000	
1996 WDA	250				250
	750				
1997 WDA	188	300			488
	562	900			
1998 WDA	140	225	200		565
	422	675	600		
1999 Presumed scrapped Disposal value	nil				
Balancing allowance	422				⎱ 991
WDA		169	150	250	⎰
Qualifying expenditure carried forward		506	450	750	

Where scrap or sale proceeds are not in practice taxed as trading receipts and can be identified but not related to particular acquisitions, they should be regarded as disposal value of the earliest period for which a short life asset pool is in existence. For example, if proceeds from the sale of all tools scrapped in 1999 were 50, the balancing allowance in the example would be 372.

Example 2

Assets held in large numbers where individual identification is possible but impracticable in the circumstances of the case.

The taxpayer uses in his trade large numbers of relatively small items such as scientific or technical instruments, calculators, or amusement machines and elects for short life asset treatment. His accounting records enable him to identify for each kind the number and cost of acquisition, and both the number and sale proceeds of disposals and the number on hand at the end of the short life asset period related to those acquisitions.

Technical instruments	Number	Cost	Disposal value
Acquisition in 1996	100	10,000	
Sold in 1998	20	500	
Sold in 1999	40	400	
On hand 2000	40		

13.80   *Short life assets*

Computation		Cost	Total allowance
1996 expenditure on 100 instruments		10,000	
WDA		2,500	2,500
		7,500	
1997 WDA		1,875	1,875
		5,625	
1998 disposal of 20 instruments			
Expenditure unallowed			
5,625 × 20/100 =	1,125	1,125	
Disposal value	500	4,500	
Balancing allowance	625		
			1,750
WDA		1,125	
80 instruments			3,375
1999 disposals: 40 instruments			
Expenditure unallowed			
3,375 × 40/80 =	1,688	1,688	
		1,687	
Disposal value	400		
Balancing allowance	1,288		
			1,710
WDA		422	
40 instruments		1,265	
2000 WDA		314	314
Expenditure unallowed			
(40 instruments)		951	
2001 transfer to main pool		951	

It is presumed in this example that all the items cost the same amount; where similar items cost different but broadly similar amounts, this method of computation may still be used.'

Disadvantages of short life asset election

13.81   As mentioned above, the election is irrevocable. It will be beneficial in most cases, but some thought must be given to likely future events before electing. The most important factor is often the expected disposal value, as the following example illustrates.

Example

13.82   Walker has a general pool of expenditure with a tax written-down value of £10,000. In his year ended December 1995, he acquired a new computer for £12,000 and elected to treat it as a short life asset. In 1997 he sold the computer for £10,000. His allowances were as follows:

		General pool	S/L asset	Total allowances
1995	B/fwd	10,000		
	Additions		12,000	
	WDA	(2,500)	(3,000)	5,500
1996	B/fwd	7,500	9,000	
	WDA	(1,875)	(2,250)	4,125
1997	B/fwd	5,625	6,750	
	Proceeds		(10,000)	
	Balancing charge		3,250	(3,250)
	WDA	(1,406)		1,406
	C/fwd	4,219	0	7,781

If Walker had not made the election, his allowances would have been as follows:

		General pool	Total allowances
1995	B/fwd	10,000	
	Additions	12,000	
		22,000	
	WDA	(5,500)	5,500
1996	B/fwd	16,500	
	WDA	(4,125)	4,125
1997	B/fwd	12,375	
	Proceeds	(10,000)	
		2,375	
	WDA	(594)	594
		1,781	10,219

Walker would therefore have received almost £2,500 more allowances if the election had not been made. This is because the balancing charge would have been absorbed by the pool. The converse can apply where there is a balancing allowance on the short life asset and a large general pool.

Chapter 14

Plant: The Meaning of the Term

Introduction

14.1　The major problem, or perhaps opportunity, arising in connection with capital allowances on plant is that the term 'plant and machinery' is not defined by statute. 'Machinery' is generally more easily identifiable than 'plant'. The former is generally thought of as some sort of device incorporating both fixed and moving parts, whereas the latter has a much wider meaning. For the purposes of capital allowances it is generally unnecessary to distinguish one from the other.

14.2　For expenditure incurred on or after 30 November 1993, the scope of the term 'plant and machinery' is further limited by *Secs 21* and *22* (see 14.62 et seq.). Nevertheless, apart from a few types of expenditure which are specifically treated as plant by statute, the eligibility of individual assets will be decided either by established custom or by decided cases.

Case law

General

14.3　Full details of relevant cases are given in Appendix 4. The following sections concentrate on the most important cases and illustrate the general principles that have developed over more than a century.

14.4　The earliest case of relevance was in 1860. Like many cases dealing with plant, *Blake v Shaw (1860) 8 WR 410* was heard long before the introduction of capital allowances as they are now known. Over the years, the definition of plant has been important for the purposes of such areas as employer's liability and compensation for war damage. The conclusions, however, remain of relevance for the purposes of capital allowances. In *Blake v Shaw*, plant was said to commonly include: 'all the matters permanently used for the purposes of the trade as distinguished from the fluctuating stock'. This distinction was taken further in the case of *Yarmouth v France (1887) 19 QBD 647* where the question arose as to whether a horse was plant. In a judgment which has come to be regarded as the most basic definition of plant, Lindley LJ said:

'There is no definition of plant in the Act but, in its ordinary sense, it includes whatever apparatus is used by a businessman for carrying on his business — not his stock-in-trade which he buys or makes for sale; but all his goods and chattels, fixed or variable, dead or alive, which he keeps for permanent employment in his business.'

14.5 Important points to extract from this are that plant is:

(*a*) used for carrying on a business, and

(*b*) kept for permanent employment (i.e. an element of durability is required).

14.6 This definition has generally withstood the test of time but, of course, after more than a century, it has been qualified by subsequent decisions. Various major themes and sub-themes have emerged over the years. These include:

  (i) durability of the asset;

 (ii) the 'functional' test;

(iii) the 'premises' test;

(iv) the 'business use' test.

14.7 To a greater or lesser extent these overlap and in fact stem from a relatively small number of cases. They are sufficiently important, however, to examine the development of each.

Durability of the asset

14.8 This is essentially the most fundamental of tax questions, i.e. the distinction between revenue and capital expenditure (see 1.6–1.22). An important case specifically on this subject is *Hinton v Maden and Ireland Ltd (1959) 38 TC 391* where the subject of the claim was expenditure on knives and lasts used by a footwear manufacturer. By a three to two majority it was held in the House of Lords that the lasts and knives were plant; this was in spite of the fact that they were numerous, small and cheap. The vital factor was the durability of the assets which in this case was between one and five years. Lord Jenkins said:

> 'The reference to "permanent employment" (in *Yarmouth v France*) in the business demands some degree of durability ... The intention no doubt is to keep and use [the knives] for so long as they are serviceable and I cannot regard the circumstance that they wear out in [a] relatively short period as investing them with so transitory a character as to take them out of the category of plant to which they would otherwise belong.'

14.9 The alternative would presumably have been to allow the cost of the knives and lasts on a renewal basis like the cost of replacement tyres for a lorry or crockery for a hotel. This argument was put forward by Lord Denning but evidently did not convince sufficient of his peers! (See 1.25 et seq. regarding the renewals basis.)

14.10 The Revenue will generally regard an asset as sufficiently durable if it has a normal working life of more than two years (CA, para 21100). However, each case must be considered on its merits.

The function test

14.11 No distinction is generally drawn between machinery and plant. The man in the street, if asked to describe machinery, would invariably accredit it with moving parts. To describe plant is more complicated. In order to qualify as plant for capital allowance purposes, there is no strict requirement that the asset should have moving parts in the nature of machinery. Indeed, it may appear to be quite passive in nature. Examples of such 'passive plant' may include a paint spray booth in a garage or the bric-a-brac popular in hotels and public houses.

14.12 The term 'passive plant' is, however, something of a misnomer; the plant can invariably be shown to perform a function of some kind. In the examples given, the spray booth will enable the spraying of vehicles to be carried out without either polluting the surrounding areas or endangering employees or members of the public. The bric-a-brac helps to create a relaxing and pleasant atmosphere necessary for the attraction of customers. However, the more obvious the function, the more readily an asset will be accepted as plant.

14.13 A starting point for considering the importance of the 'functional test' is the 1969 case of *CIR v Barclay, Curle & Co Ltd (1969) 45 TC 221*. The taxpayers constructed a dry dock. This involved not only items such as pumps and valves that were clearly machinery, but also the excavation of 200,000 tons of earth and the lining of the hole with concrete. It was held that the whole of the expenditure was incurred on the provision of plant. The dry dock was more than just a hole in the ground — it performed the active function of lifting and lowering ships and could be drained to facilitate repairs. Lord Reid said:

> 'The only reason that a structure should also be plant ... is that it fulfils the function of plant in the trader's operations ... I do not say that every structure which fulfils the function of plant must be regarded as plant, but I think that one would have to find some good reason for excluding such a structure.'

14.14 He also pointed out that the cost of providing plant could perfectly well exceed the cost of the plant itself, and that an asset was not excluded from being plant merely by virtue of size.

14.15 Another dockside case was heard in 1974 — *Schofield v R & H Hall Ltd (1974) 49 TC 538*. In this case the taxpayer erected a silo for the purpose of holding grain in a position where it could conveniently be discharged for delivery to purchasers; tankers could pass below the silo and the grain could be loaded by the operation of gravity. Before the construction of the silo, the grain had been bagged by hand, carried ashore and loaded by hand onto customers' lorries. The silo effectively carried out these functions plus the cooling, turning over and fumigation of the grain. Simple storage alone was but 'a trifling part' of the silo's function. Of course, with the progress of technology, designs may change. A modern silo might, for example, be more horizontal than vertical, with delivery effected by means other than gravity. This should not alter the fact that the whole installation qualifies as an item of plant. Dry docks and silos are relatively rare, but there are in practice a number of other types of structure which have been regarded as composite items of plant, although none of these has reached the courts.

14.16　By way of illustration, an interesting case was heard by the Australian courts (*Wangaratta Woollen Mills Ltd v Federal Comr of Taxation (1969) 1/9 CRL 1*) which has been quoted, with approval, in the House of Lords. A dye house, although a building, was held to be almost entirely an item in the nature of plant; certain unusual features meant that the dye house itself played an essential part in the dyeing process. These features included a complex ventilation system and drains to remove volatile liquids. It is, however, debatable whether the decision would have been the same, had *Secs 21–23* then been in force (see 14.62).

14.17　It is important to stress, of course, that allowances for plant are by no means restricted to businesses where an industrial process is carried on. Another useful case to consider is therefore *Leeds Permanent Building Society v Proctor [1982] STC 821*. Here, decorative screens used for window displays were held to be plant, on the grounds that by providing security, privacy and publicity they played a part in the commercial activities of the society.

The premises test

14.18　Plant was first formally contrasted with 'setting' in a 1944 case concerned, not with taxes, but with the *War Damage Act 1943, J Lyons & Co Ltd v A-G [1944] 1 All ER 477*. Uthwatt J asked:

> 'Are the lamps and fitments properly to be regarded as part of the setting in which the business is carried on, or as part of the apparatus used for carrying on a business?'

14.19　In this particular case, it was found that the majority of the lighting in a Lyons cafe was not plant. Further consideration of the eligibility of lighting for allowances is given at 15.19 et seq.

14.20　This test was developed further in the case of *Wimpey International Ltd v Warland [1989] STC 273*, where the word 'premises' was substituted for 'setting'. Fox LJ commented:

'There is a well established distinction in general terms, between the premises in which the business is carried on and the plant with which the business is carried on. The premises are not plant.'

14.21   He also approved the comment of Lord Lowry in *CIR v Scottish & Newcastle Breweries Ltd (1982) 55 TC 252* case that 'something which becomes part of the premises, instead of merely embellishing them, is not plant'.

14.22   The question of whether or not something becomes part of the premises is largely a matter of fact. Hoffman J in the *Wimpey* case proposed four considerations:

(i)   whether the item appears visually to retain a separate identity;

(ii)   the degree of permanence with which it has been attached to the building;

(iii)   whether the building or structure would be incomplete without it;

(iv)   the extent to which it was intended to be permanent.

14.23   The dividing line between plant and setting is at times a very indistinct one. In *Jarrold v John Good & Sons Ltd (1962) 40 TC 681*, movable partitions were the subject of dispute. Pennycuick J said: 'the setting in which a business is carried on, and the apparatus used for carrying on a business, are not always necessarily mutually exclusive'. The finding was determined by the requirements of the particular trade. In fact, the same asset may be plant in one business and not in another. This is considered further in 14.30 et seq. below.

14.24   One thing which is certain is that an asset is not precluded from being plant simply because of its great bulk or high cost. Lord Reid in *Barclay, Curle* (see above) said: 'one would have to find some good reason for the exclusion of [such] a structure [from the definition of plant]. And I do not think that mere size is sufficient'. Similarly, Blackburne J in *Bradley v London Electricity plc [1996] STC 1054* stated that simply because something was a substantial fixed structure, with a roof and inner and outer walls and floors, and has in it what is accepted to be plant used for the purposes of the business, does not mean that it must be regarded as premises rather than plant. Entire buildings and structures have been regarded as plant (see Chapter 15). The question of whether structures can be plant has also been considered in a number of cases. The dry dock in *Barclay, Curle* was followed into the plant category by another 'hole in the ground' — the swimming pool in *Cooke v Beach Station Caravans Ltd [1974] STC 402*. In this case, swimming pools together with their attendant machinery for purifying and heating the water were considered as a single unit. It was found that the pools performed the active function of attracting visitors to the caravan park.

14.25   Not all buildings or structures can be categorised as plant. In the following cases such treatment was not allowed, although sometimes the taxpayer appears to have been unfortunate. In *Dixon v Fitch's Garage [1975] STC 480* the item not allowed as plant was a canopy over a filling station. It was held to be part of the setting, providing light and shelter for customers. A similar shelter used for advertising purposes was held to be plant in the Irish case *O'Culachain v McMullan Bros [1991] 1 IR 363* and it may be that if *Fitch's Garage* came to court today, the decision could be reversed. Certainly the decision has been doubted twice in the House of Lords, by Lord Hailsham in *Cole Bros Ltd v Phillips [1982] STC 307* and by Lord Cameron in *Scottish & Newcastle Breweries* above. Another case, *Thomas v Reynolds [1987] STC 135*, concerning an inflatable tennis court cover, might have had a better chance of success for the taxpayer if more pertinent facts had been established before the Commissioners.

14.26 Often the court's refusal of plant status appears difficult to argue with. In the case of *St John's School v Ward (1974) 49 TC 524* the supposed items of 'plant' were a gymnasium and a laboratory. Both were prefabricated buildings, bolted together on site and with mains electricity connected. A key factor in deciding that the buildings were part of the setting rather than plant was that neither had any function to perform other than sheltering the persons who used them.

14.27 The reasoning was similar in *Brown v Burnley Football and Athletic Club Co Ltd [1980] STC 424*, where it was held that a football stand was the place 'from where' spectators watched the match rather than them watching the match 'by means of' the stand. However, it is of interest that in the Irish case of *O'Grady v Roscommon Race Committee [1992] IR 425*, an improved racecourse stand was held to be part of the means to attract patrons and was therefore plant like the swimming pool in *Cooke v Beach Station Caravans Ltd*.

14.28 Finally, in *Benson v Yard Arm Club (1979) 53 TC 67*, an old ferry boat and barge converted for use as a floating restaurant were held not to be plant. The vessels were the structure in which the business was carried on, rather than apparatus used to carry on the business. If the vessels had not been moored, but had been used for, say, dinner cruises on the river, the decision might have been different *[1974] STC 402*.

14.29 In *Bradley v London Electricity plc [1996] STC 1054*, Blackburne J thought the key question was to ask what plant-like function the structure as an entity performed in the taxpayer's trading activity:

> 'The fact that features of the structure were carefully designed to accommodate the equipment within does not convert what is otherwise plainly the premises in which the activity is conducted into the plant or apparatus with which that activity is conducted.'

The business use test

14.30 When considering 'setting' above, reference was made to *Jarrold v John Good & Sons Ltd (1962) 40 TC 681*, and to the fact that identical assets may be regarded as plant in one business and not in another. In fact, this was already an old idea having been suggested by, amongst others, Uthwatt J in *J Lyons & Co Ltd v A-G [1944] 1 All ER 477* when he speculated that certain lighting might qualify as plant if it were connected with the particular needs of the trade carried on.

14.31 In the *Jarrold* case, the items in question were movable partitions. It was successfully argued that these partitions performed a particular function in the taxpayer's business, namely that they enabled different departments to be segregated from each other, regardless of whether individual departments expanded or contracted.

14.32 The importance of the nature of the particular trade came to greatest prominence with the concept of ambience. This idea was put forward in *CIR v Scottish & Newcastle Breweries Ltd [1982] STC 296*, where the taxpayer, carrying on the trade of a hotelier, incurred significant expenditure on lighting and decor in its licensed premises. These items were successfully claimed as plant. The Special Commissioners found that the company's trade was not just the provision of food and accommodation, but also the creation of atmosphere or ambience. This view was ultimately upheld in the House of Lords.

14.33 In consequence of this decision, items of bric-a-brac festooning hotels, restaurants and public houses will qualify as plant. The same items would not, of course, be plant if purchased by anyone carrying on a trade of which the provision of hospitality (and therefore ambience) was not a fundamental part.

14.34 The comments of Lord Wilberforce in the *Scottish & Newcastle Breweries* case serve as a fitting conclusion:

'In the end each case must be resolved, in my opinion, by considering carefully the nature of the particular trade being carried on, and the relation of the expenditure to the promotion of the trade.'

Statute — eligible expenditure

General

14.35 Various types of expenditure, which would otherwise not obviously qualify as plant, are expressly stated to qualify. These include:

(i) thermal insulation (*Sec 28*);

(ii) computer software (*Sec 71*);

(iii) films, etc. (*Sch 2, para 82*);

(iv) fire safety (*Sec 29*);

(v) safety at sports grounds (*Secs 30–32*);

(vi) personal security assets (*Sec 33*).

The expenditure covered by these sections has in each case been perceived as being worthy of relief for non-tax reasons. In addition, building alterations connected with the installation of machinery or plant are treated as plant by virtue of *Sec 25* (see 13.24 et seq.).

Expenditure on thermal insulation

14.36   Thermal insulation will be treated as plant if it is added to an existing industrial building occupied for the purposes of a trade or let for such a purpose. [*Sec 28.*] If the insulation is added during the course of construction of a new industrial building, it will qualify only for IBAs.

14.37   The legislation also provides that on a disposal of the asset a disposal value of nil has to be brought into account, so as to ensure that relief is only given to the person installing the insulation. [*Sec 63(5).*] Assets likely to qualify for allowances will include:

•   roof lining;

•   double glazing;

•   draught exclusion;

•   cavity wall insulation.

(CA, para 22220)

14.38   Where expenditure is incurred on assets which serve more than one purpose (for example, double glazing which retains heat and excludes noise), allowances will nonetheless be available provided that insulation against loss of heat is *one of the reasons* why it is incurred. It does not have to be the main reason (CA, para 22220).

14.39   It should be noted that the provisions cover only prevention of the loss of heat, and not the prevention of the loss of cold, for example to assist in the creation of a low ambient temperature. Where the latter is relevant, however, it may well be that the insulation qualifies as plant under general principles. *Secs 21* and *22*, for example, envisage that cold stores, cold rooms, and air cooling equipment may be eligible as plant (see 14.63 et seq.).

Computer software

14.40   Expenditure on computer software may be treated as plant in accordance with *Sec 71* (though for expenditure on or after 1 April 2002, companies, but not individuals, must elect for the treatment to apply – see 24.14). Prior to the enactment of *Sec 71*, some doubt existed as to the availability of capital allowances in respect of expenditure on computer software, though many such claims were agreed. The perceived problem was that software was not generally purchased outright. Instead, it was (and still is) common for a payment to be made for the right to use software under licence. Under such an arrangement, it could not be said that the software was owned by the user of the software, as is required by *Sec 11(4)(b)*. For small companies, a first-year allowance of 100% may be available — see 13.5.

14.41 Allowances under *Sec 71* are extended to capital sums paid for computer software licences and software distributed by electronic means. Such software is treated as machinery or plant, and as satisfying the belonging requirement. The Inland Revenue has confirmed that allowances are only available to the grantee. Thus, if A incurs the expenditure, but requires the licence to be granted to B, no allowances will be available.

14.42 It is of course generally better to claim the cost of software as a revenue expense, thus obtaining full tax relief in the year in which it is incurred. Whether or not this is possible will depend upon the facts. When software is acquired at the same time as hardware, the Revenue will seek to treat it as capital. However, this is not a firm rule. The borderline between capital and revenue is as uncertain for 'deemed' plant such as software as it is for 'true' plant.

14.43 In most cases, an election to treat software as a short life asset under *Sec 83* will not confer any benefit. This is because under those rules, the benefit of the election is only felt where the asset is disposed of within the prescribed period (see 13.73 et seq.). It is not sufficient that the software has been taken out of use. The question arises, of course, as to whether software can physically be disposed of — unlike hardware it is not a tangible asset and so the question is not easily answered. It appears the following would qualify as a disposal:

- where software is acquired under a fixed term licensing agreement, expiry of that term;

- where dedicated software can only be used with certain items of hardware, disposal of that hardware;

- in other cases, deletion of software from hard disks and destruction of any other media.

14.44 Where, under the provisions outlined above, computer software (or the right to use such software) is treated as machinery or plant, then if a right is granted to another person to use that software, a disposal value must be brought into account. This is the case whenever a capital sum is received for the grant of such a right, regardless of whether the right granted is in respect of the whole or part only of the software.

Example

14.45   Kingston, a trader, makes up his accounts to 31 March annually. On 1 April 1996, the value of his general plant pool was £30,000. He subsequently had the following transactions:

- 30 April 1996 — purchased computer for £5,000, together with associated software for £2,000.

- 10 June 1996 — purchased for £3,000 from a young inventor the exclusive right to a specialist software package for investment analysis which he used in his trade. He also employed the young inventor.

- 30 November 1996 — granted a licence to Bowley to use the specialist package for £1,500. Bowley did not intend to use the software for trading purposes.

- 6 June 1997 — granted a similar licence to Potter for £2,000. Potter also did not intend to use the software for trading purposes.

- 10 June 1997 — granted a similar licence back to the original inventor of the software. No consideration was given.

Allowances are as follows:

Year ended 31 March 1997	£	£	
Plant pool b/fwd		30,000	
Additions: Computer	5,000		
Software	2,000		
Software	3,000		
	10,000		
		40,000	
Disposals: licence 30.11.96		(1,500)	
		38,500	
Writing-down allowance		(9,625)	
		28,875	
Year ended 31 March 1998			
Plant pool b/fwd		28,875	
Disposals: licence 6.6.97		(2,000)	
licence 10.6.97		(nil)	(Note)
		26,875	
Writing-down allowance		(6,719)	
		20,656	

NB It is assumed that the licence granted on 10 June will give rise to a Schedule E charge on the inventor, who is employed by Kingston. Market value is therefore not brought into account. See 11.42 et seq.

14.46 The Inland Revenue is understood to accept that allowances are due where a person incurs capital expenditure on writing software programs for his own use, even if these are never stored in a tangible form (e.g. disk).

Fire safety

14.47 *Sec 29* gives relief for traders incurring expenditure in taking steps to comply with a notice issued under the *Fire Precautions Act 1971, Sec 5(4)*, where the notice was issued on an application for a fire certificate in respect of premises used for the purposes of the trade and where relief would not otherwise be available. [*Sec 29.*] It may be that no formal notice is issued. However, relief is also available where a trader incurs expenditure in taking, in respect of any premises used by him for the purposes of the trade:

(*a*)   steps specified, in a letter or other document sent or given to him by or on behalf of the fire authority or an application for a fire certificate under the *Fire Precautions Act 1971* in respect of those premises, as steps that would have to be taken in order to satisfy the authority as mentioned in *Sec 5(4)* of that Act, being steps which might have been, but were not, specified in a notice under that subsection; or

(*b*)   steps which, in consequence of the making of an order under *Sec 10* of that Act prohibiting or restricting the use of the premises, had to be taken to enable the premises to be used without contravention of the order. [*Sec 29(4).*]

14.48 Under *Pt II*, relief is given to lessors who make contributions towards their tenants' or licensees' fire safety expenditure, provided the expenditure satisfies the conditions of *Sec 29* or Northern Ireland equivalents. In practice, relief is also allowed where the lessor incurs the expenditure himself, if similar expenditure by the tenant or licensee would have qualified for relief (ESC B14).

14.49 As with expenditure on thermal insulation, a disposal value of nil is deemed to be brought into account in the period in which the asset(s) represented by the expenditure is disposed of [*Sec 63(5)*], thereby ensuring that relief is only given to the person incurring the initial expenditure.

14.50 The *Fire Precautions Act 1971* does not apply in Northern Ireland. However, ESC B16 grants relief under Northern Ireland equivalents, on the same basis as in Great Britain. There are, however, two other problem areas:

(i)   Buildings covered by the relevant parts of the *Fire Precautions Act 1971* include:

(*a*)   factories;

(*b*)   offices;

(*c*)   shops;

(*d*)   railways;

(*e*)   boarding houses;

(*f*)   hotels.

Other premises, for example, hospitals and nursing homes are not included. The Revenue is believed to have denied relief for fire safety expenditure in such cases.

(ii)   As stated above, relief is strictly given only where expenditure is incurred as a result of fire authority instructions. Where a new building is being constructed, the architect will incorporate fire safety features from the first draft in accordance with the planning requirements, before there is any need for them to be specified by a fire authority. Expenditure on these safety features would not strictly qualify for relief under *Sec 29* but may constitute plant for other reasons. The potential claimant should be aware that the wording of *Sec 29* is strictly adhered to.

Safety at sports grounds

14.51   The rules under this heading are similar to those affecting fire safety, as set out above. Expenditure will be treated as plant, if incurred to comply with the terms and conditions of a safety certificate issued under the *Safety of Sports Grounds Act 1975* or certified by a local authority as falling within those requirements if such a certificate had been applied for. [*Sec 30.*] Not all sports grounds are regulated by this Act. However, safety expenditure on other (non-designated) sports grounds may qualify for similar relief if it is incurred to comply with safety certificate requirements of a local authority. [*Secs 31* and *32.*]

If the assets are disposed of, the disposal value to be brought into account is nil, so that allowances can only be given to the person originally incurring the expenditure. [*Sec 65(4).*]

Security assets

14.52   *Sec 33* gives plant allowances for expenditure on the provision of a 'security asset' where relief could not otherwise be given. A 'security asset' is one which is used to meet a 'special threat' to an individual's personal physical security, arising wholly or mainly by virtue of his trade, profession or vocation. [*Sec 33(2).*] If the expenditure is incurred partly for security and partly for other reasons, the amount qualifying under this section will be based on an appropriate proportion of the whole. [*Sec 33(5)*.] Incidental use of a security asset for other purposes (e.g. staff welfare) does not preclude the allowance being given (*Sec 33(3)* and ICAEW Technical Release TR 759). Similarly, allowances are still available where the benefit of increased security is felt not only by the trader, but also by members of his family or household. [*Sec 33(4)*.]

14.53 A Revenue Press Release of 13 April 1989 detailed the types of assets intended to be covered. These include:

(*a*) alarm systems;

(*b*) bullet-resistant windows in houses;

(*c*) flood-lighting and similar facilities.

14.54 Certain assets are excluded from being security assets:

(i) cars;

(ii) ships;

(iii) aircraft;

(iv) dwellings and grounds appurtenant to a dwelling. [*Sec 33(6)*.]

14.55 In considering whether an asset qualifies for relief, it is immaterial whether or not it becomes affixed to land (whether constituting a dwelling or otherwise). [*Sec 33(6)(b)*.] It should be noted, however, that this allowance is only available to individuals carrying on a 'relevant qualifying activity', i.e.: a trade; an ordinary *Schedule A* business; a furnished holiday lettings business; an overseas property business; or a profession or vocation. [*Sec 33(1)*.] Expenditure by a company for the benefit of an employee will not qualify for an allowance.

Demolition costs

14.56 Where any machinery or plant in use for the purposes of a qualifying activity is demolished, then:

(*a*) if that machinery or plant is replaced, the net cost of demolition is treated as expenditure incurred on the provision of the new machinery or plant; and

(*b*) if the machinery or plant is not replaced, the net cost of demolition is treated as qualifying expenditure in the chargeable period in which the demolition takes place. [*Sec 26*.]

14.57 Exceptions to (*b*) above are encountered in the context of the offshore oil industry, which is beyond the scope of this book. [*Sec 163*.]

Statute — ineligible expenditure

Background

14.58   As a result of case law, the dividing line between plant and buildings has shifted over the years in favour of the taxpayer, as a result of the courts or the Special Commissioners being convinced of the 'correctness' of taxpayers' claims, in the sense that they fell within the definition laid down by the premises, function and business use tests (see 14.11–14.34). One result of this, however, was that certain items were eligible for the accelerated allowances available for plant, despite having a life which was just as long as the building in which they were incorporated. In respect of accounting periods ending on or after 26 November 1996, this anomaly was addressed by the introduction of a lower rate of allowance for plant which is a long life asset (see 13.53).

14.59   An earlier attempt to address the issue, at least in connection with plant which is incorporated into a building, reached the statute book in what are now *Secs 21–23*. These consist largely of tables (reproduced below) which firstly list items in a building or structure which are not generally plant, then set out the circumstances in which such items may nonetheless qualify. These new rules apply to expenditure incurred on or after 30 November 1993, or in pursuance of a contract entered into before that date. [*FA 1994, Sec 117.*]

14.60   These provisions were not intended to change the treatment of assets which had been accepted as plant by the courts (Statement by the Financial Secretary to the Treasury, *Hansard*, Standing Committee A, 10 March 1994, col 602). However, this does not extend to cases where the Special Commissioners had decided in the taxpayers' favour (prior to publication of the Special Commissioners' decisions), and the Revenue has chosen not to appeal, or where the treatment of certain assets has been the subject of a long-standing agreement between taxpayer and Revenue. Thus the seemingly unfair situation can now arise where a taxpayer has incurred expenditure on, say, a lighting system in 1992, and the Commissioners have regarded the whole as expenditure on plant. If the same taxpayer incurs the same type of expenditure in 1998, the claim would have to be pressed against the background of the new (i.e. different) rules. Such an anomaly is only partly resolved by the publication of Special (but not General) Commissioners' decisions, which commenced in 1995.

14.61   The second claim made for the new rules was that they would 'help clarify the boundary between buildings, structures and land on the one hand and plant on the other'. Such a 'reclarification of boundaries' was always a Herculean task, attempting as it does to clarify a term that, as we have seen, has long defied definition by many learned judges. Modern commercial buildings have a variety of hi-tech features built into their very fabric. For example, a computer centre may incorporate a so-called 'Faraday cage' to prevent corruption of data. In the light of such technological advances, the clarification of the boundary between buildings and plant would have taxed the most competent draughtsman. One may perhaps see the 1996 rules on long life assets as recognition that *Secs 21–23*, as originally enacted, were less than fully successful in this attempted clarification.

Details of *Secs 21–23*

14.62 Buildings, structures and interests in land are all dealt with separately.

Buildings

14.63 For expenditure incurred on or after 30 November 1993, expenditure on the provision of machinery or plant does not include any expenditure on the provision of a building. [*Sec 21(1)*.] The term 'building' includes any asset in the building which is incorporated into the building or is normally so incorporated, and in particular any asset in or in connection with the building which appears in List A. [*Sec 21(3)*.] The Revenue regards 'in connection with' as merely indicating physical connection (Revenue reply to ICAEW representations on the *Finance Bill 1994*).

14.64 In addition to these general exclusions, the question of whether or not an asset is an item of plant is initially determined by List A of *Sec 21* (reproduced below). This is subject to List C in *Sec 23* (see 14.70).

'List A

Assets Treated as Buildings

1. Walls, floors, ceilings, doors, gates, shutters, windows and stairs.

2. Mains services, and systems, for water, electricity and gas.

3. Waste disposal systems.

4. Sewerage and drainage systems.

5. Shafts or other structures in which lifts, hoists, escalators and moving walkways are installed.

6. Fire safety systems.'

Structures, assets and works

14.65 For expenditure incurred on or after 30 November 1993, expenditure on the provision of machinery or plant does not include any expenditure on:

(*a*) the provision of any structure or asset in List B; or

(*b*)   any works involving the alteration of land. [*Sec 22(1)*.]

14.66   A structure means a fixed structure of any kind, other than a building. [*Sec 22(3)*.] The Revenue Press Release accompanying the draft legislation declared that 'a structure is any substantial man-made asset'. The meaning of this is not entirely clear, as no doubt many structures are less 'substantial' than many machines and items of plant.

14.67   As with buildings, the legislation gives a list of structures excluded from being plant. This is set out below. This is subject to List C in *Sec 23* (see 14.70).

'List B

Excluded Structures and Other Assets

1.   A tunnel, bridge, viaduct, aqueduct, embankment or cutting.

2.   A way, hard standing (such as a pavement), road, railway, tramway, a park for vehicles or containers, or an airstrip or runway.

3.   An inland navigation, including a canal or basin or a navigable river.

4.   A dam, reservoir or barrage, including any sluices, gates, generators and other equipment associated with the dam, reservoir or barrage.

5.   A dock, harbour, wharf, pier, marina or jetty or any other structure in or at which vessels may be kept, or merchandise or passengers may be shipped or unshipped.

6.   A dike, sea wall, weir or drainage ditch.

7.   Any structure not within items 1 to 6 other than—

   (*a*)   a structure (but not a building) within Chapter 2 of Part 3 (meaning of "industrial building"),

   (*b*)   a structure in use for the purposes of an undertaking for the extraction, production, processing or distribution of gas, and

   (c)   a structure in use for the purposes of a trade which consists in the provision of telecommunication, television or radio services.'

Land

14.68   Expenditure on the provision of machinery or plant on or after 30 November 1993 does not include expenditure on the acquisition of any interest in land. Items which are attached to land such that, under general land law, they become part of it, are not covered by this provision. [*Sec 24.*]

General exemptions

14.69 The rules in *Secs 21* and *23* do not affect:

(*a*) thermal insulation (*Sec 28* — see 14.36 et seq.);

(*b*) computer software (*Sec 71* — see 14.40 et seq.);

(*c*) films etc. (*Sch 2, para 82*);

(*d*) fire safety expenditure (*Sec 29* — see 14.47 et seq.);

(*e*) safety equipment at sports grounds (*Secs 30–32* — see 14.51);

(*f*) security assets (*Sec 33* — see 14.52 et seq.).

Specific exemptions

14.70 Lists A and B (see 14.64 and 14.67) are subject to List C (*Sec 23*). This does not mean that assets included in List C are automatically plant, but merely that they are not precluded from being plant by *Secs 21* and *22* (Lists A and B). These assets will only attract plant allowances if they meet the usual criteria, including the function, premises and business use tests (see 14.11–14.34).

'List C

Expenditure Unaffected by Sections 21 and 22

1. Machinery (including devices for providing motive power) not within any other item in this list.

2. Electrical systems (including lighting systems) and cold water, gas and sewerage systems provided mainly—

   (*a*) to meet the particular requirements of the qualifying activity, or

   (*b*) to serve particular plant or machinery used for the purposes of the qualifying activity.

3. Space or water heating systems; powered systems of ventilation, air cooling or air purification; and any floor or ceiling comprised in such systems.

4. Manufacturing or processing equipment; storage equipment (including cold rooms); display equipment; and counters, checkouts and similar equipment.

5. Cookers, washing machines, dishwashers, refrigerators and similar equipment; washbasins, sinks, baths, showers, sanitary ware and similar equipment; and furniture and furnishings.

6. Lifts, hoists, escalators and moving walkways.

7. Sound insulation provided mainly to meet the particular requirements of the qualifying activity.

8. Computer, telecommunication and surveillance systems (including their wiring or other links).

9. Refrigeration or cooling equipment.

10. Fire alarm systems; sprinkler and other equipment for extinguishing or containing fires.

11. Burglar alarm systems.

12. Strong rooms in bank or building society premises; safes.

13. Partition walls, where movable and intended to be moved in the course of the qualifying activity.

14. Decorative assets provided for the enjoyment of the public in hotel, restaurant or similar trades.

15. Advertising hoardings; signs, displays and similar assets.

16. Swimming pools (including diving boards, slides and structures on which such boards or slides are mounted).

17. Any glasshouse constructed so that the required environment (namely, air, heat, light, irrigation and temperature) for the growing of plants is provided automatically by means of devices forming an integral part of its structure.

18. Cold stores.

19. Caravans provided mainly for holiday lettings.

20. Buildings provided for testing aircraft engines run within the buildings.

21. Moveable buildings intended to be moved in the course of the qualifying activity (see 14.72).

22. The alteration of land for the purpose only of installing plant or machinery.

23. The provision of dry docks.

24. The provision of any jetty or similar structure provided mainly to carry plant or machinery.

25. The provision of pipelines or underground ducts or tunnels with a primary purpose of carrying utility conduits.

26. The provision of towers to support floodlights.

27. The provision of—

   (*a*) any reservoir incorporated into a water treatment works, or

   (*b*) any service reservoir of treated water for supply within any housing estate or other particular locality.

28. The provision of—

   (*a*) silos provided for temporary storage, or

   (*b*) storage tanks.

29. The provision of slurry pits or silage clamps.

30. The provision of fish tanks or fish ponds.

31. The provision of rails, sleepers and ballast for a railway or tramway.

32. The provision of structures and other assets for providing the setting for any ride at an amusement park or exhibition.

33. The provision of fixed zoo cages.'

14.71   The Revenue has also confirmed that the reference to 'water heating systems' includes the whole of the system, and not just heating apparatus (Revenue reply to ICAEW representations on the *Finance Bill 1994*).

14.72   For an example of the scope of Item 21, see *Anchor International Ltd v IRC [2003] STC (SCD) 115* (Appendix 4), dealing with the base for an artificial sports pitch.

Chapter 15

Plant: Treatment of Common Items in Buildings

Plant in buildings

15.1   It is true to say that many of the areas of dispute regarding plant are common to the majority of buildings, whether newly built or purchased second hand. These include:

(*a*)   mains services generally;

(*b*)   water systems;

(*c*)   gas installations;

(*d*)   electrical systems;

(*e*)   substations;

(*f*)   lighting;

(*g*)   lightning protection;

(*h*)   lift installations;

(*i*)   suspended ceilings;

(*j*)   partition walls;

(*k*)   doors (e.g. roller shutters).

15.2   What follows is a brief discussion of the treatment of such items. As ever, the merits of an individual claim will depend on the precise facts of the case, and the application of the general principles described in Chapter 14.

Mains services generally

15.3   When considering the question of machinery or plant in buildings, the first port of call must be what are now *Secs 21–23* which, with effect from 30 November 1993, sought to codify existing case law and practice. *Sec 21* rules that the term 'building' includes 'mains services, and systems, of water, electricity and gas'. Such items cannot therefore be regarded as plant, unless they are provided:

15.3 Plant in buildings

(*a*) to meet the particular requirements of the trade; or

(*b*) to serve particular machinery or plant used for the purposes of the trade.

15.4 The question had been raised by the accountancy bodies many years earlier, and an answer given by Sir William Pile, Chairman of the Board of Inland Revenue. This answer (released by the ICAEW as Technical Release 256) still provides an invaluable insight into this area, and may in some ways be seen as a commentary (albeit well in advance) of the relevant parts of *Secs 21–23*.

15.5 The specific clarification sought by the CCAB (Consultative Committee of Accountancy Bodies) was with regard to the eligibility for capital allowances of expenditure on the installation of 'main services' in new hotels. This followed the case of *St John's School (Mountford and Knibbs) v Ward (HMIT) (1974) 49 TC 524*. The Revenue's reply is set out below:

'You have asked about the treatment of expenditure on the installation of the "main services" in new hotels. You said that hitherto the Revenue had regarded such expenditure as expenditure on plant and machinery which therefore qualified for capital allowances, but that recently, in the light of a court case about school buildings, Inspectors of Taxes had begun to challenge this view and to suggest that no relief was due as such expenditure should be regarded as part of the cost of the building.

There has, in fact, been no recent change in Revenue practice in this area. What has happened is that the recent case to which you refer — *St John's School v Ward* — has focused fresh attention on the distinction which has always had to be drawn for the purposes of capital allowances between expenditure on plant and machinery and expenditure on buildings. As a result, Inspectors of Taxes have no doubt recently been looking more critically at borderline expenditure. But there has been no change in our view of what falls on either side of the dividing line, and there is, of course, no question of any "attack" on the hotel industry. It is our job to apply the law as we understand it, and the treatment of hotels and restaurants is in this respect no different from that of any other business.

It may be helpful if I summarise our practice in this area, which is based on the views expressed by the courts over the years. Expenditure on the provision of main services to buildings such as electrical wiring, cold water piping, and gas piping is regarded as part of the cost of the building, and therefore as not qualifying for capital allowances. We do, however, regard as eligible for capital allowances expenditure on *apparatus* to provide electric light or power, hot water, central heating, ventilation or air conditioning, and expenditure on alarm and sprinkler systems. Relief is also given on the cost of all hot water pipes, and on the cost of baths, washbasins, etc. although the *St John's School* case suggests that the courts might regard such expenditure as part of the cost of the building. We do not, however, propose any change of practice in this respect. Finally, to complete the picture, and since you mentioned modernisation, I should say that expenditure on alterations to *existing* buildings which is incidental to the installation of plant or machinery qualifies for relief under a separate provision [*Sec 25*].'

Hot and cold water systems

15.6   *Sec 21* regards as part of a building both a mains water system and a sewerage or drainage system. However, cold water and sewerage systems may still be regarded as plant if they are provided mainly to meet the particular requirements of the trade, or to serve particular machinery or plant used for the purposes of the trade. As discussed below, hot water installations are not generally considered to be a contentious item of plant.

15.7   Very often, analyses of building expenditure include one amount only in respect of plumbing, to cover both hot and cold water systems. The claimant should go further, and attempt to break down further this amount into a hot water element and a cold water element. The tax treatment of each can be quite different.

Hot water installations

15.8   Items included within a hot water installation were accepted as plant by the Revenue in the case of *Lupton v Cadogan Gardens Development Ltd (1971) 47 TC 1*. Water heaters were also inferred to be plant in the case of *Jarrold v John Good & Sons Ltd* (see 15.36 et seq.). In addition, apparatus to provide hot water, along with all hot water pipes, was allowed as plant in Sir William Pile's letter reported in *Accountant* magazine in August 1977, and subsequently forming part of Technical Release TR 256 of the Institute of Chartered Accountants in England and Wales (see 15.36 et seq.). The Revenue has confirmed that the reference to a 'hot water system' includes the whole of such a system, and not just the heating apparatus.

Cold water installations

15.9   In general terms, cold water installations are not usually regarded as plant. To all intents and purposes, the question of their eligibility for allowances has only once been specifically considered by the courts. A cold water installation is generally seen from the outset of a project as an asset which is part of the actual structure of the building, rather than an item of plant.

15.10   The one significant occasion of cold water systems being considered by the courts was in the *Wimpey International* case referred to above at 14.20. On that occasion, the items in dispute were cold water tanks and piping installed solely due to the requirements of Wimpey's catering trade. Due to this particular fact, the tanks and piping were allowed as plant. In the words of the published decision: 'In so far as the installations they serve are plant they too are plant. But if they form part of a general water supply such as any occupier would need they are not.' The need for special cold water installations is by no means restricted to the restaurant trade. Such a system may be necessary, for example, where there is a requirement for machinery to be constantly cooled or where water is consumed in processing or manufacturing. However, in most other circumstances, the nature of the properties and the trades carried on there does not suggest that there is any significant scope for claiming allowances in respect of general cold water installations. A claim is more likely to succeed where the installation consists of a separate potable water supply, or where it consists of pipes etc. dedicated to serving accepted items of plant (for example, a hot pressings machine).

Gas installations

15.11 These are usually treated in their entirety as items of plant or machinery. In contrast to electrical systems, the eligibility of gas installations has not been specifically considered by the courts. However, Revenue practice is again set out in Sir William Pile's letter incorporated within the ICAEW Technical Release TR 256 (see 15.4 et seq.). That letter states that 'the provision of mains services to buildings such as ... gas piping is regarded as part of the cost of the building'. However, the same letter then goes on to say that capital allowances are given for expenditure on 'apparatus to provide ... hot water [and] central heating'.

Electrical systems

15.12 The electrical system of a building is in the first instance precluded from being regarded as plant by *Sec 21*. However, a system may nonetheless be plant if it is provided mainly for one of two purposes:

(*a*) to meet the particular requirements of the trade; or

(*b*) to serve particular machinery or plant used for the purposes of the trade [*Sec 23*].

15.13 In a standard electrical system, some items will qualify and some will not. However, it is sometimes possible to claim allowances on the whole of the system, provided certain conditions are met (CA, para 21180). These are:

(i) it is specifically designed and built as a whole, and is a fully integrated entity;

(ii) it is designed and adapted to meet the particular requirements of the trade;

(iii) the end user items of the system function as apparatus in the trader's business; and

(iv) it is essential for the functioning of the business.

By way of illustration, these rules were first formulated in respect of a claim for the entire electrical system of a supermarket. The electrical installation in that case was regarded as one gigantic complex system, the function of which was a tool to enable the supermarket to sell its merchandise. It went far beyond merely providing the essential housing of the business.

15.14   If a system does not meet these criteria, a piecemeal approach will be adopted in deciding which elements are plant and which are not (CA, para 21180).

Electrical substations

15.15   Expenditure under this heading is likely to fall into two broad categories:

(*a*)   expenditure on transformers, and

(*b*)   expenditure on switch gear.

15.16   Both transformers and switch gear were considered in the case of *Cole Bros Ltd v Phillips [1982] STC 307.* The Special Commissioners had found that the transformers were plant, but that the switch gear was not. When the case went to court, the Revenue did not dispute the decision regarding transformers, however, there is some confusion regarding the treatment of switch gear. It is believed that the switch gear ancillary to the transformer was allowed as part of the cost of the transformer itself. It is likely that switch gear will qualify in full if the items it serves have been substantially allowed as plant.

15.17   Much depends on the precise nature of each relevant electrical system, and the way in which it operates. However, in most cases, it is unlikely that the cost of housings will qualify for allowances.

15.18   In order to substantiate any claim, the claimant will need precise details both of the substations and of the electrical systems which they serve. It may be that such information can only be provided by the relevant electrical engineers.

Lighting

15.19   Lighting is not generally allowed as plant. Although exceptions to this rule have been reported, these are relatively rare, and normally turn on the particular circumstances of the case. For example, lighting has been allowed as plant where it could be properly said to perform a function in the trade of a restaurateur. This, however, is often tied in with the question of 'ambience', necessary to attract custom. This particular argument is therefore unlikely to be of relevance to most claimants. Another very common example of qualifying lighting is that used for display purposes in shops. The key factor to consider is whether the lighting can be regarded as something more than part of the premises in which the trade is carried on. The leading case on this subject was for many years not a tax case at all, but rather one dealing with compensation under the *War Damages Act 1943*. This was *J Lyons & Co Ltd v A-G [1944] 1 All ER 477*, although it was acknowledged in *Wimpey International* that the *Lyons* case was dealing with 'setting' (rather than 'premises') in a very special sense. This reasoning was confirmed more recently in the case of *Cole Bros Ltd v Phillips* above, where general lighting was one of the elements claimed as plant in respect of a department store at Brent Cross.

15.20   *Sec 23* recognises that lighting systems may on occasion qualify as plant, where provided mainly to meet the particular requirements of the trade, or to serve particular machinery or plant used for the purposes of the trade. Building specifications will often refer to 'special light fittings' or some such term. In order to be successfully claimed, such fittings really must perform a special function, for example:

(*a*)   providing ambience in a trade dealing with members of the public;

(*b*)   providing daylight lamps for examining fabrics etc.;

(*c*)   display lighting in shops.

15.21   Lighting is not sufficiently 'special', for example, if it is intended solely to provide an attractive feature or focal point in the reception area of an office.

15.22   The above comments do not necessarily apply to car park and emergency lighting and floodlighting. The specific question of whether car park lighting is eligible for allowances has not been decided by the courts. It is understood, however, that an appeal is before the Special Commissioners in respect of a claim for allowances on the whole of a car park, including its attendant lighting, used in a trade of retailing. Like the restaurant trade referred to above in connection with lighting, a retail concern has fixed asset requirements which are highly specialised. This claim would seem to be based on fixed asset requirements which are unique to the restaurant or retail trades, and would therefore be of only limited scope.

15.23   Emergency lighting was claimed as plant in the case of *Cole Bros Ltd v Phillips* referred to above. The claim was not disputed by the Revenue. It seems clear that, perhaps unusually for lighting, emergency lighting will qualify for allowances as an item of plant.

Floodlighting

15.24   In general terms, there can only be two reasons for the installation of floodlighting:

(*a*) to draw attention to a property at night, to advertise its pleasant aspect and its occupiers' trades, and

(*b*) for security purposes.

15.25 In either case, it is likely that the lighting performs a function in the trade of the building's owners or tenants. Furthermore, *Sec 23* specifically provides that expenditure on the provision of towers to support floodlights may qualify for plant allowances.

Lightning protection

15.26 Systems of lightning protection will generally qualify as plant for capital allowances purposes. However, the treatment does vary and some Inspectors state that where the building is of a type or size normally equipped with such protection, it could be said to be a part of the building or 'setting', rather than an item of plant used for the purposes of a trade.

15.27 However, where the existence of lightning protection is not only normal but is also essential because of the trade carried on, it may be that the lightning protection qualifies as plant in accordance with the 'business use' test. Examples would be the explosives store of a fireworks manufacturer or the premises of an electronics manufacturer.

Lift installations

15.28 Lift cars and their attendant machinery (including wiring) are items of plant not disputed by the Revenue. They were allowed as plant in the following cases:

(*a*) *Macsaga Investment Co Ltd v Lupton (1967) 44 TC 659*;

(*b*) *Lupton v Cadogan Gardens Developments Ltd (1971) 47 TC 1*;

(*c*) *Benson v Yard Arm Club Ltd (1979) 53 TC 67*.

15.29 In the *Macsaga* case, Pennycuick J stated, 'I would say at the outset that it is, I think, perfectly clear that … lifts … are machinery or plant in any ordinary use of those words'. This was not questioned in the other cases referred to above, and has now been formally confirmed by the Revenue (CA, para 21190).

15.30 The treatment of lift shafts will depend on when the expenditure was incurred. If this was after 30 November 1993, then lift shafts are specifically prohibited from being regarded as plant by *Sec 21*, which, *inter alia*, denies machinery and plant capital allowances to expenditure on 'Shafts or other structures in which lifts, hoists, escalators and moving walkways are installed' (List A). For expenditure on or before 30 November 1993, the treatment depends on the facts. A lift shaft was specifically allowed as plant in the case of *Schofield v R & H Hall Ltd (1974) 49 TC 538*, although it has to be said that the circumstances in this case were somewhat unusual, as the whole of the structure that the lift served (a grain silo) also qualified as plant.

15.31 Where a lift is added to an existing building, for instance one added to an external wall, it is clear that the building is complete without the lift or its shaft. The shaft should qualify under *Sec 25* (as an alteration to an existing building incidental to the installation of machinery or plant). However, where the lift forms an integral part of the structural entity of the building from the start, it will be regarded as part of the structure, rather than as machinery or plant (CA, para 21190). In most cases the treatment of lift pits will follow the treatment of shafts.

Suspended ceilings

15.32 Suspended or false ceilings do not usually qualify as plant, and are regarded as part of a building by *Sec 21*. However, it is possible for them to so qualify in certain, very restricted circumstances. The leading case on this subject is *Hampton v Forte Autogrill [1980] STC 80*. In this case a company operating a number of restaurants claimed capital allowances in respect of false ceilings in areas used by the public. The basis of this claim was that:

(*a*) the ceilings served to clad or hide services such as piping and wiring, and

(*b*) the ceilings acted as support for items such as loudspeakers and ventilation grilles.

15.33 The claimant further contended that the ceilings were therefore part and parcel of the equipment which they supported and covered. Fox J said, 'It is clear that in determining whether something is plant the test to be applied is a functional test; that is to say, does that thing perform a function in the actual carrying out of the trade?' Fox J found no suggestion that the ceilings were strictly necessary for the functioning of any apparatus.

15.34 This view was generally endorsed in the later case of *Warland v Wimpey International Ltd [1989] STC 273*. However in this case there was one suspended ceiling which did qualify as plant. The reasons for this were connected with the idea of providing a particular atmosphere or 'ambience' for customers, which is a concept peculiar to the hotel and restaurant trades. This argument is unlikely to be of relevance to most potential claimants.

15.35 The other instance in which a suspended ceiling would qualify as an item of plant is where it forms an integral part of another item of plant. This is most likely to be appropriate in the case of a plenum ceiling which effectively acts as, or as part of, a duct forming part of an air-conditioning system. However, it must be the case that the air flows directly through the void created by the ceiling: it is not sufficient for the air to flow through pipes or ducts hidden by the ceiling. In buildings that have already been constructed, this will be a matter of fact. *Sec 23* reflects this possibility, permitting plant allowances for any ceiling comprised in a system of ventilation, air cooling or purification.

Partition walls

15.36   Walls have never been widely regarded as items of plant, and are regarded as part of a building by *Sec 21*, particularly where the wall's principal purpose is to enclose the interior of a building or is intended to remain permanently in place. However, *Sec 23* still allows treatment as plant, in appropriate circumstances, of 'Partition walls, where moveable and intended to be moved in the course of the qualifying activity'. This reflects the earlier case of *John Good & Sons Ltd (1962) 40 TC 681*. For partitions to qualify as plant they must fulfil two criteria:

(*a*)   they must be truly demountable or movable; and

(*b*)   they must be intended or likely to be moved in pursuance of trade.

Movable

15.37   Very often, an initial claim for allowances will include what claimants or their advisers have identified as 'demountable or movable partitions'. It has to be said that, perhaps in a majority of cases, the claim that the partitions involved are demountable is not sustainable once challenged by the Revenue. 'Demountable' may have different meanings for construction technique and for revenue law. Very often, terms such as 'demountable partitions' are attached to any internal wall that is not made of bricks and mortar. In strict terms, of course, any wall may be dismantled: it is a question of the degree of difficulty of so doing. The acid test is whether the partition or wall can be taken down and re-assembled elsewhere with relatively little effort (for example, without employing a builder), and without necessitating wholesale structural alterations or repairs. If this is not possible, then it is more likely that the partitions will be regarded as part of the structure or setting where the trade is carried on, rather than as items of plant used for carrying on the trade.

15.38   In the case of *John Good & Sons Ltd*, the partitions were required to be movable so as to accommodate fluctuations in the size of various internal departments. In order for the partitions to qualify as plant, it was not enough that they should be demountable or movable; it was also necessary that they actually had been moved or were intended to be moved.

15.39 *Plant in buildings*

15.39 It is understood that a small number of proprietary brands of partitions have been accepted by the Inspectors as being demountable. Where such partitions are installed, however, they still have to meet the second requirement, that they are *intended to be moved* in the course of a trade.

Intended to be moved

15.40 This is in many ways the more difficult criterion to meet. It is often a simple matter to identify partitions that are physically demountable, for example where they are fixed merely by screws at floor and ceiling. The question then is whether the partitions meet the second criterion to qualify as plant, namely whether it is envisaged that the partitions will be moved in the course of a trade.

15.41 If a claim is being submitted subsequent to the installation, and in the period since the partitions were installed, they have actually been moved, the claim should succeed with little difficulty. If, on the other hand, a claim is being prepared or planned alongside the construction or development of a property it will not be possible to rely on historical fact to support the claim. In these circumstances, it is important to ensure the appropriate evidence is available and it may be necessary to commission special reports solely for capital allowance purposes. In the case of demountable partitions, it may be appropriate to document formally the need for individual departments to be physically expanded or contracted, perhaps linked to budgets and forecasts based on different scenarios regarding sales or stockholding requirements. The important factor is that the partitions are intended to be moved — it is not necessary for any movement to actually take place.

Roller shutters

15.42 It is a common misconception that capital allowances for plant can be claimed on all roller shutters, especially those operated by electricity. It is often argued that, whilst a door is a pre-requisite for any building, the need for roller shutters is a factor arising from the particular trade being carried on. In the view of the Revenue this is not a valid argument, as the real test is one of what is normally provided in a building of that type, not just in a building generally. For example, it would be senseless to construct a warehouse which did not have large doorways suitable for the loading and unloading of goods. In practical terms, roller shutters or sliding doors are the only way of filling in or securing such a doorway, and might properly be regarded as nothing more than part of the structure or premises. This is certainly the approach taken by *Sec 21*.

15.43 However, there are instances, where a plant claim may be possible. For example, where the requirements of the trade decree the complete exclusion of dust, insects etc. a claim would be justified where roller shutters were added in addition to existing doors to form a sort of 'air lock'.

15.44   The Revenue has conceded to the ICAEW that any mechanism, electrical or mechanical, for opening doors is allowable as plant.

Specialised structures treated as plant

General

15.45   Prior to the implementation of what are now *Secs 21–23*, which have effect from 30 November 1993, the boundary between buildings or structures and plant had become increasingly blurred. As business operations became more complex it was increasingly possible to argue that what, at first sight, might have appeared to be a building or a structure, or a major part of one, was in fact functioning, actively or passively, as an item of plant.

15.46   In 1989 the 'premises test' (see 14.18 et seq.) was clarified in the *Wimpey* case in which Hoffman J acknowledged (at page 170) that:

'even a building or a structure … could be plant if it was appropriate to describe it as apparatus for carrying on the business or employed in the business than as premises or place in or upon which the business was conducted.'

15.47   In the light of *Secs 21* and *22*, however, it is certain that any claim that a building or structure is an item of plant will be more strongly resisted.

15.48   The Revenue announced (Inland Revenue Tax Bulletin, November 1992, page 46) the following policy relating to claims in respect of 'single entities'. It is included here because, although it deals with glasshouses, the principles set out are of much wider application.

'In the past couple of years, there has been a great deal of publicity suggesting that all glasshouses are plant and thus qualify for [plant] allowances […]. This is not the case. We consider the majority of glasshouse structures to be the premises or setting in which a grower's trade is carried on and on that basis they qualify for agricultural buildings allowance.

However, we do accept that, in some cases, a glasshouse unit and its attendant machinery are interdependent, forming a single entity which will function as apparatus within a grower's business and as such will be plant.

These units will be of extremely sophisticated design, including extensive computer controlled equipment, without which the structure cannot operate to achieve the optimum artificial growing environment for the particular crops involved. The equipment will have been permanently installed during construction of the glasshouse and will normally include a computer system which monitors and controls boiler and piped heating systems, temperature and humidity controls, automatic ventilation equipment and automatic thermal or shade screens.'

15.49 *Specialised structures treated as plant*

15.49 In *Gray v Seymours Garden Centre (Horticulture) [1995] STC 706*, a plant claim in respect of a glasshouse failed on the grounds that '[the glasshouse concerned] falls well on the premises side of the line wherever it may be drawn'. It was clear that the glasshouse lacked the 'extremely sophisticated design' etc. on which the position of qualifying glasshouses is founded.

15.50 The door for such claims was not closed completely, however, despite the requirements of *Secs 21* and *22* (see 14.58 et seq.), and the decision in *Attwood v Anduff Car Wash Ltd [1996] STC 110* that so-called 'single units' must still satisfy the premises test.

15.51 Blackburne J in *Bradley v London Electricity plc [1996] STC 1054* stated that just because something was a substantial fixed structure, with a roof and inner and outer walls and floors, and has in it what is accepted to be plant used for the purposes of the business, does not mean that it must be regarded as premises rather than plant.

15.52 The Revenue admits, in the case of cold stores, that whilst some stores will consist of a building housing an insulated 'box' (in which case only the box will qualify as plant), others may be incapable of independent existence as a building, in which case the entire store may qualify for plant allowances (CA, para 1366). Cold stores were accepted as plant in the New Zealand case *CIR v Waitaki International Ltd [1990] 3 NZLR 27*.

Structures protecting plant

15.53 A claim for plant allowances in respect of a housing for an item of plant is made more difficult by *Secs 21* and *22*, but may still be possible, if it can be shown that the housing is an integral part of the plant installation. Despite new legislation, the underlying principles have changed little since they were set out in a Revenue Press Release of March 1953, in the context of allowances for the iron and steel manufacturing industry:

'Where an installation of machinery or plant is protected or sheltered by a structure which is an integral part of the installation in the sense —

   (i)   that the structure with its supports could not be adapted to any other use, and

  (ii)   that the machinery or plant could not be removed without demolishing the structure,

the structure may be treated for Income Tax purposes as plant eligible for the same rate of wear and tear as the protected or sheltered installation.'

Example

15.54   Smith constructs a new automated storage facility, controlled entirely by computers. As a result, the goods can be accepted, identified, stored, sorted by date or type, made up into delivery batches and ejected in customer batches and in order of lorry routes, all under the control of a computer. The method of construction is that the foundation slab is cast first, the frame of the storage racks follows with the roof and cladding being added last. The latter are fastened to and supported solely by the racking. In such circumstances, it is likely that the cost of any purely structural elements would be minimal, with the result that the whole, or substantially the whole, would qualify as plant.

15.55   It must be emphasised, however, that each case will be decided on its facts, and the structural items claimed to be plant must be a genuinely integral and essential part of the plant which they house and protect, rather than being a structure first and foremost. A recent claim (ultimately unsuccessful) was in respect of an underground electrical substation in *Bradley v London Electricity plc [1996] STC 1054*. Following an extensive review of relevant cases, Blackburne J thought the key question was to ask what plant-like function the structure as an entity performed in the taxpayer's trading activity:

'The fact that features of the structure were carefully designed to accommodate the equipment within does not convert what is otherwise plainly the premises in which the activity is conducted into the plant or apparatus with which that activity is conducted.'

Chapter 16

Vehicle Fleet

Introduction

16.1 The treatment of company vehicles will depend on whether they are cars or other vehicles and, if they are cars, whether they cost in excess of £12,000. The legislation begins by defining a car as 'any mechanically propelled road vehicle'. There are, however, a number of exclusions, the first being those vehicles which are of a construction primarily suited for the conveyance of goods. [*Sec 81.*] Lorries and vans are therefore generally excluded from the special treatment accorded to cars. Some vehicles can be designed either for goods or for passengers, and the tax treatment will depend on the precise construction of the relevant vehicle. The Revenue has confirmed that Land Rovers are capable of falling within this exclusion, Range Rovers and estate cars are not. Exclusions from the scope of the term 'motor car' are considered at 16.16 et seq. below.

16.2 If the relevant vehicles are not cars costing more than £12,000, they are dealt with in the same manner as most other items of plant, i.e. as part of the general pool (see 13.3 et seq.).

Cars

16.3 The treatment of a particular car depends on its original cost as sepa rate rules govern cars costing in excess of £12,000. Cars were historically excluded from the general pool of qualifying expenditure (see 13.3 et seq.). This changes for cars costing up to £12,000 from April 2000 (see 16.5).

16.4 The long life assets rules (see 13.53) do not apply to expenditure on cars (including those which are hired out, and are generally not regarded as cars for capital allowances purposes by virtue of *Secs 74(2), 82*).

Inexpensive cars

16.5 The term 'inexpensive cars' does not appear in the statute, but is here used to indicate those cars with a cost to the present taxpayer of £12,000 or less (£8,000 for expenditure prior to 1 April 1992). From 1 June 1980, all new expenditure on such vehicles was deemed to be incurred for the purposes of a notional trade separate from the actual trade carried on. Allowances given were nonetheless treated as arising in the course of the actual trade. The effect of this was that all such expenditure was put into a separate pool (often colloquially called the 'car pool') and allowances could be used in the same way as those from the general pool.

The requirement for separate pooling is abolished for chargeable periods ending on or after 1 April 2000 for corporation tax, or 6 April 2000 for income tax. The taxpayer may formally elect to delay the effect of the abolition by one year.

The closing written-down value of the separate pool for the last chargeable period before abolition is to be added to the opening written-down value of the general pool in the following chargeable period.

[*FA 2000, Sec 74.*]

Expensive cars

16.6   Cars costing in excess of £12,000 are not included in the 'car pool'. Instead, each such car is kept in its own single asset pool. [*Sec 74.*] It follows from this that, unlike disposals from the general or car pools, a balancing adjustment will arise where the individual 'expensive' car is disposed of.

16.7   *Sec 74* refers to capital expenditure exceeding £12,000. Therefore, a car costing £12,000 exactly will be included in the car pool. 'Cost' is stated to be cost when new, inclusive of factory-fitted extras. In practice, a car acquired second hand for under £12,000 will not be treated as 'expensive', even if its cost when new was over that limit.

16.8   Additions made to a car after it has been brought into use, being additions not contracted for or paid for by the time of the acquisition of the car, do not form part of the cost of the car and will be added to the general pool.

16.9   Expensive cars qualify for a writing-down allowance but this is restricted to £3,000 p.a. [*Sec 75*], proportionally adjusted where the accounting period is more or less than a full year.

16.10   Because of the fact that balancing adjustments are made on the disposal of an expensive car, it may be worth paying slightly more to ensure that a new car is deemed to be 'expensive'. In general terms, it will be advantageous to do this where it is anticipated that the car will be sold after a relatively short time for a low value.

Example

16.11   X Ltd has a brought forward car pool of £20,000. In 1998 it intends to purchase a new car. Two models are considered, one costing £11,500 and

16.11 Expensive cars

the other £12,500. It is expected that each car will be sold in 2000 for one-quarter of its original cost. The capital allowances position will be as follows:

	Option 1		Option 2	
	Pool	Pool	Expensive car	Total allowances under option 2
Pool b/fwd	20,000	20,0000		
Additions	11,500		12,500	
	31,500	20,000	12,500	
WDAs	(7,875)	(5,000)	(3,000)	
	23,625	15,000	9,500	
1998 WDAs	(5,906)	(3,750)	(2,375)	6,125
	17,719	11,250	7,125	
1999 WDAs	(4,430)	(2,812)	(1,781)	4,593
	13,289	8,438	5,344	
2000 proceeds	(2,875)		(3,125)	
	10,414			
WDA/bal allowance	(2,604)	(2,109)	(2,219)	4,328
C/fwd	7,810	6,329	nil	

16.12 Total allowances given over the four years will be £20,815 if the cheaper car is purchased, £23,046 for the more expensive one. This is because the 'balancing allowance' for the cheaper car remains in the pool and is effectively allowed over an infinite number of years. This principle is normally clouded by the numerous other movements in the pool.

16.13 However it is a fact that in these circumstances, the dearer car has turned out to be the cheaper of the two in terms of relief for capital expenditure. This may be tax planning for the sake of it, in the case of a business with only two or three cars, because the potential gain is in any case dependent upon the ratio of purchase price to sale price. In the case of a large fleet user, it is a point which might be exploited.

Further restrictions on allowances

16.14 The writing-down allowance is proportionally reduced in the following circumstances:

(a)   where the chargeable period is less than one year [Sec 75(2)];

(b) where the person carrying on the trade receives a subsidy towards the qualifying expenditure [*Sec 532*];

(c) if the car is used partly for purposes other than the purposes of the actual trade [*Sec 77*];

(d) if the person carrying on the trade is paid an amount in respect of wear and tear [*Sec 78*];

(e) where a person contributes towards an expensive car, the allowances he may claim will be restricted to such proportion of £3,000 as his contribution bears to the total expenditure;

(f) the Revenue may also seek to restrict allowances where it appears that the purchase of an expensive car was determined partly by personal choice and only partly by the needs of the trade.

Leasing expensive cars

16.15 The £3,000 limit on the annual writing-down allowance for expensive cars is only a deferment of relief. This is in contrast to the treatment of lease rental payments on cars costing more than £12,000. In the latter case, there is a permanent disallowance calculated annually in accordance with the following formula set out in *TA 1988, Sec 578A*:

$$\text{Rental payments in year} \times \frac{(\text{cost less } \pounds12,000)}{2}$$

Where an 'expensive car' is sold in connection with a 'relevant transaction' for anti-avoidance purposes (*Sec 213* — see 17.27, 19.6), the disposal value brought into account is the lower of market value and original cost. [*Sec 79.*]

This disallowance does not apply if the car is either an electric car or one with low CO_2 emissions (*FA 2002, Sec 60*), provided the expenditure is incurred on or after 17 April 2002 on a car first registered on or after that date. The period of hire must begin on or before 31 March 2008.

Vehicles excluded from special treatment

16.16 Many vehicles continue to be dealt with within the general pool, including:

(a) cars costing £12,000 or less (with effect for chargeable periods ending after 5 April 2000 or one year later if an election is made) — see 16.5;

(b) vehicles constructed in such a way that they are primarily suited for the conveyance of goods or burden of any description [*Sec 81(a)*];

(c) vehicles of a type not commonly used as a private vehicle and unsuitable to be so used (for example, driving school cars fitted with dual controls, in *Bourne v Auto School of Motoring (Norwich) Ltd (1964) 42 TC 217) [Sec 81(b)]*; and

(*d*) 'qualifying hire cars' *[Sec 74(2)(a)]*. These are defined as vehicles provided wholly for hire to, or for the carriage of, members of the public in the ordinary course of trade, provided the following conditions are met *[Sec 82]*:

(i) the vehicle must normally be on hire to (or used for the carriage of) the same person for less than 30 *consecutive* days, and for less than 90 days in any period of 12 months *[Sec 82(2)]*, or

(ii) the vehicle is provided for hire to a person who will himself use it so as to comply with the above conditions *[Sec 82(3)]*.

The restrictive provisions given above relating to the hire of vehicles do not apply where the vehicles are made available wholly or mainly for the use of persons in receipt of mobility allowance or supplement. *[Sec 82(4).]*

(*e*) cars with low CO_2 emissions, and electric cars (see 16.20).

16.17 Mini-vans licensed as goods vehicles and used as such were held to be of a type not commonly used as private vehicles and unsuitable to be so used (*Roberts v Granada TV Rental Ltd (1970) 46 TC 295*). However, the opposite conclusion was reached in respect of the mini-van of a radio dealer (*Tapper v Eyre (1967) 43 TC 720*) and an electrical contractor's van which was not adapted in any way for business use (*Laing v IRC (1967) 44 TC 681*).

Employees' cars

16.18 Special rules apply where an employee incurs capital expenditure on a 'mechanically propelled road vehicle' which is used partly for the purposes of the office or employment and partly for other purposes. The rules are set out in *Sec 80*. These rules remove the requirement that the asset must have been *necessarily* provided for use in the performance of the duties of the office or employment (see 13.29 et seq.) and set out the calculation of a balancing allowance in the event of sale, etc.

Car registration plates

16.19 A registration plate is not plant unless it is attached to a vehicle. In particular, personalised or 'cherished' number plates are not accepted by the Revenue as plant, but merely as evidence of certain intangible rights, not qualifying for allowances (CA, para 21250). Arguably, amortisation of the cost will qualify for relief under *FA 2002, Sch 29* – see Chapter 24. If a car is acquired for a price which reflects the fact that a cherished plate is already fitted, it is in practice unlikely that allowances will be denied on the part of the expenditure attributable to the plate.

Electric cars, and cars with low carbon dioxide emissions

16.20 Electric cars, and cars with low carbon dioxide emissions are exempt from the single asset pool requirement, and qualify for 100% first year allowances (*FA 2002, Sec 59*).

This is provided the expenditure on such cars is incurred in the period from 17 April 2002 to 31 March 2008, the car is unused, not second-hand, and is first registered on or after 17 April 2002, and the asset is not precluded from qualifying for first year allowances by *CAA 2001 s 46* (see 13.9).

A qualifying car is one which has a UK approval certificate, or an EC certificate of conformity, showing that the carbon dioxide emissions do not exceed 120 grams per kilometre.

The provisions apply to taxis, but not to motorcycles.

Chapter 17

Leasing and Hire-purchase

Machinery and plant on hire-purchase

General

17.1   In the absence of specific legislation, a person acquiring plant under a hire-purchase (HP) agreement would not immediately be able to fulfil the 'ownership' requirement of *Sec 11(4)(b)* (see 13.41 et seq.), because title will not generally pass until all instalments have been paid. However, special rules apply where a trader incurs capital expenditure on plant *under a contract* providing that he *shall or may* become the owner of that plant *on the performance of that contract*. The scope of these special rules goes beyond HP alone, but it is in connection with HP that they are most commonly met. Where expenditure could be subject both to the fixtures rules in *Secs 172–204* and the 'hire-purchase' provisions of *Sec 67*, it is the former which take precedence [*Sec 69*].

17.2   The Revenue's view is that expenditure is *incurred under a contract* if and only if the contract is legally binding, and the contract commits the taxpayer to incur that expenditure (CA, para 23310). In such cases, the legislation deems two effects:

(*a*)   the 'belonging' requirement is treated as satisfied at any time when the trader is *entitled to the benefit of the contract* [*Sec 67(2)*]; and

(*b*)   all capital expenditure to be incurred under the contract after the plant has been brought into use is treated as having been incurred at that time. [*Sec 67(3)*.]

17.3   With effect for chargeable periods ending on or after 2 July 1997, the provisions of (*b*) do not apply where the machinery or plant is to be let under a finance lease. [*Sec 229(3)(a)*.] This means that, in such circumstances, expenditure on an asset will only qualify for allowances when it is incurred, and not when (as would otherwise be the case) when the asset is brought into use. This restriction does not apply where the expenditure was incurred before 2 July 1997, or is incurred within 12 months of that date in pursuance of an earlier contract. [*F(No 2) A 1997, Sec 45(2)*.]

17.4   It must be noted that *Sec 67* applies to a contract only if it provides that the intended purchaser 'shall or may become the owner ... on the performance of the contract'. If the contract provides for ownership to pass before all the payments have been made (as in some ship construction contracts) *Sec 67* does not apply because in those circumstances the ownership does not pass 'on the performance of the contract'.

17.5 The second effect [*Sec 67(3)*] deals only with expenditure incurred after the plant has been brought into use. Any expenditure incurred in advance of that time is dealt with under the normal rules for determining the date it is incurred (see 1.36 et seq.). This was confirmed by the Revenue in May 1996 (ICAEW Technical Release 580).

17.6 Where a person to whom any plant is treated as belonging by virtue of *Sec 67(2)* ceases to be entitled to the benefit of the contract (without in fact becoming the owner) the following rules apply:

(i) the plant is treated as ceasing to belong to him at the time when that entitlement ceases;

(ii) if the plant has already been brought into use, the disposal value cannot exceed the total capital expenditure which he would have incurred if he had wholly performed the contract; and

(iii) subject to that limitation, the disposal value consists of so much of the capital expenditure as he has not in fact incurred, and any compensation, damages or insurance moneys. [*Secs 67(4), 68.*]

Example

17.7 Cartons Ltd buys a carton printing machine on a hire-purchase contract. The total price, inclusive of finance charges of £9,600, is £91,200 and is payable in 24 instalments of £3,800 on the first day of each month beginning 1 June 1994. The machine was delivered on 1 June 1994 but was not brought into use until 1 October 1994. The company's accounting date is 31 August. The finance charges of £9,600 will be allowable under Case I of Schedule D over the period of the agreement. The expenditure qualifying for capital allowances will be £91,200 − £9,600 = £81,600 i.e. £3,400 per month. The qualifying expenditure will be as follows:

	£
Year ended 31 August 1994	
Instalments due June, July and August 1994 —	
(*Sec 5(5)* applies) £3,400 × 3 =	10,200
Year ended 31 August 1995	
Instalment due September 1994 —	
(*Sec 5(5)* applies)	3,400
Instalments due October 1994 to May 1996 —	
(*Sec 67(3)* applies) £3,400 × 20 =	68,000
	81,600

Leasing machinery or plant

Introduction

17.8   It is a requirement for claiming capital allowances on plant that the plant must be owned by the person incurring the expenditure. [*Sec 11(4)(b)*.] Where plant is merely leased, this requirement will not be met by the lessee. This applies whether the agreement takes the form of an operating lease or a finance lease. In each case, the lessee will obtain tax relief other than by using capital allowances, by means of rental payments, finance charges or depreciation calculated in accordance with SSAP 21.

17.9   The entitlement to allowances therefore remains with the lessor. However, when negotiating leasing agreements, it is important that the intending lessee is aware of the allowances available to the lessor, so he may understand the economics of the transaction.

Plant allowances are available under *Sec 15* for a number of qualifying activities — these include trades, Schedule A businesses, etc., which could be relevant to leasing, and also a category called 'special leasing' (see 17.20, etc.).

Leasing as a trade or as part of another 'qualifying activity'

17.10   Expenditure on plant and machinery does not fail to attract capital allowances simply because the plant is leased out, rather than used for some other type of trade. However, there are a number of restrictions. Assets used for leasing do not generally qualify for first-year allowances although an exception is where the asset is energy-efficient, and a claim made under *Sec 45A* or *FA 2002, Sec 59* (see 13.14 and 16.20). [*Sec 46(2)*.] In addition, writing-down allowances are given at a reduced rate of 10% [*Sec 109*] where, at any time in the 'designated period' (broadly, the ten years following first use by the lessor) [*Sec 106*], the asset is leased to a person who:

(a)   is not resident in the United Kingdom; and

(b)   does not use the asset for the purposes of earning profits subject to UK tax [*Sec 105*].

17.11   Lessees should therefore expect to be asked to provide the lessor with a copy of their certificate of incorporation, and to enter into an agreement not to sub-lease the assets to a non-resident. Inland Revenue Tax Bulletin 40 confirms that, with effect from 19 April 1999, *Sec 109* will apply not only where the ultimate lessee, but also any intermediate lessee, is not resident in the United Kingdom.

17.12   Allowances on leased assets can be denied altogether if the lease to a non-resident falls within the following list [*Sec 110*]:

'List

Leases in Relation to which Allowances are Prohibited

1. The lease is expressed to be for a period of more than 13 years.

2. The lease, or a separate agreement, provides for—

    (*a*) extending or renewing the lease, or

    (*b*) the grant of a new lease,

    making it possible for the plant or machinery to be leased for a period of more than 13 years.

3. There is a period of more than one year between the dates on which any two consecutive payments become due under the lease.

4. Any payments are due under the lease or a collateral agreement other than periodical payments.

5. If payments due under the lease or a collateral agreement are expressed as monthly amounts due over a period, any payment due for that period is not the same as any of the others.

    But, for this purpose, ignore variations made under the terms of the lease which are attributable to changes in—

    (*a*) the rate of corporation tax or income tax,

    (*b*) the rate of capital allowances,

    (*c*) any rate of interest where the changes are linked to changes in the rate of interest applicable to inter-bank loans, or

    (*d*) the premiums charged for insurance of any description by a person who is not connected with the lessor or the lessee.

6. The lessor or a person connected with the lessor will, or may in certain circumstances, become entitled at any time to receive from the lessee or any other person a payment, other than a payment of insurance money, which is—

    (*a*) of an amount determined before the expiry of the lease, and

    (*b*) referable to a value of the plant or machinery at or after the expiry of the lease.

    For this purpose, it does not matter whether the payment relates to a disposal of the plant or machinery.'

17.12   Leasing machinery or plant

There are exemptions for 'protected leasing' [*Sec 110(2)*] — broadly, short-term leasing or certain leasing of ships, aircraft and transport containers [*Sec 105(5)*].

Finance lessors — restriction of allowances in first year

17.13   For most claimants, allowances will be given in full in the year the expenditure is incurred, even if the expenditure was incurred on the final day of the year. However, it was historically common practice for finance lessors to set up a group of perhaps four or even 12 companies with staggered year ends so that new assets could be purchased by the company closest to its year end. In this way, the group could minimise the delay between incurring the expenditure and obtaining the allowance.

17.14   With effect for accounting periods ending on or after 2 July 1997, where expenditure is incurred on assets to be used for leasing under a finance lease, the allowances in the first year will effectively be time-apportioned. Thus if relevant expenditure is incurred mid-way through a 12-month accounting period, allowances in the first year will be at the rate of half of 25%. [*Sec 220.*] This restriction does not apply where the expenditure was incurred before 2 July 1997, or is incurred within 12 months of that date in pursuance of an earlier contract. [*F(No 2) A 1997, Sec 44(5)*.]

Lessor's expenditure — fixtures

17.15   Where machinery or plant which becomes a fixture is owned neither by the owner of the building nor by a tenant, but rather is leased to the tenant by a third party (i.e. an equipment lessor) a problem arises. This is that allowances are not available to the property owner or the tenant (because they have not incurred capital expenditure), nor are they available to the equipment lessor (because he has no interest in the building, and hence under general land law, the fixtures do not belong to him). Where the lessee is using the fix-tures for the purposes of a trade, the problem may be alleviated by an election under *Sec 177* whereby the fixture may be treated as belonging to the equip-ment lessor. Such an election must be made jointly by the lessor and lessee, in writing, within two years of the end of the chargeable period in which the expenditure is incurred. The owner of the building, if different, is not a party to the election.

See pro forma election, Appendix 5.

17.16   The election is not possible where the equipment lessor and the lessee are connected as set out in *TA 1988, Sec 839* (see 19.13–19.19) [*Sec 177(1)(b)*], nor where the plant is leased for use in a dwelling-house. [*Sec 178(c)*.] In connection with this latter point, the Revenue accepts that plant is not leased for use in a dwelling-house if it is installed in a block of flats, and serves the whole of the block (e.g. a central heating system). To the extent that such plant serves individual flats, it will not qualify for allowances, unless such use is less less than 25% of the total use (CA, para 2708). This rule is relaxed for expenditure on boilers, heat exchangers, radiators or heating controls installed in residential property where such plant is leased under the Affordable Warmth Programme. [*Secs 177(1)(a)(iii), 180*].

To qualify, expenditure must be incurred after the passing of *FA 2000*, and before 1 January 2008. [*Sec 180, Sch 3, para 33.*]

17.17   Allowances are available only if the lessee is carrying on a qualifying activity (see 13.18). By definition, this must be within the charge to tax. [*Sec 15(1)*]. If the lessee is yet to commence a qualifying activity, then the plant is only deemed to belong to the lessor once the activity has commenced. [*Sec 177(3).*] If the building has mixed use (trading and non-trading premises), the expenditure on plant common to the whole building must be apportioned (CA, para 2726).

17.18   Following the *Decaux* case (see 10.15 et seq.), where affixation to the land is merely incidental, allowances are available on leased fixtures irrespective of whether the lessee is carrying on a trade. However, for this to apply, the following conditions must be met:

(*a*)   the plant is fixed to land (and not to a building);

(*b*)   the equipment lessee has an interest in that land at the time he takes possession of the plant;

(*c*)   the plant may be severed from the land (and will belong to the lessor) at the end of the lease;

(*d*)   the plant is of a type which may be re-used following such severance;

(*e*)   the lease is accounted for as an operating lease.

[*Secs 177(1)(a)(ii), 179.*]

17.19   These events may take place in any practical order.

Special leasing

Lessor's expenditure

17.20   One of the qualifying activities [*Sec 15*] for plant allowances is 'special leasing', which is defined as hiring out plant or machinery other than in the course of any other qualifying activity. [*Sec 19(1).*] Each such hiring out is treated as a separate qualifying activity. [*Sec 19(4).*]

An example of 'special leasing' is the letting of 'investment assets' by a life assurance business. [*Sec 545.*]

17.21 Because each non-trade leasing is deemed to be a separate trade beginning on the commencement of the lease, capital allowances in the first year may need to be time-apportioned, because the qualifying activity will not have been carried on for a full year (*Sec 56(4)* — see 13.14 et seq.).

17.22 The term 'lease' includes an agreement for a lease where the term to be covered by the lease has begun, and any tenancy, but does not include a mortgage, and 'lessee' and 'lessor' are construed accordingly. [*Sec 70(6)*.]

17.23 An asset used for special leasing cannot be a short life asset (see 13.70). [*Sec 84, Table, item 2*.] Some assets within the scope of *Sec 19* attract a writing-down allowance of only 10%. They are machinery or plant which is leased to a person who is not resident in the United Kingdom and who does not use the asset for the purposes of a trade carried on in the United Kingdom or for earning profits chargeable to tax under *TA 1988, Sec 830(4)* (exploration or exploitation activities etc.). Certain leasings of ships, aircraft or transport containers and certain short-term leasings of other assets are exempt from this restriction of writing-down allowances. [*Sec 109*.]

Lessee's expenditure

Non-fixtures/chattels

17.24 It may be that a lessee is required to incur capital expenditure on plant under the terms of the lease. If that plant does not become a fixture, it is treated as belonging to him as long as it is used for the purposes of his qualifying activity. [*Sec 70(1)(2)*.] On determination of the lease, no disposal value need be brought in by the lessee. [*Sec 70(3)*.] On a subsequent sale, etc., *Sec 61* has effect as if the capital expenditure had been incurred by the lessor and not by the lessee. [*Sec 70(4)*.] Consequently, a disposal value may be brought into account by the lessor, even though he had not incurred any capital expenditure. This assumes, of course, that the machinery or plant is not removed by the lessee when the lease ends.

Fixtures

17.25 Allowances may be available where the lessee of a building incurs expenditure on plant which becomes a fixture (see 10.19 et seq.).

Energy services providers

17.26 On occasions, an 'energy services provider' may install and operate plant and machinery in a building in which he does not have a legal interest. In such circumstances, the normal requirement for an interest in land is removed. [*FA 2001, Sec 66* and *Sch 18.*] The plant may not be formally leased, in which case an election under *Sec 177* (see 17.15) is not possible.

This provision is part of a wider package of measures aimed at helping businesses reduce their energy consumption, and so help the United Kingdom reduce emissions of greenhouse gases.

An energy services provider is essentially a person providing services under an energy services agreement, as defined by *FA 2001, Sec 175A(1)*.

The plant is effectively deemed to belong to the energy services provider, provided a joint election is made by the energy services provider and the 'client'.

This election is not possible where the client would not be entitled to an allowance if he incurred the expenditure himself. Typically, this will apply where the client is not within the charge to tax. An exception to this is where the plant is of an energy-saving nature, as specified by Treasury order.

Where a subsequent purchaser of the property pays a capital sum to discharge obligations under the energy services agreement, the plant is treated as ceasing to belong to the energy services provider, and the capital sum is treated as expenditure qualifying for allowances.

Sale and leaseback of plant

17.27   Sale and leaseback arrangements were unsuccessfully challenged by the Inland Revenue in *Barclays Mercantile Business Finance Ltd v Mawson [2002] EWCA Civ 1853, [2003] STC 66* and *BMBF (No 24) Ltd v IRC [2002] EWHC 2466 (Ch) [2002] STC 1450*. In essence, a finance lessor may obtain allowances, even though the availability of those allowances is a fundamental reason for the acquisition of the plant.

17.28   However, special rules apply where plant is sold, but continues to be used in the vendor's trade or that of a connected person. [*Sec 216.*] The primary effect is the same as where vendor and purchaser are connected, namely that the qualifying expenditure of the purchaser is restricted to the disposal value brought into account by the vendor. [*Sec 218(2).*] Where no disposal value falls to be brought into account (for example, because the vendor is a non-taxpayer) the purchaser's qualifying expenditure is the smallest of:

(*a*)   the open market value of the machinery and plant;

(*b*)   the capital expenditure incurred by the seller on the provision of the machinery or plant; and

(*c*)   any expenditure on the provision of the machinery or plant incurred by any person connected (see 19.13–19.19) with the seller. [*Sec 218(3).*]

17.29   *Sec 216* also applies, with necessary adaptation, where a person enters into a contract under which, on the performance thereof, he will or may become the owner of machinery or plant belonging to another person, or is the assignee of such a contract. [*Sec 213.*]

17.30   Where plant which is used for non-trading activities is sold and leased back under a finance lease, *Secs 221–226* impose, generally with effect from 2 July 1997, two further restrictions on the finance lessor. Firstly, no allowances will be given to the lessor if the terms of the lease or of related transactions are such that he has substantially divested himself of any risk that the lessee will not comply with his obligations. Guarantees from persons connected with the lessee are ignored. [*Sec 225.*] Secondly, even if the finance lessor has not divested himself of risk, his qualifying expenditure will be limited to the 'notional written-down value' of the plant, if no disposal value is required to be brought into account by the vendor (or market value, if lower). [*Sec 224(2)(3).*] These rules do not apply where expenditure is incurred before 2 July 1998 in pursuance of an earlier contract. [*F(No 2)A 1997, Sec 46(3).*]

17.31   The requirement to restrict the lessor's qualifying expenditure to open market value under *Sec 222* (see 17.27) or notional tax written-down value under *Sec 224* (see 17.29) is relaxed where certain conditions are met and the buyer and seller make a joint election. This election must be in writing, not more than two years after the date of the sale. [*Sec 227.*] Such an election will deem the disposal value, and hence the lessor's qualifying expenditure, to be the cost to the lessor or the cost to the lessee, whichever is the lower.

The conditions are:

- The seller incurred capital expenditure on the asset (rather than treating it as trading stock).

- The asset was new when acquired by the seller. 'New' means unused and not second-hand.

- The asset was not acquired from a connected person, or as part of a transaction whose main benefit was to obtain an allowance.

- The sale is within four months of the asset first being used for any purpose by any person.

- The seller has not claimed allowances on the asset or included it in a pool of qualifying expenditure.

Acquisition of a lease portfolio

17.32   Where assets are acquired together with rental agreements, it is likely that expenditure qualifying for allowances will be challenged by the Revenue if it exceeds the original cost of the assets concerned (CA, para 12200).

Chapter 18

Research and Development, Patents and Know-how

Introduction

18.1   This chapter deals with allowances due for expenditure on:

(*a*)   research and development (see 18.4);

(*b*)   patents (see 18.27); and

(*c*)   know-how (see 18.43).

18.2   Each of the three, perhaps, represents a different stage in the acquisition and exploitation of knowledge. However, the capital allowances treatment differs greatly between the pure intangibles, patents and know-how, where the allowances are similar to those on plant, and research and development, where a 100% initial allowance is available, and comparisons with enterprise zone allowances are inevitably drawn.

18.3   There are similarities between allowances on research and intangibles, and the more commonly encountered allowances on plant and buildings. However, the allowances are not identical, and the taxpayer should not assume that the treatment of an item or event will be the same as for the allowances with which he is more familiar.

With effect from 1 April 2002, most expenditure on intellectual property (including patents and know-how) incurred by a company, attracts relief under *FA 2002, Sch 29* – see Chapter 24.

Research and development

General

18.4   Capital expenditure in connection with research and development ('R&D') is one of the few remaining instances where a 100% first year allowance is still available. However, there is still an incentive to classify expenditure as revenue rather than capital, as revenue expenditure may qualify for relief at more than 100% (see 18.5). R&D allowances are by no means as rare as might be imagined, and many taxpayers have realised, belatedly, that a potential claim has been overlooked.

18.4   *Research and development*

For accounting periods ending on or after 1 April 2000, the legislation was amended to substitute the term 'research and development' for 'scientific research', wherever it occurs. [*FA 2000, Sec 68(2), Sch 19.*] This was intended to be a change of nomenclature only, with no impact on the allowances available.

Revenue Expenditure

18.5   Expenditure on research and development may qualify for tax relief at a rate equal to 125% of the actual expenditure incurred (150% for small or medium-sized enterprises – 'SME') (*FA 2002, Sch 12, FA 2000, Sch 20*). This is provided the expenditure is not capital in nature (*FA 2002, Sch 12, paras 4 and 9*).

The additional relief must be claimed (*FA 2002, Sch 12, para 11*). A large company may only claim the 125% relief where its R&D expenditure exceeds £10,000 (previously £25,000) per annum. The reduction in threshold has effect for accounting periods ending on or after 9 April 2003 for large companies.

A SME can obtain the 'large company' R&D tax credit where it is acting as sub-contractor to a large company. This relief is extended to cases where the expenditure is subsidised, and would not therefore qualify for the SME R&D tax credit. Such expenditure now counts towards establishing the £10,000 minimum expenditure.

Relief at 150% is available to small and medium-sized enterprises for expenditure incurred on or after 1 April 2000 (*FA 2000, Sch 20*). Relief at 125% is available to large companies for expenditure incurred on or after 1 April 2002 (*FA 2002, Sch 12, para 20*).

18.6   Relief is available for the cost of materials and labour. From 2003, employee costs qualify for relief in proportion to the time spent on R & D. Previously, no relief was available if an employee spent less than 20% of his time on research and development, but the whole cost qualified for relief if the percentage was greater than 80%.

Also from 2003, a further category of expenditure will qualify for relief, this being the cost of 'externally provided workers', i.e. those provided by an agency or other intermediary.

The amount qualifying depends in the first instance on whether the research company and the intermediary (the 'staff provider') are connected. If not, and if no election is made under para 8D (see below), then 65% of the cost incurred by the company will qualify for relief. If the parties are connected, the qualifying amount will be the lower of the cost to the research company and the cost to the staff provider. This may be greater than the 65% available for unconnected persons, who would therefore be at a disadvantage.

Consequently, an unconnected research company and staff provider may jointly elect to be treated under the connected person rules (see pro-forma at Appendix 5). The election is irrevocable and must be made within two years of the end of the research company's accounting period in which the staff provision contract is entered into.

Capital expenditure

18.7   Where the expenditure is of a capital nature, it will not be allowed as a deduction from trading profits. There is no alternative to the 100% allowance, for example by way of writing-down allowances. [*Sec 441(1).*] The deduction is given for the chargeable period in which the expenditure was incurred or, if it was incurred before the commencement of the trade, it is given for the chargeable period beginning with that commencement. [*Sec 441(2).*]

18.8   The 100% allowance is available where a person carrying on a trade incurs capital expenditure on R&D related to that trade and undertaken either directly by him or on his behalf. [*Sec 439.*] Relief is equally available where the trade begins following the R&D. [*Sec 441.*] It is important to note, however, that allowances are only available to a trader, and not to a person carrying on a profession or vocation. Research is related to the trade if:

(*a*)   it may lead to or facilitate an extension of that trade or class of trades; or

(*b*)   it is research of a medical nature having particular relevance to workers employed in that trade or class of trades.

18.9   If an asset is acquired for a different purpose, and only subsequently begins to be used for R&D, no R&D allowances are due.

Groups

18.10   Often, research will be carried out by one company for the sole benefit of others in the same group and will constitute that company's sole activity. There is some doubt that the 100% deduction would be given for expenditure incurred by the research company itself, because that company may not have a trade and any expenditure cannot therefore comply with *Sec 439*. In practice the 100% deduction will be available, provided any receipts from other group members for carrying out the research are included within trading profits. Any payments made by the group members will qualify for the deduction under normal principles as the research need only be undertaken by the trader himself or 'on his behalf'. The words in *Sec 439(1)* — 'directly undertaken by him or on his behalf' — were considered in the case of *Gaspet Ltd v Ellis [1987] STC 362.* A claim failed because the link between the person incurring the expenditure and the work undertaken was not sufficiently close. The mere provision of finance was not enough.

18.11 *Research and development*

Property companies

18.11 For a variety of commercial reasons, a group property company is often used to hold all the various properties occupied and used by the trading members of a group. Where such a company incurs expenditure on an asset to be used for research, no R&D allowances will be due. *Sec 439* requires the existence of a trade — a Schedule A business is not sufficient for this purpose.

Exclusions from allowances

18.12 No allowance is available in respect of expenditure on an interest in land, except where all or part of the expenditure may be apportioned to the acquisition of a building or other structure already constructed on the land, or to plant and machinery forming part of such a building. [*Sec 440.*]

18.13 As with industrial buildings, (see 7.68 et seq.) no allowance is available for expenditure incurred on a dwelling, unless:

(*a*)   the dwelling forms part of a building otherwise used for R&D, and

(*b*)   the expenditure justly apportioned to the dwelling is not more than 25% of the total expenditure on the building. [*Sec 438(3).*]

18.14 If expenditure is incurred which is only partly attributable to R&D, a just apportionment of the total expenditure may be made. [*Sec 439(4).*] This would be of relevance, for example, where a new building was to be used partly for research and partly for manufacture.

18.15 References to expenditure incurred on R&D do not include any expenditure incurred in the acquisition of rights in, or arising out of, research. [*Sec 438(2).*] Such rights would include patents etc. Capital allowances may be available (though at a lower rate) for expenditure on patents or know-how (see 18.27, 18.43). In this, the legislation appears to recognise that in order for, say, patents to be an issue, the scientific research must have already reached the stage where a marketable product can be identified. Expenditure at this stage carries a lower commercial risk and is therefore less likely to require the 'encouragement' of a 100% deduction.

Definition of research and development

18.16 The question of what constitutes scientific research (now called 'research and development') was dealt with in the House of Commons (by written answer) on 6 July 1994. The text was as follows:

'*CAA 1990 s139(1)* defines scientific research as covering any activities in the fields of natural or applied science for the extension of knowledge.

Whether any particular activities fall within this definition will depend on the facts of the case. However, in general terms, activities constitute scientific research if they involve the application of new scientific principles in an existing area of research or the application of existing principles in a new area of research. The essential test is innovation.

Scientific research is generally regarded as including the development of a piece of fundamental research up to the production stage. Expenditure on construction of prototypes, pilot plant and so on qualifies for scientific research allowances if the prototypes are used to test the result of the basic research or the possibility of applying the results of the basic research to manufacture.'

18.17 This has now been incorporated into Revenue instructions (CA, para 60200). Although the term 'research and development' is now used, and the definition in *CAA 1990, Sec 139(1)* has not been replicated in *CAA 2001*, the above statement is indicative of the underlying principles.

18.18 As stated above, expenditure on prototypes constructed to test the results of the basic research will qualify for allowances, but no allowances are due if the prototypes concerned are constructed solely to explore commercial possibilities. For example, research into the possibility of environment-friendly aerosols would qualify as research. Once such a device was commercially viable, and was being produced and marketed, any further expenditure incurred would be towards the development of a product. This would be a normal trading activity not qualifying for any special relief (but potentially qualifying for industrial buildings allowances as the manufacture of goods or materials [*Sec 274, Table A, item 1*]).

18.19 Research and development is now defined as being those activities which are treated as such under normal accounting practice. [*Sec 437(2)*; *TA 1988, Sec 837A.*] The Special Commissioners have held that research into the dramatic construction of films, albeit carried out in a manner that was analytical and, in the common sense of the word, 'scientific', nonetheless did not qualify as scientific research (*Salt v Golding [1996] STC (SCD) 269*).

Inland Revenue approach

18.20 The availability of a 100% deduction for capital expenditure is likely to mean that any claim will be closely scrutinised. The Revenue's official instructions formerly told the Inspector to seek an explanation, in plain language, of the research activities to be carried on. In particular, it suggests the following questions:

(*a*) What are the objectives of the research?

(*b*) What features of the research are new or involve new applications of existing principles?

18.20 *Research and development*

(c) What is the current state of knowledge in the area and how is the research designed to expand that knowledge?

(d) To what extent does the work differ from what is being done elsewhere, either privately or by government bodies?

(e) What is the background, training and qualifications of the people involved?

(f) Is the 'research' carried out by persons who are otherwise employed in the trade, at their normal workstations?

(g) To what extent will the results of the work be published?

18.21 The Inspector may also wish to visit the site to see the research at first hand.

Practicalities

18.22 With this in mind, a well-constructed claim may stress, *inter alia*, the following features:

(a) the objectives, and in particular the innovative nature of the research;

(b) whether DTI or other grants are received for research and innovation;

(c) the anticipated period of time before research results in a marketable product;

(d) the fact that research is carried out by specific members of staff, who are not involved in production generally;

(e) whether the research is carried out by science graduates;

(f) specific identification of the need to 'take out the thinking side' — i.e. to remove research staff from the production environment;

(g) specific examples of desired aims and results;

(h) whether production testing will be kept separate, either in an existing building, or in a separate building;

(i) the fact that prototypes are constructed, not to explore commercial viability, but rather to test the results of basic research, or to investigate the possibility of manufacture;

(j) past history of successful innovation and research.

18.23 Even where expenditure does validly qualify for R&D allowances, the claim may fail if the true nature of the research is not adequately identified. The steps to be taken vary from the simple (for example not inadvertently describing genuine research as 'product development' on plans and in board minutes) to the more complex. As with any claim for capital allowances it is important to establish adequate evidence. In the case of research, it may be appropriate to commission one or more reports on the nature and purpose of the research by experts in the field. Such scientists will be in the best position to understand the nature of the research — yet another example of the principle that capital allowances claims are not purely the domain of accountants, surveyors and lawyers.

Disposal

18.24 In a similar way to industrial buildings, a balancing adjustment may arise when an asset qualifying for R&D allowances is disposed of. There is no provision for balancing allowances. Where part of the initial allowance has been disclaimed, and proceeds are less than the 'residue of expenditure' or 'unclaimed allowance' [*Sec 441(3)*], a loss has arisen, but no balancing allowance is possible. A balancing charge is calculated in accordance with *Sec 442*, in much the same way as for industrial buildings. In effect, it will be equal to the excess of disposal proceeds over the tax written-down value of the asset, restricted, of course, to the allowances actually given. Where an asset is destroyed, rather than sold, insurance proceeds or costs of demolition must be taken into account. [*Sec 443.*]

Avoiding the balancing charge

18.25 Particularly in the early years of an asset's life, a balancing charge may be much more damaging when the asset sold was one qualifying for R&D allowances rather than for, say, industrial buildings allowances. This is because more allowances will have been given, and can therefore be clawed back.

18.26 In some cases it may be possible to avoid a balancing charge by not selling the whole interest in the asset, but by granting some minor interest, for example a long lease. This idea is discussed further in connection with industrial buildings (see 11.22 et seq.). The capital value rules applying in enterprise zones (see 11.26 et seq.) do not apply to R&D, and it is therefore still possible to avoid a balancing charge in this way.

Change of use

18.27 No balancing adjustment is made where an asset which has qualified for allowances subsequently ceases to be used for a qualifying purpose. Thus, for example, if a building constructed to house research facilities is turned over to commercial production after, say, one year, there is no claw-back of the 100% allowance given (CA, para 60600). The taxpayer may therefore be able to maximise his allowances by proper planning of the use to which a new building will be put. If a manufacturer with existing premises constructs a new building to carry out R&D, the new building will qualify for R&D allowances. If, on the other hand, he plans to move his manufacturing operations into the new building and use the old one for research, no R&D allowances will be due.

Patents

General

18.28 The treatment of expenditure on patents will depend on whether the expenditure is incurred by the 'inventor', or whether an existing patent is being purchased from the inventor or a subsequent owner. In addition, expenditure incurred on or after 1 April 2002 *by a company* qualifies for relief under *FA 2002, Sch 29*, rather than by way of capital allowances (see Chapter 24). The remainder of this chapter deals with the allowances available before 1 April 2002, and which are still available to individuals.

18.29 The distinction between capital and revenue is as relevant to expenditure on patents as to expenditure on other assets, and the taxpayer should not seek to build up a capital allowances claim where a revenue deduction would be more appropriate. Important cases in this respect are *British Salmson Aero Engines Ltd v IRC (1938) 22 TC 29* and *Desoutter Bros Ltd v J E Hanger & Co Ltd [1936] 1 All ER 535*.

18.30 Expenditure, whether capital or revenue, related to the assets which are subject to the patent, rather than to the patent itself, is dealt with in accordance with normal principles, for example, by giving capital allowances in respect of any expenditure on machinery or plant. Allowances can be claimed when the expenditure on the patents has been incurred by a person who:

(*a*)   uses or intends to use the rights for the purposes of a trade which is within the charge to tax ('qualifying trade expenditure') [*Secs 467–469*]; or

(*b*)   is otherwise liable to income tax or corporation tax on any income from the rights ('qualifying non-trade expenditure').

New patents

18.31 Any fees or expenses incurred in creating or registering one's own patent are treated as a revenue deduction, in accordance with the *TA 1988, Sec 83*, if the patent is for the purposes of the trade. Otherwise, such costs are allowed by virtue of *TA 1988, Sec 526*.

18.32 The cost of renewing or extending the term of a patent are allowed as a trading deduction, as is the cost of an unsuccessful application to register a patent (CA, para 75300).

Existing patents

18.33 For all expenditure incurred on or after 1 April 1986 on acquiring an existing patent, an allowance is given of 25% p.a. on a reducing balance basis. [*Sec 472(1)*.] Prior to that date, allowances were given over a maximum period of 17 years. This unusual writing-down period reflected the life of the patents which between 1949 and 1977 was for an initial period of 16 years with provision for extension. [*Sch 3, para 95.*]

Rights purchased from a connected person

18.34 In the case of rights purchased from a connected person the expenditure qualifying for allowances is restricted to the relevant amount, namely:

(*a*) where a disposal value falls to be brought into account, that disposal value;

(*b*) where no disposal value falls to be brought into account, any capital sum received by the seller and chargeable to tax under *TA 1988, Sec 524*;

(*c*) in any other case, the smallest of:

  (i) the price which the rights would have fetched in the open market;

  (ii) any capital expenditure incurred by the seller on acquiring the rights;

  (iii) any capital expenditure incurred by any person connected with the seller. [*Sec 481.*]

Definition of patent rights

18.35 Allowances are given for capital expenditure incurred on the purchase of 'patent rights'. 'Patent rights' are defined as 'the right to do or authorise the doing of anything which would, but for that right, be an infringement of that patent'. [*Sec 464(2).*] Any reference to a purchase or sale of patent rights includes a reference to an acquisition or grant of a licence in respect of a patent. [*Sec 466.*] Expenditure also qualifies where it is incurred in obtaining a right to acquire, in the future, patent rights in respect of an invention for which the patent has not yet been granted. [*Sec 465.*]

18.36 Expenditure on patent rights incurred prior to the commencement of a trade is treated as incurred on the first day of trading, unless the rights have been resold before that day. [*Sec 468(3).*] In such circumstances it appears there is no provision for allowances, and if the rights were sold at a profit, tax could be charged under Schedule D Case VI.

Allowances due

18.37 In most respects, allowances for patents mirror those available for plant. All 'new' expenditure is pooled and an annual allowance is given equal to 25% of the written-down value of the pool (i.e. on a reducing balance basis). This is proportionately reduced if the chargeable period is less than a full year or if the trade has been carried on for only part of the chargeable period. [*Sec 472(2)(3).*]

18.38 *Patents*

Disposals

18.38 A disposal value must be 'brought into account' (i.e. deducted from the pool) whenever patent rights are sold, in whole or in part, or when a licence is granted in respect of such rights. [*Sec 476(2)*.] If the disposal proceeds are less than the amount of the pool, the writing-down allowance will be given on the net amount. If, on the other hand, the disposal proceeds exceed the value of the pool but not the original cost, there will be a balancing charge equal to the excess. [*Sec 472(5)(6)*.] A balancing allowance will be given if the trade is discontinued, or the last of the patent rights included in the pool expire and are not revived. [*Sec 471(6)*.] The taxpayer more familiar with plant allowances should note this second event, where the treatment differs from that of plant, where no balancing allowance is given, even if the last plant in a pool has been disposed of.

Example

18.39 On 31 March 1992, Monty incurred £30,000 on the purchase of patents rights for use in his trade. The rights had a life of five years. Trade commenced on 30 June. Allowances are given as follows:

		£
Year ended 31.12.92	Expenditure	30,000
	WDA: 25% × 6/12	(3,750)
		26,250
Year ended 31.12.93	WDA: 25%	(6,563)
		19,687
Year ended 31.12.94	WDA: 25%	(4,922)
		14,765
Year ended 31.12.95	WDA: 25%	(3,691)
		11,074
Year ended 31.12.96	WDA: 25%	(2,769)
		8,305
Year ended 31.12.97	Balancing allowance	(8,305)
		0

Had Monty sold the rights on 30 June 1995 for £15,000, he would have suffered a balancing charge of £235 (£15,000−£14,765). The disposal value brought into account will be restricted to original cost.

18.40 Where the disposal proceeds exceed not only the written-down value of the pool but also the original cost, the excess over cost is taxable under Schedule D Case VI, in equal parts in each of the next six years, beginning with the year in which the proceeds are received. [*TA 1988, Sec 524(1)*.] The

210

taxpayer may elect within two years for the whole of the excess to be taxed in the year in which the proceeds are received. [*TA 1988, Sec 524(2)*.] Where the election is not made and tax is charged over a period of six years, it is possible that one of a number of events may take place. These include:

(*a*)   the death of an individual taxpayer,

(*b*)   the winding-up of a taxpayer company, or

(*c*)   a change in the members of a partnership.

18.41   When one of these events occurs, there are two consequences prescribed by *TA 1988, Sec 525*:

(i)   no amount will be charged to tax for any chargeable period subsequent to that in which the event occurs, and

(ii)   the amount charged to tax in that period will be increased by any amounts which would otherwise be charged to tax in subsequent periods.

Sale in exchange for shares

18.42   Under ESC B17, where an inventor sells the patent rights in his invention to a company under his control for less than market value, the assessment on the inventor is limited to actual proceeds, providing the company undertakes to only claim allowances on that amount.

18.43   Where the rights are sold in exchange for shares in that company, the Revenue is believed to have accepted that the vendor's tax liability should be computed on the basis that the value of the consideration was the nominal value of the shares, again provided the company undertook to restrict its capital allowances claim by reference to the same figure.

Know-how

General

18.44   The capital allowances described in this section apply generally to individuals and others chargeable to income tax, and to companies only for expenditure incurred before 1 April 2002. From that date, expenditure incurred by a company qualifies for relief under *FA 2002, Sch 29* (see Chapter 24) rather than by means of capital allowances.

'Know-how' is, almost by definition, secret knowledge or information. It cannot, therefore, be subject to the same public disclosure and hence protection as patents. However, the capital allowances treatment of know-how is, with one important exception, identical to the treatment of patents. All expenditure on know-how is pooled (but pooled separately from other types of asset such as plant or patents). Allowances are given at the rate of 25% p.a., on a reducing balance basis. [*Sec 458*.] Allowances are not given in respect of expenditure incurred on acquiring know-how if the parties to the transaction are connected. [*Sec 455(2)(3).*]

Disposals

18.45   The significant difference between patents and know-how is that when know-how is sold, all disposal proceeds are deducted from the pool. There is no restriction to original cost as with patents where any excess over cost is taxed under Schedule D Case VI. In the case of know-how, therefore, any excess of proceeds over written-down value will give rise to a balancing charge, taxable in most instances under Schedule D Case I. [*Secs 458(5), 462(2).*]

Definition of know-how

18.46   'Know-how' is defined by *Sec 452* as:

'any industrial information and techniques likely to assist in—

(*a*)   manufacturing or processing goods or materials,

(*b*)   working a source of mineral deposits (including searching for, discovery or testing mineral deposits or obtaining access to them), or

(*c*)   carrying out any agricultural, forestry or fishing operations.'

18.47   Excluded, therefore, is know-how connected with other fields, for example marketing or financial services.

18.48   This area was the subject of an Inland Revenue Press Release of August 1993 which stated:

'We are sometimes asked whether capital allowances are available for capital expenditure incurred on the acquisition of *commercial* know-how.

In our view there are no capital allowances available for such expenditure because of the statutory definition of know-how.

[*Section 452*] permits capital allowances to be given on capital expenditure incurred on the acquisition of know-how. "Know-how" is defined at [*Section 452(2)*] as "… any industrial information and techniques likely to assist in manufacturing or processing goods or materials …"

The terms of this definition accordingly restrict allowances to capital expenditure incurred in acquiring information relevant only to industrial or technical processes. Information relevant to commercial processes is not included.

Our view is that know-how which does not assist directly in the manufacturing and processing operations is commercial know-how. Examples include information about marketing, packaging or distributing a manufactured product. Such information does not assist directly in the manufacture of that product. Rather it is concerned with selling the product once it has been manufactured.

As such it is not in our view within the definition of know-how in [*Section 542(2)*] and so cannot qualify for allowances under [*Section 540*].'

Computer software

18.49   Where know-how is held or transmitted by means of computer software, capital expenditure could be eligible for allowances under either heading. The taxpayer will be able to choose which claim is made, which could be important with regard, for example, to a short life asset election, which is not possible where know-how is concerned. Note that, after 1 April 2002, a company wishing to claim capital allowances on computer software has to elect to disapply (*FA 2002, Sch 29*) (see 24.14).

Acquisition of know-how with a trade

18.50   Where know-how is purchased along with the trade (or part of the trade) to which it relates, any part of the consideration attributed to the know-how is not treated as qualifying for allowances, but rather as a payment for goodwill and therefore not qualifying for tax relief at all (other than on a subsequent sale on which a chargeable gain or loss arises). The person disposing of the know-how is also treated as receiving a sum in respect of goodwill. [*TA 1988, Sec 531(2)*.] This treatment does not apply in two circumstances:

(*a*)   to the purchaser if the trade was previously carried on wholly outside the United Kingdom, or

(*b*)   to either the seller or the purchaser if an election is made jointly by the purchaser and the vendor within two years of the sale. [*TA 1988, Secs 531(3); CAA 2001, Sec 454(1)(c)*.]

See pro forma election, Appendix 5.

18.51   Neither of the above exceptions will apply where the purchaser and vendor are connected or are under common control. [*Sec 455(2)*.]

18.52   Where a trade is acquired, the purchaser should investigate whether any part of the consideration may properly be apportioned to know-how, rather than merely to goodwill. Even if the know-how is not of a type qualifying for allowances as such (that is, industrial information and techniques), it may be arguable that it qualifies as plant. In *Munby v Furlong [1977] STC 232*, the definition of plant was said to encompass 'the intellectual storehouse which any professional man has in the course of carrying on his profession'.

Restrictive covenants

18.53   Where, in connection with any disposal of know-how, a person gives an undertaking (whether absolute or qualified, and whether legally valid or not) to restrict his or another's activities in any way, any consideration received in respect of the undertaking is treated as consideration for the disposal of know-how. [*TA 1988, Sec 531(8)*.] However this is only true as far as the vendor is concerned and does not apply to the purchaser (CCAB memorandum on the Finance Bill 1968). Any such expenditure will not, therefore, qualify for know-how allowances. Furthermore such a payment is open to be regarded as not made wholly and exclusively for the purposes of the trade and may therefore be denied tax relief under general principles by virtue of *TA 1988, Sec 74(a)* – see *Associated Portland Cement Manufacturers Ltd v Kerr (1945) 27 TC 103*. From a tax point of view, such payments should be avoided though it is recognised that they can be a commercial necessity.

Chapter 19

Transactions Within Groups and Between Connected Persons

Transfer of assets

Assets other than machinery and plant, know-how and patents

19.1   A general anti-avoidance measure applies (subject to the exceptions referred to below), where either:

(*a*)   the buyer is a body of persons over whom the seller has control, or the seller is a body of persons over whom the buyer has control, or both the buyer and the seller are bodies of persons and some other person has control over both of them or the buyer and the seller are connected (see below) with each other (i.e. 'the control test') [*Sec 567(2)*]; or

(*b*)   it appears with respect to the sale, or with respect to transactions of which the sale is one, that the sole or main benefit which might be expected to accrue to the parties or any of them was the obtaining of an allowance or deduction, the obtaining of a greater allowance or deduction or the avoidance or reduction of a charge (i.e. 'the tax advantage test'). [*Sec 567(4)*].

19.2   In these circumstances the sale is deemed to have taken place for a consideration equal to the open market value, even if one of the parties to the transaction is resident outside the United Kingdom. The term 'body of persons' includes a partnership. [*Sec 567(3).*]

19.3   The transaction nevertheless remains a sale. Consequently, for industrial buildings allowance purposes the writing-down allowance must be re-computed by reference to the number of years remaining out of a period of 25 (or 50) years (see 4.5 et seq.).

Election by connected persons

19.4   Where the sale is one between connected persons, but no tax advantage as described above is sought, the parties to the sale may elect, within two years of the date of the sale (not within two years of the year end), that the tax written-down value (for example, for industrial buildings, the residue of expenditure immediately before the sale), if it is lower, be substituted for the market value. [*Sec 569.*] The effect is to transfer any balancing charge, which otherwise would have fallen on the seller, to the buyer and this will manifest itself in the form of reduced allowances and perhaps, ultimately, a balancing charge.

19.5   An election cannot be made:

(*a*)   if the circumstances of the sale (including those of the parties to it) are such that, although falling within the scope of the *CAA 2001*, allowances or charges falling to be made will be incapable of being so made (for example, because one of the parties is outside the scope of UK tax) [*Sec 570(2)(a)*];

(*b*)   if the buyer is a dual resident investing company [*Sec 570(2)(b)*]; or

(*c*)   in the case of a qualifying dwelling-house, unless both the seller and the buyer at the time of the sale are or at any earlier time were approved bodies, as defined in the *Housing Act 1980, Sec 56(4)*. [*Sec 570(4)*.]

Plant or machinery

19.6   *Secs 567–570* do not apply to plant or machinery. Instead, where one of the conditions below applies, no first-year allowance can be made and the purchaser's qualifying expenditure (including any additional VAT) is limited to the disposal value brought into account by the seller. [*Sec 218.*] The conditions are:

(*a*)   the purchaser and the seller are connected with each other (see 19.13–19.19),

(*b*)   the plant or machinery continues to be used for the purposes of a qualifying activity carried on by the seller or a person connected to the seller [*Sec 216*], or

(*c*)   it appears with respect to the sale, or with respect to transactions of which the sale is one, that the sole or main benefit which, but for this section, might have been expected to accrue to the parties or any of them was the obtaining of a first-year, writing-down or balancing allowance. [*Sec 215.*]

19.7   Where no disposal value falls to be brought into account (for example because the vendor is not within the scope of UK taxation) the purchaser's qualifying expenditure is the smallest of:

(i)   the market value of the plant and machinery;

(ii) the capital expenditure incurred by the seller on the provision of the machinery or plant; and

(iii) any expenditure on the provision of the plant and machinery incurred by any person connected (see 19.13–19.19) with the seller. [*Sec 218(3)*.]

19.8   *Sec 218* also applies, with necessary adaptation, where a person enters into a contract under which, on the performance thereof, he will or may become the owner of machinery or plant belonging to another person, or is the assignee of such a contract. [*Sec 213.*]

19.9   Nothing in *Sec 218* applies to a short life asset. Where short life assets are transferred between connected persons, special rules apply (see 13.77 et seq.).

19.10   Where plant which is used for non-trading activities is sold and leased back under a finance lease, *Sec 222* imposes, generally with effect from 2 July 1997, two further restrictions on the finance lessor (see 17.27 et seq.).

Know-how

19.11   *Secs 567–570* do not apply to sales of know-how. There is therefore no requirement to substitute market value for actual consideration. This is a question of practicality, as the market value of know-how, which by its very nature is kept secret and not revealed to any market, would be difficult to establish.

Note too that for expenditure by companies on or after 1 April 2002, *FA 2002, Sch 29* applies – see Chapter 24.

Patents

19.12   *Secs 567–570* do not apply to sales of patents. Instead, the legislation provides that, in such circumstances, the purchaser's qualifying expenditure is fixed as:

(*a*)   where a disposal value falls to be brought into account, that disposal value;

(*b*)   where no disposal value falls to be brought into account, any capital sum received by the seller and chargeable to tax under *TA 1988, Sec 524*;

(*c*)   in any other case, the smallest of:

    (i)   the price which the rights would have fetched in the open market;

    (ii)   any capital expenditure incurred by the seller on acquiring the rights;

    (iii)   any capital expenditure incurred by any person connected with the seller. [*Sec 481.*]

Note too that for expenditure by companies on or after 1 April 2002, *FA 2002, Sch 29* applies – see Chapter 24.

Definition of connected persons

Individuals

19.13   An individual is connected with a person if that person is the individual's wife or husband, or is a relative, or the wife or husband of a relative of the individual or of the individual's wife or husband. Relative means brother, sister, ancestor or lineal descendant. 'Lineal descendant' will include any descendant of the spouse by a previous marriage though not a later marriage. [*TA 1988, Sec 839(2)(8)*.]

Example

19.14   'Person' is connected with all of the individuals in the following chart.

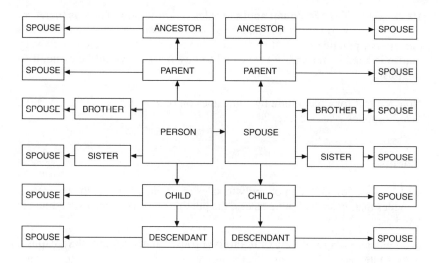

Settlements

19.15   A trustee of a settlement is connected with any individual who is a settlor in relation to that settlement, with any person who is connected with that settlor and with a body corporate which under *TA 1988, Sec 681* is deemed to be connected with that settlement. [*TA 1988, Sec 839(3)*.] A body corporate is deemed to be connected with a settlement in any year of assessment if at any time in that year:

(*a*)   it is a close company (or only not a close company because it is not resident in the United Kingdom) and the participators then include the trustees of the settlement; or

(*b*)   it is controlled (within the meaning of *TA 1988, Sec 840*) by a company falling within (*a*) above. [*TA 1988, Sec 681(5)*.]

Partnerships

19.16   Except in relation to acquisitions or disposals of partnership assets pursuant to bona fide commercial arrangements, a person is connected with any person with whom he is in partnership, and with the wife or husband or relative of any individual with whom he is in partnership. [*TA 1988, Sec 839(4)*.]

Companies

19.17   A company (including any body corporate or unincorporated association) is connected with another company:

(*a*)   if the same person has control of both, or a person has control of one and persons connected with him, or he and persons connected with him, have control of the other; or

(*b*)   if a group of two or more persons has control of each company, and the groups either consist of the same persons or could be regarded as consisting of the same persons by treating (in one or more cases) a member of either group as replaced by a person with whom he is connected. [*TA 1988, Sec 839(5)*.]

19.18   A company is connected with another person if that person has control of it or if that person and persons connected with him together have control of it. [*TA 1988, Sec 839(6)*.] In a winding-up, it is the liquidator rather than the shareholders who exercises control.

19.19   Any two or more persons acting together to secure or exercise control of a company are treated in relation to that company as connected with one another and with any person acting on the directions of any of them to secure or exercise control of the company. [*TA 1988, Sec 839(7)*.] 'Control' has the wide meaning given to it by *TA 1988, Sec 416* [*TA 1988, Sec 839(8)*] (principally on the basis of voting rights taking into account the rights of associates). It is the circumstances *at the time of the sale* which are important. In most cases, a company pension fund will *not* be connected with the company itself.

Chapter 20

Claiming and Disclaiming Allowances

Introduction

20.1   Allowances are only given if claimed. [*Sec 3(1)*.] In most circumstances, the taxpayer will wish to make the maximum claim for capital allowances. However, individual circumstances may mean that it is better to reduce the amount claimed in any particular year, typically in order to make better use of other reliefs. It must be remembered that allowances disclaimed are not lost forever; rather the benefit of them is deferred into subsequent years.

20.2   Following the case of *Elliss v BP Tyne Tanker Co Ltd* (see 20.12), it has been well known that the benefit of plant allowances may be deferred in this way. However, it was for a long time thought that any writing-down allowances on industrial buildings were lost if not taken immediately. This was because the legislation generally implied that the term of 25 years over which industrial buildings allowances (IBAs) are given was a fixed one. *Sec 314(4)*, for example, removes the possibility of a balancing allowance or charge arising beyond the end of the period of 25 years from the date the expenditure is incurred.

20.3   The wasting of allowances in this way certainly appeared inequitable, and a different approach, namely that allowances may be deferred to subsequent years (even beyond the normal 25-year 'life'), has been set out in the Revenue's guidance manual. If this results in a balance of unrelieved expenditure at the end of normal writing-down period of 25 or 50 years, the writing-down allowances will continue until all expenditure has been written off. It is understood that where the building or structure is in an enterprise zone, the deferred allowances will still be available at the rate of 25% p.a. In contrast, writing-down allowances on agricultural buildings, which one might expect to be treated in the same way, are indeed lost if not taken immediately.

Time limits for claims

General

20.4   A claim for capital allowances by an individual must be made in a return of income for income tax purposes. [*Sec 3(2)(3)*.] This return of income will normally be due on 31 January following the fiscal year in which an accounting period ends.

20.5   Companies are required to submit a formal tax return within 12 months of the period end. Any claim for capital allowances will in most cases be included in this return.

20.6   For accounting periods ending on or after 1 July 1999, companies come within the self-assessment regime. Capital allowances must be claimed in the annual return of profits (*FA 1998, Sch 18, para 79*), which must be submitted within 12 months of the end of an accounting period (*FA 1998, Sch 18, para 2*). However, the claimant then has a further 12 months to amend that return (*FA 1998, Sch 18, para 82*). The effect is therefore that the existing two-year time limit is retained in most circumstances.

20.7   Where the Revenue amends a return, the company appeals against such amendment, or where the return is subject to a Revenue inquiry, the claim may be revised up to 30 days after notification of the amendment, determination of the appeal, or conclusion of the inquiry. [*FA 1998, Sch 18, para 82.*]

20.8   Where plant is acquired, then in addition to the time limits for making a claim, the purchaser for a number of years had an obligation to notify the Inspector of the relevant expenditure within, broadly, two years. This notification is considered further at the end of this chapter (see 20.46 et seq.).

Amendments to claims

20.9   Claims may be withdrawn or varied at any time up to the later of:

(*a*)   two years after the end of the relevant accounting period, and

(*b*)   the date that the profits or losses of that period are determined (i.e. when the assessment for that period becomes final and conclusive).

20.10   Under self-assessment, a revised claim may only be made by inclusion in an amended return of profits. [*FA 1998, Sch 18, para 81.*] Previously, Statement of Practice SP 9/93 permitted revised claims to be made in the form of a letter, provided that letter included all relevant details, including the circumstances giving rise to the amendment, and an estimate of the additional tax payable or repayable.

20.11   Prior to the introduction of corporate tax self-assessment, no variation was permitted more than six years after the end of the relevant accounting period. If six years elapsed without determination of the relevant profits or losses, a further claim was permitted in the following three months if the claim was conditional on matters relevant to the determination. [*CAA 1990, Sch A1.*] The Board admitted later claims only where the claim could not have been made within the statutory time limits for reasons beyond the company's control. This six-year limit is removed under corporate self-assessment.

Allowances are not mandatory

20.12 It was formerly suggested by the Revenue that the giving of allowances was mandatory. This contention was examined in *Elliss v BP Tyne Tanker Co Ltd (1986) 59 TC 474* (see Appendix 4). It was held that the company was not obliged to accept capital allowances. Thus, so long as the relevant allowance has not been included in a tax computation (such inclusion would constitute a formal claim), the allowance does not need to be formally disclaimed.

The legislation is now explicit that all types of allowances may be wholly or partly disclaimed. The relevant provisions are:

Section	Allowance
52(4)	Plant (FYAs)
56(5)	Plant (WDAs)
306(2)	Industrial buildings (initial allowances)
309(2)	Industrial buildings (WDAs)
441(3)	R&D allowances
458(4)	Know-how allowances
472(4)	Patent allowances.

Choice of claims

20.13 If expenditure could qualify under two or more headings (for example, as plant and as R&D), double allowances are not possible, but the taxpayer may choose which type of allowances to claim. An exception is where expenditure is incurred on second-hand fixtures on or after 24 July 1996. In outline, such expenditure cannot qualify for allowances (as expenditure on plant) if the fixtures have previously been included in a claim for another type of allowance, for example IBAs or R&D allowances. [*Sec 9.*] This rule is disapplied, however, where a claim for IBAs or R&D allowances had previously been made and *Sec 186* or *187* (see 4.19) operates to define the amount which a subsequent purchaser may include in a claim for allowances on plant. [*Sec 9(2).*] Where expenditure on a fixture has once been included in a claim for plant allowances, it will henceforth (for example, in the hands of a subsequent purchaser) only qualify for allowances as plant, and not under any other heading. [*Sec 9(3).*]

20.14 No capital allowances are available in respect of expenditure for which a trading deduction is allowed. [*Sec 4(2).*] This will apply, for example, to deductions under *TA 1988, Sec 87* in respect of short lease premia.

Disclaiming or not claiming allowances

20.15   At first sight, it may appear odd that a taxpayer should decline to take advantage of an allowance granted to him. However the tax system operates in such a way that it can be advantageous either to disclaim allowances formally, or simply not to claim all that is due.

Avoiding a trading loss

20.16   It may be that capital allowances serve merely to create a trading loss which can only be carried forward to be set against future profits of the same trade. It can happen that losses remain unrelieved, whilst at the same time tax is payable on other sources of income.

Example

20.17   Snape Ltd had income and allowances as follows:

	£
Year ended 30 June 1997	
Schedule D Case I profits (before capital allowances)	150,000
Schedule D Case III interest	200,000
Capital allowances	1,000,000
Year ended 30 June 1998	
Schedule D Case I profits (before capital allowances)	750,000
Schedule D Case III interest	200,000
Capital allowances	750,000

If full allowances were claimed, the two years' tax computations would be as follows:

	£
Year ended 30 June 1997	
Schedule D Case I	150,000
Capital allowances	(1,000,000)
	(850,000)
Schedule D Case III	200,000
Loss carried forward	(650,000)
Year ended 30 June 1998	
Schedule D Case I	750,000
Capital allowances	(750,000)
	0
Schedule D Case III	200,000
	200,000
Tax @ 31%	62,000
Loss carried forward*	(650,000)

20.17 Disclaiming or not claiming allowances

* The loss carried forward may only be offset against trading profits, and not against income generally. [*TA 1988, Sec 393(1)*.] A current year loss may be set off against other income under *TA 1988, Sec 393A(1)*.

If some of the 1997 allowances were disclaimed, the position could be as follows:

	£
Year ended 30 June 1997	
Schedule D Case I	150,000
Capital allowances	(350,000)
	(200,000)
Schedule D Case III	200,000
Loss carried forward	0
Year ended 30 June 1998	
Schedule D Case I	750,000
Capital allowances	(912,500)
	(162,500)
Schedule D Case III	200,000
	37,500
Tax @ 31%	11,625

In this example, tax of £50,375 is saved.

Note	£
Capital allowances:	
(a) as previously stated	750,000
(b) on increased expenditure b/fwd	
(£650,000 × 25%)	162,500
	912,500

Desire to use a trading loss

20.18 There may be trading losses brought forward, which it is thought appropriate to utilise in the current year, rather than carry them forward. This could result from a variety of special circumstances.

Example

20.19 Clarke Ltd had the following income and allowances.

31 March	*Profit/loss*	*CAs*	*Net profit*
	£	£	£
1995	500	400	100
1996	200	300	(100)
1997	200	200	—

20.20 At the end of March 1997, the shares in Clarke were sold to an unconnected person in circumstances such that any losses carried forward were likely to be lost, by operation of *TA 1988, Sec 768*. Rather than waste losses of £100,000, Clarke could disclaim allowances in 1997, so that the position in that year was as follows:

	£	£
Profits before CAs		200,000
CAs	200,000	
Less: disclaimed	(100,000)	
		(100,000)
Schedule D Case I		100,000
Losses b/fwd		(100,000)
		0

20.21   In this way, no losses will be wasted. In effect, the losses will have been converted into an increased general pool of expenditure to give increased capital allowances in the future. This might even increase the value of the company, and hence the amount the purchaser is willing to pay.

Generating or avoiding a balancing adjustment

20.22   On occasions, the taxpayer may know or believe that an asset is shortly to be sold, giving rise to a balancing allowance or charge. Disclaiming allowances will increase the tax written-down value of the asset carried forward and hence reduce a balancing charge (or increase a balancing allowance). A disclaimer is often worthwhile where a balancing charge would cause tax to be paid at a higher rate.

Example

20.23   Bowen Ltd makes up accounts to 31 December each year. Its profits for 1997 and 1998 are as follows:

	£
1997	100,000
1998	180,000

20.24   It plans to sell one of its properties in 1998. At the start of 1997, this property has a residue of expenditure of £500,000 and the annual allowance is £250,000. It is expected the property will be sold for around £620,000. If full allowances are claimed, tax will be payable as follows:

1997	£	
Profits (before capital allowances)	100	
IBAs	(250)	
Loss c/fwd	(150)	Tax payable nil

225

20.24 *Disclaiming or not claiming allowances*

1998

Profits	180
Balancing charge	
(620,000 − 250,000)	370
	550
Loss b/fwd	(150)
	400

Tax payable £99,000

£300,000 @ 21%	63
£100,000 @ 33%	33
	99

If the 1997 annual allowance were not claimed, the position would be as follows:

£

1997

Profits	100

Tax payable @ 21% = £21,000

1998

Profits	180
Balancing charge	120
(620,000 − 500,000)	
	300

Tax payable @ 21% = £63,000

20.25 It will be seen that although in each case the profits over two years total £400,000, the effect of not claiming has been to reduce tax payable from £99,000 to £84,000 — a fall of over 15%. This is because profits up to £300,000 are taxed at a lower rate than profits above that amount.

Impact of foreign taxes

20.26 Disclaiming allowances to increase profits may be advisable where some income has arisen abroad and has been charged to foreign tax. This foreign tax can normally be offset against UK tax, but where the foreign tax is greater, the excess is lost.

Example

20.27 Hughes Ltd, in the year ended 31 December 1997, has the following sources of income.

£

Trading profits	115
(before capital allowances)	
Less capital allowances	(100)
	15

20.28   Foreign tax of £8,000 has been paid on £40,000 of these profits. If no disclaimer of allowances is made, the position will be as follows:

	£
Taxable profits	15
UK tax	3.15
Less foreign tax	(3.15)
Tax payable	nil

20.29   However the balance of the foreign tax (£4,850) is wasted. Hughes will effectively have paid tax on its total income at a rate of over 53%. If sufficient allowances were disclaimed, this could be avoided.

	£
Profits	115.0
Capital allowances	(76.9)
Taxable profits	38.1
UK tax	8
Less foreign tax	(8)
Tax payable	nil

20.30   Tax suffered is still £8,000 but the value of the capital allowances pool (and hence tax saved in the following year) is greater.

Use of ACT

20.31   Advance corporation tax (ACT) has been abolished (subject to transitional 'shadow ACT' provisions) from 6 April 1999. In some cases, however, a company may disclaim allowances so as to preserve sufficient profits so that the maximum amount of ACT can be offset. This is most appropriate where there is a risk of not being able to use surplus ACT in the future.

Example

20.32   Tait Ltd, in the year ended 30 June 1997, had the following amounts relevant to its tax computation.

20.32   *Disclaiming or not claiming allowances*

	£
Profits before capital allowances	300
Capital allowances	(200)
	100
Tax payable	21
ACT paid	(40)
Surplus ACT carried forward	15

20.33   The surplus ACT may be used to reduce a tax liability in future years, but for the time being, Tait has suffered tax at a rate of 40%. If allowances were partially disclaimed, the position could be as follows:

	£
Profits	300
Capital allowances	(140)
	160
Tax payable	40
ACT paid	(40)
	nil

20.34   Tax paid is still £40,000 but the opening value of the capital allowances pool in the following year will be £60,000 higher, reducing tax in that year.

Non-trade charges

20.35   Excess charges on income may only be carried forward to set against future profits where such changes are made wholly and exclusively for the purposes of the trade. [*TA 1988, Sec 393(9)*.] A problem will arise, therefore, where the charges in question are, for example, covenanted payments to charity other than for a trading purpose. If this is the case, these payments will not attract any tax relief.

Example

20.36   Tindall Ltd's tax computation for the year ended 31 December 1997 showed the following figures:

	£
Profits	150
Capital allowances	200
Donation to charity	20

20.37   The loss carried forward would normally be only £50,000, i.e. excluding the non-trade charge. If allowances were disclaimed, the position could be as follows:

	£
Profits	150
Capital allowances	(130)
	20
Donation to charity	(20)
Taxable profits	nil

20.38   The capital allowances pool carried forward will be increased by £70,000. Overall, tax relief has been increased because the covenanted payment has been disclaimed.

Using group relief

20.39   A company in a group may be able to take advantage of group relief in one year but not in the next, and a disclaimer of allowances will ensure that the fullest advantage can be obtained.

Example

20.40   Moss Ltd and Boyd Ltd are in a 75% group until the end of the year ended 30 June 1997, when Boyd Ltd is sold. Relevant figures are as follows:

	1997	*1998*
	£	*£*
Moss Ltd		
Profits	100	300
Capital allowances	(80)	(140)
	20	160
Tax payable (after group relief)	nil	33.6
Boyd Ltd		
Profits	20	
Capital allowances	(80)	
Available for group relief	60	

20.41   If Moss Ltd does not disclaim allowances, it will have 1997 profits of only £20,000. Potential group relief from Boyd Ltd of £40,000 will be lost. Tax payable in 1998 will be £33,600 (at 21%). Allowances could be disclaimed in 1997, however, to ensure the following position.

20.41 *Disclaiming or not claiming allowances*

Moss Ltd 1997	£
Profit (before capital allowances)	100
Capital allowances	(40)
	60
Group relief	(60)
	nil

1998	
Profit (before capital allowances)	300
Capital allowances (note)	(150)
	150
Tax payable @ 21%	£31,500

Note Capital allowances:	£
As previously stated	140
Increase arising from disclaimer in previous year (£40,000 @ 25%)	10
	150

Tax of £2,100 has been saved.

Making use of personal allowances

20.42 For an individual, it is possible that a full capital allowances claim may result in the wastage of personal allowances.

Example

20.43 In 1997–98 Wild was assessed on profits of £8,000 and had capital allowances available of £6,000. However the net amount £2,000 was insufficient to make full use of his single person's allowance of £4,045. If capital allowances of £2,045 were disclaimed, this would be avoided, and higher allowances would be available in the following year.

Pension planning

20.44 An individual's personal pension plan contributions will qualify for tax relief only to the extent that they do not exceed a fixed percentage (dependent on age) of that person's net relevant earnings. Disclaiming allowances can therefore be used to increase this figure, and hence increase the funding of the individual's pension.

Conclusion

20.45   Listed above are some of the most common instances of when it may be beneficial not to claim the maximum allowance due. However, there will be others, emanating from the taxpayer's individual circumstances, and the final claim should only be submitted after the taxpayer has considered whether the making of a capital allowances claim ties in with the overall minimisation of his tax liability.

Notification of expenditure on plant and machinery

General

20.46   Between 30 November 1993 and 31 March 1998, there was, in addition to the rules for making an actual claim for allowances, a further requirement that expenditure on plant and machinery could only qualify for allowances if it was notified to the Inspector within the prescribed time. For accounting periods of companies ending on or after 30 November 1993, the time limit was two years after the end of that period. [*FA 1994, Sec 118(3)*.] For individuals, etc. operating under the system of self-assessment, the deadline for notification was 12 months after the 31 January following the year of assessment in which the period of account ends.

Example

20.47   Potts carries on a trade, and first comes within the scope of self-assessment in respect of his year ended 30 April 1996. This year of assessment, 1996–97, ends on 5 April 1997, so notification is necessary by the following 12 months after the following 31 January, that is, by 31 January 1999.

Notification requirements

20.48   With effect from 30 November 1993, no expenditure may form part of a person's qualifying expenditure unless the 'relevant condition' is fulfilled. The 'relevant condition' essentially refers to a requirement that the Revenue has been informed of the expenditure. This requirement applies only to machinery and plant, and not to other types of asset.

The notification requirement was abolished with effect for accounting periods ending on or after 1 April 1998 for companies (6 April for individuals). [*FA 2000, Sec 73*].

20.49 *Notification of expenditure on plant and machinery*

Form of notification required

20.49 Statement of Practice SP 6/94 gives guidance on notification procedures. The relevant parts of that statement are as follows:

'Form of Notification Required by the Board

5. In view of the great variety of circumstances, the Board do not propose to specify in detail the form notifications should take. Generally, the requirement to notify the Inspector will be satisfied where the expenditure is included in a computation prepared for any tax purpose (provided the time limits set out earlier are met). However, it will be advisable to give enough information in the computations to identify the asset for which notification is given, as well as the amount of the expenditure. This does not mean that it will be necessary to list each and every item where large numbers of similar assets are purchased.

6. Where the expenditure is included within the calculation of taxable trading profit (ie as revenue expenditure) but is subsequently recategorised as being expenditure on machinery and plant, the original tax computation will be regarded as notice for the purposes of the new rules.

7. Inclusion of expenditure in a document prepared primarily other than for tax purposes (eg annual accounts of a business, valuation reports, quantity surveyor's reports etc) will not satisfy the requirement.'

20.50 In correspondence with the Chartered Institute of Taxation, the Revenue has confirmed that where expenditure is originally claimed as a revenue deduction but is subsequently recategorised as plant or industrial buildings, the original computation will be regarded as notice for the purposes of the notification rules.

Effect of missing time limit

20.51 Where notification is not made in time, the expenditure may not be included in a claim for capital allowances for that chargeable period. The expenditure may be included in a claim in a subsequent period (in respect of which the notification deadline has not expired), but only if the machinery or plant on which the expenditure was incurred still belongs to the taxpayer at some time in that subsequent period. [*FA 1994, Sec 118(6)*.]

This remains the case, following the abolition of the notification requirement — a claim may only include expenditure from an earlier year if the relevant assets are still owned at some time in the period for which the claim is made.

Extension of time limits

20.52 The board may extend the notification period if it appears appropriate to do so. [*FA 1994, Sec 118(5)*.] Statement of Practice SP 6/94 sets out the Board's policy in this respect. The relevant paragraphs are set out below:

'Board's Policy on Extending Time Limits

8. The time limits allowed for giving written notification of qualifying expenditure on machinery and plant described above should generally be adequate and the Board will not make routine use of its powers to extend the notification period outside of these limits. But there may be exceptional circumstances in which notification cannot be made within the time specified. Applications to allow further time in accordance with the power referred to at paragraph 1 [section 118(5)] above will be considered under the following criteria.

9. In general terms the Board's policy will be to extend the notification time limit only where there is good reason, arising out of circumstances beyond the taxpayer's and his agent's control, why notification could not be given within the statutory time limits.

10. Sometimes a large construction project involving expenditure on a variety of assets, including machinery and plant, extends over several years and it is impossible to complete the final allocation of expenditure between different classes of asset when the normal time limit expires. In such cases, the Board will accept a refinement of the allocation of the overall expenditure between machinery and plant and other assets after the time limit has passed provided:

- reasonable estimates have been made of the expenditure attributable to machinery and plant within the time limit; and

- there is no undue delay in finalising the details.

11. The application for extension and notification of the expenditure involved must be made within a reasonable period (normally not more than three months) after the expiry of the circumstances giving rise to the late notification.

12. What constitute acceptable reasons for late notification will depend upon the particular circumstances of each individual case. Such circumstances do *not* include the following:

- oversight or negligence on the part of the taxpayer or his agent;

- delay, whether due to pressure of work, the complexity of the facts or to other causes except where the circumstances come within paragraph 9 above;

- the taxpayer was absent or ill, unless:

  - the absence or illness arose at a critical time and prevented the giving of notification within the normal time limit, and

  - there was good reason why notification was not given before the time of absence or illness, and

  - in the case of absence, there was a good reason why the taxpayer was unavailable, and

- there was no other person who could have given notification on the taxpayer's behalf within the normal time limit.

Procedure

13. The application to extend the notification period outside the statutory time limits should be sent to the Inspector dealing with the taxpayer and must include an explanation as to why notification could not have been given within the statutory time limit.'

Chapter 21

Interaction With Other Taxes

VAT

Introduction

21.1   The impact of value added tax on capital allowances is often not fully considered by taxpayers or their advisers. Not only will the VAT amounts themselves be large ($17\frac{1}{2}\%$ of the net asset cost) but there is also the risk of stringent penalties and interest should the rules be misapplied. Taxpayers who are unable to recover their input VAT fully should particularly take note of the impact of the capital items scheme, where the capital allowances effect of adjustments is often overlooked.

General

21.2   Where input VAT has been reclaimed, it has not ultimately been borne by the taxpayer. It will not therefore attract tax relief, as a revenue deduction, or as expenditure qualifying for capital allowances. Consequently no allowances will be due in respect of the VAT element of any purchase consideration in such circumstances. However, some taxpayers may be making supplies which are exempt from VAT, and be unable to reclaim any input VAT. Where VAT has been charged on assets qualifying for capital allowances, that VAT will form part of the qualifying cost. Where a property is acquired second hand, and the qualifying expenditure on fixtures is based on an apportionment of the purchase price, that apportionment should take account of any irrecoverable VAT incurred by the vendor.

Partially exempt businesses

21.3   If the taxpayer is making a mixture of taxable and exempt supplies (i.e. a partially exempt business), the input VAT must be apportioned between taxable (i.e. recoverable) and exempt (non-recoverable) supplies. In fixing the appropriate proportion of the VAT on purchases which is not recoverable, and will therefore qualify for allowances, the deciding factor is not the nature of the goods, assets or services acquired, but rather the mix of the purchaser's sales or other outputs, and the use made of these goods, assets etc. There are three possibilities:

(*a*)   Assets will be solely used in relation to the making of taxable supplies. The VAT on these assets should be recoverable in full, and will not therefore qualify for capital allowances.

(b)   Other assets will be used only for making exempt supplies. The VAT on these will not be recoverable, and will therefore be added to the net cost of the assets for capital allowance purposes.

(c)   Some assets will be of general or mixed use. The VAT on these will be recoverable in part, with the irrecoverable part qualifying for allowances.

21.4   For expenditure after 1 April 1990 on computers and on land and buildings, the recovery of input VAT by partially exempt businesses is subject to a set of rules known as the capital items scheme.

Capital items scheme

21.5   The capital items scheme is set out in the VAT Regulations 1995. [*Regs 112–116.*] It relates to two types of asset:

(a)   computers or items of computer equipment worth £50,000 or more; and

(b)   land and buildings worth £250,000 or more.

21.6   In the absence of the capital items scheme, it would be possible for a partially exempt business to acquire such assets in a period when VAT recovery was abnormally high, for example, by using the assets only for producing taxable supplies in the first year, before resorting to more general use subsequently, once the VAT had been recovered. Consequently, in the case of items covered by the scheme, an adjustment is made to the recoverable portion of the VAT (and hence the amount qualifying for capital allowances) where the composition of a partially exempt business's use of the asset changes within a set period of time, this being five years for computers, and ten years for land and buildings. This may apply whether the change is an increase or a decrease in the taxable output as a percentage of the total. The amount qualifying for allowances may therefore, in the case of a building, increase or decrease up to ten years after the original expenditure was incurred.

Example

21.7   Manning Ltd purchased a factory for £500,000 plus VAT. The company makes a variety of supplies, 60% of which are taxable for VAT purposes. The total VAT charged on the building will be £500,000 × $17\frac{1}{2}$% = £87,500. Of this 60% will be recoverable. The balance will be added to the cost of the building for capital allowance purposes.

	£
Net cost	500,000
VAT (40% × £87,500)	35,000
	535,000

Industrial buildings allowance @ 4% = £21,400.

21.8 In the following year the mix of sales changes, such that the recoverable VAT fraction rises to 75%. An adjustment is made to the VAT recoverable on the building as follows. Original VAT × change in recoverable proportion × 1/10. £87,500 × (75% − 60%) × 1/10 = £1,313. This amount will be repaid to Manning. The impact on capital allowances is as follows:

	£
Balance b/fwd (£535,000 − £21,400)	513,600
VAT rebate	(1,313)
	512,287

Industrial buildings allowance (£512,287 ÷ 24) = £21,345.

21.9 In year three, the mix of sales changes again, taxable supplies accounting for only 55% of the total. The VAT adjustment due under the capital items scheme is as follows. £87,500 × (60% − 55%) × 1/10 = £438. Because the recoverable VAT fraction has fallen below what it was on the purchase of the building, this further amount will be payable by Manning. Capital allowances will be:

	£
Brought fwd (£512,287 − £21,345)	490,942
VAT liability	438
	491,380

Industrial buildings allowance (£491,380 ÷ 23) = £21,364.

21.10 These annual adjustments will continue for ten years (unless, of course, the building is sold before the end of that time). If a building is sold, say, in year eight, the final adjustment for VAT will take into account that part of the ten-year period not yet expired.

Effective date of VAT rebate or additional liability

21.11 The general rule is that the date in question is the last day of the 'rele vant VAT period of adjustment'. [*Sec 548(1)*.] These are those periods (normally one year) for which adjustments are made under the capital items scheme, and the relevant one is the one in which a particular adjustment is made. [*Sec 548(1)*.] This date is the key one, therefore, for determining, *inter alia*, whether the event arises in the life of an enterprise zone, or whether the asset (if plant) has belonged to the claimant at the right time.

21.12 Because an additional liability or rebate will arise, in practice, some time after the event which triggered it and in a VAT interval not likely to coincide with a chargeable period, a number of practical difficulties have to be coped with. Consequently, a supplementary set of rules applies and applies for this purpose only.

21.13 An additional VAT liability or rebate is, for determining the chargeable period for capital allowances purposes, regarded as incurred or made at a time determined in accordance with the following paragraph. For all other purposes (for example, determining the rate of allowance), the liability or rebate continues to be treated as incurred or made on the last day of the 'relevant VAT period' (see above). The chargeable period is derived from the following table [*Sec 549*]:

'TABLE

ACCRUAL OF VAT LIABILITIES AND REBATES

Circumstances	*Chargeable period*	*Time of accrual*
The liability or rebate is accounted for in a VAT return.	The chargeable period which includes the last day of the period to which the VAT return relates.	The last day of the period to which the VAT return relates.
The Commissioners of Customs and Excise assess the liability or rebate as due before a VAT return is made.	The chargeable period which includes the day on which the assessment is made.	The day on which the assessment is made.
The relevant activity is permanently discontinued before the liability or rebate is accounted for in a VAT return or assessed by the Commissioners.	The chargeable period in which the relevant activity is permanently discontinued.	The last day of the chargeable period in which the relevant activity is permanently discontinued.

… In the Table—

(a) "VAT return" means a return made to the Commissioners of Customs and Excise for the purposes of value added tax, and

(b) "the relevant activity" means the trade or, in relation to *Part 2*, the qualifying activity to which the additional VAT liability or additional VAT rebate relates.'

21.14 Where any allowance or charge is restricted under any capital allowance provision to a proportion only of the capital expenditure or to a proportion only of what an allowance or charge would otherwise have been then the allowance or charge in respect of any additional VAT liability or rebate is similarly restricted. [*Sec 550.*] This will most commonly be seen in the context of non-trade use by individuals.

Example

21.15 Watts Bros makes up its accounts to 30 April each year. In January 1997, £70,000 was spent on a new computer and VAT was reclaimed in the quarter ended 31 March 1997. In the year to 31 December 1997, the taxable outputs of the business fell, and a further VAT liability of £3,000 became payable. This was accounted for in a return to Customs and Excise for the quarter to September 1998. For the purpose of deciding in which year the £3,000 qualifies for allowances, it is necessary to look at when it was accounted for to Customs and Excise, i.e. 30 September 1998. The amount will therefore first attract capital allowances in the year to 30 April 1999. [*Sec 549.*] However, for other purposes, including determining what rate of allowance is available, the question is governed by *Sec 548*, so that 31 December 1998 is the relevant date. Any additional VAT liability arising in respect of computer equipment will qualify for first-year allowance if the capital expenditure to which it relates also qualifies.

Capital gains tax

General

21.16   For most taxpayers faced with a large or unusual transaction, it is tempting to put different taxes (or different aspects of tax) into separate compartments, and deal with each in isolation. Consideration of capital gains tax (CGT) is necessary, however, in those instances where the capital allowances treatment and the capital gains treatment differ, or where one has an impact on the other. The term CGT is used throughout this section to denote both capital gains tax proper, and also corporation tax on gains, which is the equivalent for companies.

Time of disposal

21.17   For capital allowance purposes, the time of disposal is the earlier of the date of completion and the date possession is given (*TA 1988, Sec 832(1)*); *Sec 451* for R&D allowances). However, for CGT purposes, disposal takes place at the time the contract is made (and not, if different, the time at which the asset is conveyed or transferred). [*TCGA 1992, Sec 28(1)*.] If the contract is conditional (and in particular if it is conditional upon the exercise of an option), the time of disposal is the time the condition is satisfied. [*TCGA 1992, s 28(2)*.] The effect of these rules is that it is possible for the vendor of an asset to have a chargeable gain on that asset in one period and then a balancing charge in the next.

Example

21.18   Warren Ltd, which makes up accounts to 31 March each year, sold an industrial building in such circumstances that gave rise to a balancing charge and a chargeable gain. Contracts were exchanged on 18 March 1997, and completion took place two weeks later. The chargeable gain will arise in the year ended 31 March 1997, and tax will be payable on 1 January 1998. However, the balancing charge (and the additional tax payable as a result) will not arise until one year later, as completion took place after an accounting year end.

Capital sums derived from assets

21.19   For CGT purposes, the realisation of a capital sum is in various circumstances deemed to be a disposal. This includes:

(*a*)   compensation for damage to assets, or for loss, destruction, dissipation or depreciation of assets;

(*b*)   insurance proceeds;

(*c*)   capital sums received for forfeiture or surrender of rights; and

(*d*)   capital sums received for the use or exploitation of assets. [*TCGA 1992, Sec 22(1)*.]

21.20   In such cases, the time of disposal for CGT purposes is the time at which the capital sum is received. Again, this could result in the CGT and capital allowances disposals being taken into account in different accounting periods, although in this case the capital allowances disposal would normally precede the chargeable gain.

Example

21.21   Stanley Ltd makes up accounts to 31 March each year. In March 1998 his factory burned down. Insurance proceeds were received six months later. The balancing adjustment for IBA purposes will be made in the year ended 31 March 1998. However, the chargeable gain will only arise in the following year upon receipt of the proceeds.

The amount of expenditure qualifying for relief

21.22   There is, of course, a fundamental difference between the time that tax relief is given for capital allowances purposes, and the time relief is given from CGT. Capital allowances are generally given over a period beginning with the acquisition of an asset; as far as CGT is concerned, relief is only given when the asset is disposed of, and various costs may be deducted from the proceeds.

21.23   The CGT cost may differ from the cost for capital allowances purposes. For example, it is unlikely that capital allowances would be available in respect of any right over an asset.

21.24   Alternatively, the cost of a second-hand industrial or agricultural building qualifying for capital allowances may be limited to the original construction cost. This will not be the case for CGT. For CGT purposes, the deductible costs are:

(*a*)   the amount or value of the consideration given wholly and exclusively for the acquisition of the asset, or for the provision of the asset;

(*b*) costs incidental to the acquisition of the asset such as fees, commission or remuneration paid for the professional services of any surveyor, valuer, auctioneer, accountant, agent or legal adviser; costs of transfer or conveyance (including stamp duty), and advertising costs;

(*c*) the amount of any expenditure wholly and exclusively incurred on the asset for the purpose of enhancing its value;

(*d*) expenditure incurred on establishing, preserving or defending title to, or a right over, the asset. [*TCGA 1992, Sec 38.*]

21.25 The capital allowances legislation contains no equivalent provisions to define incidental costs.

Restriction of capital losses by reference to capital allowances

21.26 The fact that expenditure has attracted capital allowances does not prohibit deduction of that expenditure in a capital gains computation. However, special rules apply where the result would be a capital loss. [*TCGA 1992, Sec 41.*] In the computation of a capital loss, there is excluded from the sums allowable as a deduction any expenditure to the extent that capital allowances have been made in respect of it. The allowances referred to comprise not only first-year or writing-down allowances, but also any balancing allowance or charge brought about as a result of the disposal itself. [*TCGA 1992, Sec 41(6).*]

21.27 Where the asset involved is an item of plant which has been included in the pool of expenditure, a balancing adjustment will not generally arise. In such cases, allowances are deemed to have been given of an amount equal to the difference between the acquisition cost and the disposal proceeds. In most cases, this is tantamount to including a notional balancing allowance or charge.

Example

21.28 Andrew purchased a machine for use in his business in March 1982 at a cost of £30,000. Capital allowances were claimed and the machine was sold in May 1998 for £10,000. Due to the restriction of capital losses, as set out above, these transactions do not give rise (as would otherwise be the case) to an unindexed loss of £20,000. Instead, the result is as follows:

	£	£
Proceeds		10,000
Less: cost	30,000	
CAs	(20,000)	
		(10,000)
Unindexed 'loss'		0

21.29   For disposals prior to 30 November 1993, it was possible to create an indexed loss equal to the indexation allowance. [*TCGA 1992, former Sec 53(1)(c)*.]

Andrew would have a capital loss calculated thus:

	£
Unindexed loss (as above)	nil
Indexation allowance	
(say) 80% × £10,000	(8,000)
Allowable loss	(8,000)

21.30   This loss could be offset against other chargeable (i.e. capital) gains. However, this is no longer possible for disposals on or after 30 November 1993. [*TCGA 1992, Secs 41, 53(2A)*.]

Chapter 22

International Matters

Overseas assets

General

22.1 Assets are often acquired for use abroad. This fact alone does not normally affect the calculation of capital allowances. An exception is where plant is used for overseas leasing, where the rate of writing-down allowance is 10%, rather than the more usual 25%. However, plant allowances will only be available for plant which is used for a trade, etc. taxable in the United Kingdom. [*Sec 15(1)*.] (See 13.18.) Where overseas, rather than UK, allowances are relevant, see 22.22.

22.2 Any local grant or subsidy has to be taken into account in just the same way as a grant or subsidy from a UK source (see 1.70 et seq.). However, any equivalent of capital allowances computed for the purposes of foreign taxes does not affect the UK allowances.

Buildings and structures

22.3 Industrial buildings allowances are still available in respect of a building or structure outside the United Kingdom, so long as it is in use for purposes of a trade, the profits or gains of which are computed in accordance with the rules applicable to Case I of Schedule D. [*Sec 282*.] The Inland Revenue's view is that this requires those profits to be actually subject to UK tax (CA, para 32850). A company with an overseas trade or vocation chargeable to corporation tax under Case V of Schedule D or a person with an overseas trade, profession or vocation chargeable to income tax under Case V of Schedule D can still claim, however, because such profits are required to be computed in accordance with the rules of Case I of Schedule D. [*TA 1988, Secs 65(3), 70(2)*.]

Assets purchased in a foreign currency

22.4 As a general rule, where the amount of expenditure is denominated in a foreign currency, the exchange rate to be used for conversion into sterling is the rate for the date on which the expenditure is treated as incurred for capital allowances purposes.

22.5 So far as the relevant expenditure is incurred under a hire-purchase contract, the rate to be used is therefore, with two exceptions, the rate in force when the asset is brought into use (CA, para 11750). The two exceptions are as follows:

(*a*)   Where the assets acquired are to be used for finance leasing (see 17.13 et seq.), in which case the exchange rate to be used is that for the day on which each block of expenditure is actually incurred, regardless of the date the asset is brought into use.

(*b*)   Where expenditure is incurred prior to the commencement of a trade. Such expenditure is generally treated as incurred on the first day of trading (see 1.63). However, for the purpose of conversion from a foreign currency, the rate to be used is that in force on the date the expenditure is actually incurred, and not that for the first day of trading (CA, para 11750).

Immigration of trade

Machinery and plant

22.6   When an existing trade comes within the scope of UK taxation, for example, because the company carrying it on has become resident in the United Kingdom, or begun to operate through a branch or agency, capital allowances are available in respect of machinery and plant subject to satisfaction of the normal conditions.

22.7   As regards assets already owned (and previously used abroad), the qualifying cost is deemed to be their market value on the date the trade comes within the scope of UK taxation. The authority for this practice is cited as *Sec 13*, which refers to plant or machinery being brought into use for the purposes of a qualifying activity. In the circumstances described the plant or machinery will have already been in such use (albeit outside the United Kingdom), however the occasion of a trade first coming within the charge to UK tax is deemed to be a commencement of that trade. [*TA 1988, Sec 337(1)*.] Although *Sec 337* only applies to companies, the same treatment is in practice applied to individuals and partnerships.

Industrial buildings and structures

22.8   Writing-down allowances will commence when liability to UK tax commences (or, if later, when the building or structure comes into use) and will cease at the end of the writing-down period (usually 25 years from the date of first use). It is not the case that the whole of the original cost may be written off over the period from immigration to the end of the 25 years. For example, if a trade using an industrial building first comes within the charge to UK taxation 15 years after the building's construction, it is *not* possible for the entire cost to be written off over the remaining ten years, as if the immigration of the trade were a balancing event. Though the legislation is unclear, the Revenue would argue strongly that the original cost should be reduced to reflect notional allowances arising in the years before immigration to the United Kingdom.

Intangible fixed assets

22.9 Where a company becomes resident in the United Kingdom, any intangible which it owns shall be treated as acquired for its accounting value at that time (*FA 2002, Sch 29, para 110*).

Emigration of trade

Plant and machinery

22.10 When a company ceases to be within the charge to corporation tax in respect of a trade, that trade is deemed to have been discontinued. [*TA 1988, Sec 337.*] *Sec 61, Table, items 6* and *7* then applies to require a disposal value to be brought into account (see 11.39). Although *TA 1988, Sec 337* deems there to have been only a discontinuance whereas *Sec 61* requires there to have been a *permanent* discontinuance, no attempt to differentiate the two is made in practice.

22.11 There are no provisions similar to *Sec 337* applicable to persons subject to income, rather than corporation, tax. However, in most such cases there would be an actual discontinuance requiring a disposal value to be brought into account (see 11.38).

Industrial buildings and structures

22.12 When a company ceases to be within the charge to corporation tax in respect of a trade, that trade is deemed to have been discontinued. [*TA 1988, Sec 337.*] Such an event is not, however, an event giving rise to a balancing allowance or charge (see 11.4). The writing-down allowances will cease unless, for example, continued use of the building creates a UK tax liability by reason of there being a 'permanent establishment' in the United Kingdom. On ultimate disposal, a balancing allowance or charge would arise, but as the company will by that time not be within the scope of UK taxation, the event will in practice be ignored.

22.13 Although *Sec 337* only applies to companies, the same treatment is in practice applied to individuals and partnerships.

Intangible fixed assets

22.14 Where a company ceases to be resident in the United Kingdom, any intangible which it owns shall be treated as realised for its market value at that time (*FA 2002, Sch 29, para 108*).

Timing of disposals

22.15 Where a trade is leaving the United Kingdom, it may be that some of the assets used in that trade will not be transferred abroad, but will be sold or scrapped in the UK. If such disposal would give rise to a balancing allowance, the disposal should take place *before* emigration; if, on the other hand, a balancing charge would arise, the disposal should be deferred until *after* emigration. It should not be forgotten that if the trade carried on after emigration is substantially different from the previous UK trade, the UK trade will be regarded as having actually ceased, and not just deemed to have ceased.

Transfer of a UK trade within the European Union

General

22.16 EEC Mergers and Divisions Directive (90/434/EEC) is intended to ensure (*inter alia*) that no immediate capital allowance consequences arise on the transfer of a *business* within the EU. The resultant UK legislation [*Sec 561*] is, however, restricted to the transfer of *trades* (and not any of the other activities which qualify for plant allowances — see 13.18). The legislation effectively, but not overtly, ensures that transfers of trade between members of different member states are treated similarly for capital allowances purposes to a transfer between two UK companies under *TA 1988, Sec 343*.

Conditions

22.17 *Sec 561* applies when:

(*a*) a qualifying company (A) resident in one EU member state transfers to another qualifying company (B) resident in another member state the whole or part of a trade carried on in the United Kingdom, and

(*b*) *TCGA 1992, Sec 140A* applies, causing the transfer of the assets to be treated as made without gain or loss.

22.18 If company B is not resident in the United Kingdom immediately after the transfer it must be carrying on a trade (including whatever trade is transferred to it) in the United Kingdom through a branch agency (so that B is subject to UK taxation). A 'qualifying company' is a body incorporated under the law of a member state. [*Sec 561(1)(c).*]

22.19 Relief under *Sec 140A* is conditional upon the transfer taking place on bona fide grounds and the avoidance of tax must not be the main or one of the main reasons for the transaction. It should be noted that the relief must be claimed jointly by both parties.

Effect

22.20   The application of *Sec 561* has a twofold effect.

(*a*)   The transfer does not give rise to either a balancing allowance or a balancing charge.

(*b*)   Company B takes over the capital allowances history of the assets so that when it disposes of the assets (other than in circumstances to which *Sec 561* also applies) there will be a balancing adjustment calculated on the basis that the assets had remained in one ownership spanning the date of the transfer. [*Sec 561(2)*.]

22.21   Where *Sec 152B* applies the following provisions do not apply:

(i)   *Sec 266* (successions to trades: connected persons);

(ii)   *Sec 560* (insurance companies: transfers of business);

(iii)   *Secs 567–570* (sales without change of control or between connected persons);

(iv)   *TA 1988, Sec 342(2)* (companies in liquidation).

Overseas capital allowances equivalents

22.22   UK capital allowances are available only where the trade or qualifying activity is taxable in the United Kingdom. Where this is not the case, for example, because overseas assets are held in a foreign subsidiary, the prime concern will be to obtain tax relief in the local jurisdiction. Most countries do not recognise the term 'capital allowances' (Ireland and some commonwealth countries being exceptions). However, an equivalent deduction is usually available, generally in the form of tax depreciation.

It is useless to set out details of overseas tax depreciation systems, as legislation and practice is constantly changing in each jurisdiction, and action based on out-dated information can be dangerous. Specialist professional advice should be sought. Although local tax specialists should be involved, most foreign countries do not have capital allowances specialists, and coordination by a UK-based specialist is likely to optimise the claim.

It should be helpful, however, to have a checklist of relevant issues. The following has proved useful in preparing claims under a number of European and other jurisdictions.

1	**Entitlement**	Is entitlement to depreciation based on economic or legal ownership?
		Do different rules apply for fixtures and moveable plant?
		How are the terms 'moveable' and 'fixed' defined (by tax law, land law or commercial practice)?
		Are fixtures automatically treated as part of the building, and depreciated over the same period?
		Is depreciation permissible for leased property?
		Is depreciation possible where a property as a whole is expected to increase in value?
		What is the interaction with other taxes, e.g. VAT, stamp duty/transfer tax, capital gains tax or local taxes?
2	**Basis**	Does the depreciable cost include all costs of making an asset ready for use, including prime cost, transport, commissioning, etc.?
		Can professional fees be depreciated?
		Is it possible to depreciate taxes incurred on an acquisition (e.g. transfer tax/stamp duty)?
		Can the whole cost be depreciated, or merely the net amount, after taking into account the estimated realisable value?
3	**Timing**	Does depreciation run from the time the asset is acquired, or when it is brought into use?
		Where a project runs over a year-end, what is an acceptable basis for splitting the expenditure on a time basis?
		Can estimated interim claims be submitted?
4	**Calculation**	In the year of acquisition, can a full year's depreciation be claimed?
		If not, is expenditure apportioned on a time basis, or do other rules apply? (e.g., some countries allow a full year's depreciation for expenditure in the first six months, but only half of the full year's depreciation for expenditure in the second half of the year).

5	**Method**	Is depreciation calculated on a straight line or reducing balance basis, or on some other basis?
		Does the taxpayer have a choice of depreciation method?
		Can the method be changed during the asset's life?
		Are second-hand assets subject to different rates?
6	**Accounts**	Is it necessary for depreciation to be reflected in the accounts, in order to qualify for tax relief?
		Must the accounts and tax depreciation be identical? (In some countries, less than the whole of the accounts depreciation may be claimed for tax purposes.)
		If depreciation gives rise to a loss, can that be set against other income, carried back or forward, or surrendered to group companies?
		What are the appropriate accounts categories?
		How much detail must be filed or merely retained?
		What are the filing deadlines?
		Is there a requirement to make payments of tax 'on account' before the final accounts are filed?
		Can rates of allowances be changed retrospectively?
		What is the procedure and timescale for a claim to be 'agreed'?
		Is there any procedure for obtaining an advance ruling on borderline issues?
7	**Rates**	Are permissible rates of depreciation set out by statute, or by commercial practice?
		What are the permissible rates of depreciation?
		Does depreciation of a building depend on the use to which it is put?

7	Rates (contd)	Is accelerated depreciation possible where an asset is used more than usual (e.g. where a factory operates in shifts, on a 24-hour basis)?
		Many countries specify a range of depreciation rates for certain assets. How much discretion does the taxpayer have within that range?
		Can depreciation be deferred if it is not needed, due to losses, etc.?
8	Incentives	Are incentives, such as increased or accelerated rates of depreciation, available for small businesses?
		Is accelerated depreciation available for expenditure in prescribed geographical areas or development areas, or for certain types of businesses?
		Are there incentives for energy-efficient or environmentally-friendly assets or expenditure?
9	Disposal	Is there a claw-back of depreciation on disposal?
		Can the claw-back be 'rolled over' if replacement assets are acquired?
10	Planning	Opportunities for planning should be discussed with a local tax specialist. Various elections may be advisable.
11	Other	Local specialists should be asked for details of other 'quirks' peculiar to a particular jurisdiction.

Chapter 23

Contaminated Land

Introduction

23.1   Tax relief at the rate of 150% is available for expenditure on cleaning up contaminated land ('Land Remediation Relief'). Although this relief is not strictly a capital allowance, it is available equally on revenue and capital expenditure, and should not, therefore, be overlooked when acquiring land or constructing a building.

The legislation operates firstly by allowing capital expenditure to be treated as revenue expenditure, and secondly by granting a deduction equal to 150% of relevant revenue expenditure (including any capital expenditure treated as such under these provisions).

23.2   The relief is only available where the expenditure is incurred on or after 11 May 2001 [*FA 2001, Sch 22, para 32*].

Deduction for capital expenditure

23.3   Capital expenditure on land remediation may be deducted in computing the profits of a trade [*FA 2001, Sch 22, para 1*] or Schedule A business [*FA 2001, Sch 23, para 1*], provided the taxpayer elects in writing for such treatment within two years of the end of the relevant accounting period. This will generally be the period in which the expenditure is incurred, unless the trade is yet to commence, in which case the expenditure is deemed to have been incurred on the first day of trading [*FA 2001, Sch 22, para 1*].

See pro forma election, Appendix 5.

Qualifying expenditure

23.4   Expenditure qualifies for the deduction if it relates to employee costs, direct materials, or sub-contractors' costs incurred on relevant land remediation undertaken by the company or on its behalf [*FA 2001, Sch 22, para 2*].

23.5   The relevant land must be *contaminated*, which means that, because of substances in, on or under the land, there is actual or potential harm being done (including water pollution) [*FA 2001, Sch 22, para 3*].

23.6 *Exclusions*

23.6 Qualifying land remediation has the purpose of preventing, remedying or mitigating the effects of any harm which contaminates the land, or of returning the land to its former state. Expenditure for this purpose will qualify for the deduction, along with any associated preparatory work, for example, in assessing whether land is contaminated. However, it should be noted that preparatory work of this nature only qualifies for the deduction where the land does, in fact, prove to be contaminated [*FA 2001, Sch 22, para 4*]. The relief is available for qualifying work on buildings, as well as land itself. Consequently, 150% tax relief may be claimed, for example, on the cost of removing asbestos.

Exclusions

23.7 The deduction is not available where:

- the land is contaminated due to anything done, or omitted to be done, by the company or a connected person [*FA 2001, Sch 22, paras 1, 12*];

- the expenditure has already attracted a tax deduction in a previous accounting period [*FA 2001, Sch 22, para 1*];

- the expenditure would have been incurred irrespective of the contaminated land issue [*FA 2001, Sch 22, para 2*];

- the expenditure is subsidised [*FA 2001, Sch 22, para 2*];

- the land in question is a nuclear site [*FA 2001, Sch 22, para 3*]; or

- the expenditure qualifies for capital allowances [*FA 2001, Sch 22, para 1*].

The final exclusion means that expenditure on plant cannot qualify for the deduction.

Employee costs

23.8 The costs which qualify for the deduction are all emoluments, pension contributions and secondary Class 1 National Insurance.

23.9 Where an employee spends only part of his time in dealing with land remediation, his remuneration etc. qualifies for the deduction in accordance with the following table:

Proportion of time spent dealing with land remediation	*Proportion of remuneration etc. qualifying for deduction*
20 % or less Between 20 and 80% 80% or more	Nil The appropriate proportion 100%

23.10 The deduction for employee costs does not extend to administrative or secretarial functions.

[*FA 2001, Sch 22, para 5*].

Sub-contractors

23.11 Provided the company and the sub-contractor are not connected, the whole of the company's payment to the sub-contractor will qualify for the deduction [*FA 2001, Sch 22, para 11*].

23.12 If the company and the sub-contractor are connected, the whole of the company's payment to the sub-contractor will only qualify if:

- the sub-contractor has brought the payment into account in calculating his profits; and

- the whole of the expenditure incurred *by* the sub-contractor has been brought into account in computing profits, ie it is not capital in nature, is not subsidised, and has been incurred on materials or employee costs.

[*FA 2001, Sch 22, para 10*].

Relief at 150%

23.13 Where a company has acquired land in the United Kingdom for the purposes of a trade or Schedule A business, and then incurs land remediation expenditure, it may make a claim to treat that expenditure as if it were 150% of the actual amount. This applies initially to revenue expenditure, but covers also capital expenditure allowed as a deduction by *FA 2001, Sch 22*. [*FA 2001, Sch 23, para 1*].

23.14 A claim for this relief must be made in the relevant tax return, and can only be amended by amending the return [*FA 2001, Sch 23, para 4*].

23.15 The detailed rules relating to claims, and penalties for fraudulent or negligent claims, are in *FA 1998, Sch 18, Part 9B*. One important factor is that the amount of the claim must be quantified at the time it is made.

Loss relief

23.16 If the land remediation relief (ie the 150% deduction) gives rise to a loss, the company may claim a 'land remediation tax credit' equal to 16% of the loss. The company may claim for the tax credit to be repaid to it.

The loss for this purpose is reduced by any set-off (including group relief) in the current year, but no account is taken of losses brought forward or carried back.

[*FA 2001, Sch 22, para 14, 15*].

Chapter 24

Goodwill and Other Intangible Fixed Assets

Introduction

24.1   Prior to 1 April 2002, expenditure on most intangible fixed assets did not qualify for tax relief, other than in calculating a gain or loss on a subsequent sale. The only exceptions were computer software (see 14.40) patents and know-how (see 18.27 and 18.43).

24.2   For companies chargeable to corporation tax, with effect from 1 April 2002 (para 117), relief is given for expenditure on such assets (including goodwill) on the basis of amortisation shown in accounts, or (on election) at a fixed rate of 4% per annum. This applies to patents and know-how, such that the 'old' capital allowances are not available for new expenditure incurred by a company. The allowances remain in place for individuals and others chargeable to income tax.

24.3   Certain assets are specifically excluded from these rules (see 24.12).

24.4   *FA 2002, Sch 29* sets out a complete system for dealing with both debits and credits relating to intangibles – this chapter concentrates primarily on the debits, to the extent that, like capital allowances, they aim to provide relief for capital expenditure. It should be remembered, however, that the amortisation of intangibles is not a capital allowance as such, and consequently the general principles outlined in other chapters may not apply where intangible assets are concerned.

24.5   Statutory references in this chapter are to *Finance Act 2002, Sch 29*.

Relief for company expenditure on intangibles

24.6   With effect from 1 April 2002, amortisation under *Sch 29* is the only way that relief is given for capital expenditure by a company on intangibles. So far as patents and know-how are concerned, *Sch 29* amortisation replaces the capital allowances previously available (para 1(3)). However, *Sch 29* applies only to companies, consequently 'old style' allowances are still available to individuals, etc. chargeable to income tax.

24.7 The amount relieved is:

- the amount of expenditure written off in the accounts on the acquisition of an intangible asset (para 8);

- the amortisation shown in the accounts, pro-rated if the cost for tax purposes differs from the cost in the accounts (para 9); or

- fixed rate amortisation (whether or not charged in the accounts), provided an election is made (para 10 – see 24.8).

The accounts must be drawn up in accordance with generally accepted accounting practice – if they are not, such amortisation will be permitted as would have been the case if generally accepted accounting practice had been applied (para 5).

24.8 The taxpayer can elect to write down the cost of an intangible fixed asset at a fixed rate of 4% per annum, whether or not the asset is written down for accounting purposes.

This election must be made within two years of the end of the accounting period in which the asset is acquired or created, and once made, is irrevocable (paras 10, 11).

See pro forma election, Appendix 5.

Definition of intangible fixed asset

24.9 An intangible asset is one which is regarded as such by generally accepted accounting practice, whether or not the asset is in fact capitalised in the accounts. It is a fixed asset if it is acquired or created for use on a continuing basis in the course of a company's activities (para 2). An option to acquire such an asset is treated in the same way as the asset itself is, or would be, treated (para 3).

24.10 The definition of an intangible asset specifically includes intellectual property, including:

- patents, trade marks, registered designs, copyright or design rights;

- foreign rights equivalent to the above;

- any other information or technique having industrial, commercial or other economic value; and

- a licence or other right relating to any of the above.

(para 2).

24.11 *Sch 29* also applies to goodwill, determined in accordance with generally accepted accounting practice (para 4).

Excluded assets

24.12 A number of assets are excluded from the application of *Sch 29* in whole or in part (para 2(3)). The excluded assets include:

- rights over tangible assets;

- oil licences;

- financial assets;

- rights in companies, trusts, etc;

- assets held for non-commercial purposes;

- assets held for the life assurance business of an insurance company;

- assets held for the purposes of a mutual trade or business;

- films and sound recordings;

- computer software treated for accounting purposes as part of the cost of related hardware;

- other computer software (on election).

(paras 72–83).

Computer software

24.13 Computer software acquired with hardware, and accounted for as part of the cost of the hardware, will qualify as plant for capital allowances purposes, and is exempt from *Sch 29* (para 81).

24.14 Other computer software qualifies for capital allowances under *Sec 71* (see 14.40). However, from 1 April 2002, new expenditure on software will initially qualify for relief under *Sch 29*, provided it is incurred by a company. If the company wishes to exempt such expenditure from *Sch 29*, it must make an election within two years of the end of the accounting period in which the expenditure was incurred. Such an election is irrevocable (para 83).

See pro forma election, Appendix 5.

24.15 For taxpayers other than companies, *Sch 29* does not apply, and consequently, capital allowances are given without the need for an election.

24.16 Companies therefore can effectively choose between capital allowances under *Sec 71* and amortisation under *Sch 29*. Capital allowances will be more generous than fixed rate amortisation under para 10 (see 24.8), but less generous than an immediate write-off under para 8 (see 24.7).

Where amortisation is charged in the accounts, the advisability of making an election will depend on the period over the accounting policy used, i.e. the period over which the expenditure is written off. Ideally, the correct accounting policy should be determined first, without considering the choice of tax relief, then the advisability of making an election will be determined by a discounted cash flow calculation.

Qualifying expenditure

24.17 Expenditure which qualifies for relief is:

• the cost of acquiring or creating an intangible asset;

• the cost of establishing, preserving or defending title to an intangible asset;

• royalties in respect of the use of an asset (para 132).

24.18 Where expenditure is incurred only partly for the above purposes, the amount qualifying under *Sch 29* is to be determined by a just apportionment (para 132).

24.19 Where a qualifying intangible asset is acquired together with other assets, the amount qualifying under *Sch 29* shall be the value allocated by the company in accordance with generally accepted accounting practice. If there is no such allocation, the qualifying amount is determined by a just and reasonable apportionment (para 105).

This is the case wherever assets are acquired as a result of a single bargain, even if there are, or purport to be, separate acquisitions or separate prices agreed between the parties.

Realisation of intangible assets

24.20 *Sch 29* provides for debits or credits to be brought into account when an intangible asset is realised (para 18). Realisation is defined as a reduction in the accounting value of an asset, including the asset ceasing to be recognised in the accounts. Assets without a balance sheet value are treated as if they did have a balance sheet value (para 19).

24.21 A debit or credit (effectively a loss or gain) is brought into account, calculated as the difference between proceeds and net book value. If the asset is not shown in the balance sheet, the credit will be equal to the proceeds (paras 20–23).

24.22 Where assets are sold together, the proceeds are to be allocated on the basis of a just and reasonable apportionment (para 105).

24.23 Where proceeds are reinvested (within a period running from one year before the disposal to three years afterwards), the company may claim to

24.23 *Connected persons, etc.*

reduce both the proceeds of the old asset and the cost of the new asset as follows:

	Amount of relief
(1) cost of new assets equals or exceeds the proceeds of realisation of the old asset	the amount by which proceeds of realisation exceed the cost of the old asset
(2) cost of new assets is less than the proceeds of realisation of the old asset	the amount by which the new expenditure exceeds the cost of the old asset

(para 41).

See pro forma election, Appendix 5.

24.24 A claim for this relief must specify the old assets to which the claim relates, details of the new expenditure and the amount of the relief claimed (para 40).

Connected persons, etc.

24.25 Where an intangible fixed asset is transferred between connected persons or related parties, the transfer will generally be treated as taking place at market value (para 92). However, there are a number of exceptions, where the transfer is treated as being tax-neutral. These include intra-group transfers (para 55) and certain transfers of a business (para 84).

Emigration and immigration

24.26 Where a company ceases to be resident in the United Kingdom, any intangible which it owns shall be treated as realised for its market value at that time (para 108).

24.27 Where a company becomes resident in the United Kingdom, any intangible which it owns shall be treated as acquired for its accounting value at that time (para 110).

Tax avoidance

24.28 Arrangements aimed mainly at securing a debit (or avoiding a credit) are ignored for the purposes of *Sch 29* (para 111).

Rates of Allowances

Buildings

Initial allowances

	%
Industrial buildings, commercial buildings and structures in enterprise zones	100
Industrial buildings, etc. in other geographical areas	Nil
Buildings used for scientific research	100

Writing-down allowances

Industrial buildings, commercial buildings and structures in enterprise zones (when initial allowance is disclaimed)	25
Industrial buildings, etc. in other geographical areas	4
Commercial (non-industrial) buildings not in an enterprise zone	Nil
Qualifying hotels	4
Agricultural buildings	4

Machinery and plant

First-year allowances (all enterprises)

Expenditure incurred on or after 1 April 2001 on energy-saving plant or machinery	100
Expenditure incurred on or after 17 April 2002 on electric cars or cars with low CO_2 emissions, or on gas refuelling stations	100
Expenditure incurred on or after 17 April 2002 in a ring-fence trade	100
Expenditure incurred on or after 17 April 2002 in a ring-fence trade (long life assets)	24
Expenditure incurred on or after 1 April 2003 on environmentally beneficial plant or machinery	100

First-year allowances (for small or medium-sized enterprises only)

Expenditure incurred 2 July 1997 to 1 July 1998	50
Expenditure incurred 2 July 1997 to 1 July 1998 (long life assets)	12

Appendix 1

Expenditure incurred on or after 2 July 1998   40
Expenditure incurred by *small* enterprises on information and
communications technology, in four years ending 31 March 2004   100

Writing-down allowances

Long life assets   6
Plant used for overseas leasing   10
Other plant   25
(NB writing-down allowance on expensive cars restricted to £3,000 p.a.)

Examples of Machinery and Plant

It is impossible to compile a comprehensive list of items qualifying for allowances as plant. This is because a claim is dependent upon many features, not least of which is the context in which the asset is used. At best such a list can act as a catalyst in the compilation of an actual claim. The following items are listed for that purpose only.

A

Advertising signs, billboards, and hoardings
Aerials
Air compressors and services
Air-conditioning including ducting and vents
Aquaria
Arc welding plant
Automatic exit doors and gates

B

Battery chargers
Beehives
Bicycle holders or racks
Blast furnaces
Blast tunnels
Blinds and curtains
Boilers
Bowser tanks
Brick elevators
Brick kilns
Bullet resistant screens
Burglar alarms
Bus bars

C

Cable TV provision and ducting
Cameras
Canteen fittings and equipment
Car park illumination and barrier equipment
Carpets and other loose floor coverings
Car wash apparatus, including housing
Cash dispensers (ATMs)

Catwalks
Ceilings — suspended, but only when performing a function, e.g. an integral part of a ventilation or air-conditioning system
Checkouts
Chilling equipment and insulation
Cleaning cradles (including tracks and anchorages)
Compressed air systems
Computers and associated specialised flooring and ceilings
Communications equipment
Conduit for security alarm systems
Conveyor installations
Cooler rooms
Cold water systems for drinking and air-conditioning
Counters and fittings
Cranes, gantries and supports
Crush barriers for safety at sports grounds

D
Dark rooms (demountable)
Derricks
Distribution systems
Document hoists and other hoists
Dry dock
Dry riser installation
Dumb waiters
Dust extraction equipment
Dynamos

E
Electric fences
Electric scoreboards
Electrically operated doors
Electrically operated roller shutters
Electrical substations and generators
Electrical wiring serving an accepted item of plant
Electrical systems designed to suit a particular trade
Emergency lighting

F
Fairground and similar amusements
Fans and heaters
Fascia lettering and signs
Fire alarms
Fire protection systems and sprinklers
Fire safety equipment to comply with the requirements of a fire authority
Fitted desks, writing tables and screens
Floodlighting
Floor covering (specialised)
Flooring (demountable)

Flooring (raised but only where incorporating special features necessary for trade)
Freezer rooms
Furnaces

G
Gas installations
Generators

H
Hand dryers
Heating installations, fittings, pipes and radiators
Hoses and hose reels
Hot water services and related plumbing

I
Incinerators
Intercom installations
Internal signs

K
Kitchen equipment

L
Laundry equipment and sluices
Lifts and hoists
Lifting and handling equipment
Light fittings and lamps (certain trades, e.g. hotels, for ambience)
Lighting to control day length or supplement natural light (for growing plants)
Lightning protection systems
Loose floor coverings and doormats
Loose furniture

M
Mechanical gates
Mechanical vehicle barriers
Mezzanine storage platforms (movable)
Movable partitions (where required by trade)
Murals (certain trades, e.g. hotels, for ambience)

O
Ornaments (certain trades, e.g. hotels, for ambience)

P
Passenger lifts
Paging systems
Pictures (certain trades, e.g. hotels, for ambience)
Portable toilets

Power installations
Public address and piped music systems

R
Racking, cupboards and shelving (removable)
Radio and television receivers
Refrigeration installations and cold stores

S
Safety equipment and screens
Sanitary installations
Screens in a window display (movable)
Security screens
Silos
Smoke detectors and heat detectors
Soft furnishings
Software purchased at the same time as the hardware of a computer system
Sound attenuation baffles
Spray and valeting booths
Sprinkler systems
Storage racks, etc.
Strong rooms
Switchboards
Switch gear

T
Tea and coffee dispensers, vending machines
Telephone booths and kiosks
Telex and fax systems
Thermal insulation regarding industrial buildings
Transformers
Turnstiles

V
Vacuum cleaning installations
Ventilation equipment
Vents
Vibration control
Video equipment

W
WC partitions (if demountable)
Wash basins and associated plumbing
Waste disposal units
Water tower
Water treatment plant
Weigh bridge
Wet and dry risers
Winches

Window display lighting in shops
Window displays (movable)
Wiring and trunking to accepted items of plant
Works of art (at a museum, or hotel, etc.)

Location of Enterprise Zones

The complete list of zones created, together with their expiry dates, is as follows:

Lower Swansea Valley (No.1)	10 June 1991
Corby	21 June 1991
Dudley	9 July 1991
Langthwaite Grange (Wakefield)	9 July 1991
Clydebank	2 August 1991
Salford Docks	11 August 1991
Trafford Park	11 August 1991
City of Glasgow	17 August 1991
Gateshead	24 August 1991
Newcastle	24 August 1991
Speke	24 August 1991
Hartlepool	22 October 1991
Isle of Dogs	25 April 1992
Delyn	20 July 1993
Wellingborough	25 July 1993
Rotherham	22 September 1993
Scunthorpe (Normanby Ridge and Queensway)	15 August 1993
Dale Lane and Kinsley (Wakefield)	22 September 1993
Workington (Allerdale)	3 October 1993
Invergordon	6 October 1993
North West Kent (Nos.1–5)	30 October 1993
Middlesbrough (Britannia)	7 November 1993
North East Lancashire	6 December 1993
Tayside (Arbroath)	8 January 1994
Tayside (Dundee)	8 January 1994
Telford	12 January 1994
Glanford (Flixborough)	12 April 1994
Milford Haven Waterway (North Shore)	23 April 1994
Milford Haven Waterway (South Shore)	23 April 1994
Dudley (Round Oak)	2 October 1994
Lower Swansea Valley (No.2)	5 March 1995
North West Kent (Nos.6 and 7)	9 October 1996
Inverclyde	2 March 1999
Sunderland — Hylton and Southwick	26 March 2000
Sunderland — Castleford and Doxford Park	26 March 2000
Lanarkshire (Hamilton)	31 January 2003
Lanarkshire (Monkland)	31 January 2003

Lanarkshire (Motherwell)	31 January 2003
Dearne Valley (Nos.1–6)	2 November 2005
East Midlands (NE Derbyshire)	3 November 2005
East Midlands (Bassetlaw)	16 November 2005
East Midlands (Ashfield)	21 November 2005
East Durham (Nos.1–6)	29 November 2005
Tyneside Riverside (No.1)	19 February 2006
Tyneside Riverside (Nos.2–7)	26 August 2006
Tyneside Riverside (Nos.8–10)	21 October 2006

Case Summaries

Re Addie & Sons (1875) 1 TC 1

The very first case in *Volume One* of *Tax Cases* was on the subject of relief (or the lack of it) for capital expenditure. The taxpayers carried on an iron and coal business, and owned a number of mineral fields. They claimed that there should be deducted from their profits for tax purposes amounts in respect of sinking pits and depreciation of buildings and machinery. These amounts were calculated on a percentage basis, not dissimilar to modern capital allowances. The Lord President observed: 'No sum shall be set against or deducted from ... profits or gains on account of any sum employed or intended to be employed as capital in a trade'. Almost identical provisions are now found in *TA 1988, Sec 74(f)*. No allowance was therefore due, though of course this apparent injustice was to be remedied in subsequent years.

Caledonian Railway Co v Banks (1880) 1 TC 487

This early case does not sit easily alongside the complex modern system of capital allowances. The *Customs and Inland Revenue Act 1878* introduced statutory allowances for wear and tear. The company claimed that it was entitled to such allowances in addition to a deduction for sums actually expended on repairs and renewals. It was held that this was not the case. Lord Gifford opined:

> '... the Railway Company cannot get deduction for deterioration twice over — first by deducting the actual expenses of repair and renewal, and then by deducting an additional estimated sum for the same thing.'

However, although relief could not be given twice over, the taxpayer was entitled to choose by which method relief was obtained. The method must be consistently applied, i.e. it is not possible to claim 'capital allowances' in respect of some assets whilst dealing with others on a 'renewals basis'.

The importance of this case now is in its confirmation, unchallenged, that the renewals basis remains a permissible alternative to formal capital allowances.

Yarmouth v France (1887) 19 QBD 647

This case, though dealing with employer's liability, is renowned as being the source of the most commonly used definition of plant. The asset in question was a horse. Lindley LJ stated:

'There is no definition of plant in the Act: but, in its ordinary sense, it includes whatever apparatus is used by a businessman for carrying on his business, not his stock-in-trade which he buys or makes for sale; but all goods and chattels, fixed or moveable, live or dead, which he keeps for permanent employment in his business.'

John Hall Jr & Co v Rickman [1906] 1 KB 311

The term 'plant' was held to encompass a hulk, which had formerly been a sailing ship, but which had been dismantled and had had its rudder removed and was now used as a floating warehouse for coal. This was not the main point considered by the court, and indeed was barely referred to at all. That the hulk qualified as plant cannot be said to be the outcome of protracted reasoning.

Earl of Derby v Aylsner (Surveyor of Taxes) (1915) 6 TC 665

In this case the taxpayer claimed an annual allowance to represent the gradual diminution in value of two stallions used for breeding purposes. The relevant legislation at that time only envisaged allowances where the assets were subject to wear and tear. Rowlett J decided that the horses did not fall in value by reason of wear and tear, but merely by reason of the passing of time. He compared a horse to machinery which, if it were not used, would not diminish in value. The horses did not fall within the provisions of the legislation as it then stood and hence allowances were not granted. NB this case is often interpreted as showing that horses cannot be 'plant or machinery'.

This interpretation is wrong. Rowlatt J specifically declined to consider whether a horse could ever be plant or machinery. In practice, horses will normally be treated as plant where they perform some function in a business, for example, brewery dray horses, or even showjumpers used for advertising purposes. Capital allowances are not available for production animals dealt with under the herd basis set out in *TA 1988, Sch 5 [Sec 38]*.

Law Shipping Co Ltd v CIR (1923) 12 TC 621

The taxpayer company purchased a second-hand ship at a time when the ship's periodical Lloyd's survey was overdue, but had been deferred pending completion of a voyage. Six months later the survey was carried out, and the company was obliged to spend a large sum on repairs. It was held that only part of the expenditure was properly chargeable to repairs, being in respect of repairs necessitated by the use of the ship since it was acquired by Law Shipping. The cost of repairs attributable to the period before Law Shipping acquired the ship was to be properly regarded as capital. The need for repairs would have been reflected in a lower purchase price upon acquisition. It is interesting, however, that if the ship had not changed hands, the repairs would have been allowable, even though they had been allowed to build up, and might represent more than one year's wear and tear. The Lord President (Clyde) said: 'Accumulated repairs are, in fact, nonetheless repairs necessary to earn profits, although they have been allowed to accumulate.'

Daphne v Shaw (1926) 11 TC 256

A solicitor incurred expenditure on his law library and claimed that this constituted expenditure on plant for capital allowances purposes. Daphne, who appeared for himself, referred to 'Coke upon Littleton', where there is reference to 'the utensils or instrument of [a] trade or profession, [such] as the axe of the carpenter, or the bookes of a scholler'. Sir Edward Coke (1552–1633) was a barrister, Chief Justice and some time Speaker of the House of Commons, remembered for his commentary on the *Treatise on Tenures* written by Sir Thomas Littleton in the sixteenth century. This must be one of the older authorities called upon in cases on the subject of capital allowances! The claim was rejected, with regret, by Rowlatt J and no appeal was made by the taxpayer. Rowlatt J attached great weight to the ordinary meaning of the word 'plant'. A flaw in this case was perhaps that no reference was made to *Yarmouth v France*. Although that case was heard in 1887 (39 years before *Daphne v Shaw*) it had related to the question of employer's liability and had never yet, in 1926, been referred to in a revenue context.

The decision in *Daphne v Shaw* stood for some 50 years, until it was overturned by *Munby v Furlong* (qv) in 1977.

Lyons J & Co Ltd v A-G[1944] 1 All ER 477

This case considered whether lamps and light fittings were 'land' under the *War Damage Act 1943*. That Act included within 'land' any plant and machinery as defined by rating legislation, so in effect the question was whether the lamps etc. were 'plant'. Uthwatt J laid down the following principle:

> 'In the present case, the question at isssue may, I think, be put thus: Are the lamps and fitments properly to be regarded as part of the setting in which the business is carried on, or as part of the apparatus used for carrying on the business? In this case the lamps and their fitments are owned by a caterer and used in premises exclusively devoted to catering purposes. But the presence of lamps in this building is not dictated by the nature of the particular trade these carried on, or by the fact that it is for trade purposes that the building is used. Lamps are required to enable the building to be used where natural light is insufficient. The actual lamps themselves, so far as the evidence goes, present no special feature either in construction, purpose or position and, being supplied with electricity from public suppliers, they form no part of an electric lighting plant in or to the hereditament.
>
> In my opinion, these lamps are not, in these circumstances, properly described as "plant" but are part of the general setting in which the business is carried on. They would not, I think, in any catalogue of this trader's assets, fall under the heading "machinery and plant" ...'.

Abbott v Albion Greyhounds (Salford) Ltd (1945) 26 TC 390

A company operating a greyhound track maintained a kennel of its own dogs for racing purposes. It claimed the dogs were trading stock, whilst the Revenue contended that the dogs were truly part of the fixed capital of the business. Wrottesley J mentioned in passing that the dogs were not plant or machinery. His comment, it appears, was not a particularly considered one, and capital allowances were not the subject of the case. The case is therefore of limited use as an authority on this subject.

CIR v Lambhill Ironworks Ltd (1950) 31 TC 393

IBAs were claimed, and given, in respect of a drawing office. The drawing office in question occupied one floor of a two-storey building some 200 yards from the industrial buildings used for the purposes of a trade of structural steel engineering. The buildings were not physically connected. The people employed in the drawing office numbered between 20 and 35. Of these, two prepared drawings to be used for tenders sent to prospective customers; the remainder made drawings and lists necessary to the carrying out of orders received. The Lord President (Cooper) said '... the drawing office is ... to all outward semblance and in real substance an integral, and indeed a vital part of the industrial premises'. Further, the drawing office was not used for a purpose ancillary to the purposes of the general office — 'a drawing office is no more an "office" within the meaning of the Act than a machine shop is a "shop"'. Lord Keith inferred that an office must be something which clearly has not got anything of an industrial character, or is not directly ancillary to the industrial operations conducted in the rest of the works.

Dale v Johnson Bros (1951) 32 TC 487

Johnson Brothers acted as a selling agent for the products of various companies. Being required to have in stock certain quantities of each product, it constructed a warehouse for such purpose. Industrial buildings allowances were claimed under the equivalent of *Sec 274, Table A, item 3(c)*, i.e. 'the storage of goods or materials ... not yet delivered to any purchaser'. The claim was denied, and two important principles were laid down.

First, to qualify for IBAs, there must be a trade of storage — storage incidental to a wider trade was not sufficient: 'It will not do that the trade is storage plus something else or something else plus storage' stated Sheil J. Second, it was held that Johnson Brothers (by virtue of the transfer of title to it), even though it was a selling agent or intermediary, was nonetheless a purchaser within the meaning of the legislation.

CIR v George Guthrie & Son (1952) 33 TC 327

The taxpayer made a payment to a motor dealer for a car to be used entirely for business purposes. However, he then discovered that the same car had already been sold to another person, and the car was subsequently delivered to that person. The motor dealer then went into liquidation and the taxpayer was unable to recover any of the money spent on the car which was never delivered. He claimed capital allowances in respect of this expenditure, whilst the Revenue argued that allowances were not due, as the 'provision' of the plant had never, in fact, taken place. The Lord President (Cooper) thought it significant that the effect of the legislation was:

'not that the benefits (ie the allowances) shall be claimable by the person who *provides* the prescribed improvement, but by the person who *incurs capital expenditure on its provision*'.

Allowances were rightly claimable, it being appropriate to look at the object of the expenditure, and not at the question of whether the intended object was actually realised.

Kempster v McKenzie (1952) 33 TC 193 and *Chambers (GH) (Northiam Farms) Ltd v Watmough (1956) 36 TC 711*

These two cases are important in respect of what are now *Secs 205–207*. Those sections operate to reduce the amount of any allowance in respect of assets which are used partly for the purposes of the trade and partly for other purposes. The allowances shall be reduced 'to such extent as may be just and reasonable having regard to all the relevant circumstances'.

These cases both dealt with cars used by farming businesses. In one case, allowances were not reduced to take account of the 'personal choice or preference' of the driver; in the other case they were, as the car (a Bentley) was far more expensive and luxurious than would have been necessary simply to meet the needs of the trade.

CIR v National Coal Board (1957) 37 TC 264

The National Coal Board built a number of dwelling-houses for occupation by colliery workers, and claimed IBAs in accordance with the predecessor of *Sec 277(2)(3)*, under which a dwelling-house is not excluded from being an industrial building by *Sec 277(1)* if it is:

'for occupation by ... persons employed at, or in connection with the working of, a mine, oil well or other source of mineral deposits ... if the building or structure is likely to have little or no value to the person carrying on the trade when the mine [etc.] is no longer worked'.

It was held (in the House of Lords) that the houses did not qualify for IBAs. On the supposition that the mine closed (immediately) the houses did have an alternative use as general dwellings, and were therefore not 'of little or no value'.

The courts did not favour the National Coal Board's contention that it was necessary to look ahead to the date (2141) when the pit was likely to be exhausted, and quantify the value of the houses at that time. As Lord Radcliffe observed, by that time the houses would have ceased to exist.

The legislation is intended to compensate the taxpayer for the need to construct dwellings which have no value other than in connection with a trade; it is not intended to compensate for loss of value due to normal physical decay.

Hinton v Maden and Ireland Ltd (1959) 38 TC 391

Knives and lasts used by a shoe manufacturer, having an average life of three years, were held to be plant. The durability of the assets was sufficient to ensure that expenditure on them was capital in nature.

Jarrold v John Good & Sons Ltd (1962) 40 TC 681

A company operating as a shipping agent and warehouse keeper, installed a quantity of movable partitions, which to all extents and purposes functioned as internal walls, albeit not load-bearing. The partitioning consisted of metal ribs into which insets of either hardboard sheeting, doors or windows were installed. It was then screwed to the floor and ceiling to form a room of any desired size. The taxpayer claimed these partitions were necessary for the functioning of its trade, as departments could expand or contract, appear or disappear according to the volume of trade. At the planning stage, special instructions were given to the architects that the portion of the building to be devoted to offices was to be capable of the greatest degree of elasticity. A key observation was made by Pennycuick J regarding the concept of setting: 'It appears to me that the setting in which a business is carried on, and the apparatus used for carrying on a business, are not always necessarily mutually exclusive.' The partitions were not excluded from being plant merely by virtue of the fact that they might be 'setting', and on the facts of the case, allowances were deemed to be available.

Though not directly relevant to this case, another interesting comment was made by Ormerod LJ in the Court of Appeal: 'I am not satisfied that it is proper to say that the word "plant" in the Income Tax Acts must be construed as something capable of being the subject of wear and tear.'

Bourne v Auto School of Motoring (Norwich) Ltd (1964) 42 TC 217

The taxpayer made a claim for a now obsolescent investment allowance in respect of vehicles used in his trade as a driving instructor. The allowance was not generally available for motor cars, unless they were 'of a type not commonly used as private vehicles and not suitable to be so used' or alternatively were used 'wholly or mainly for hire to or for the carriage of members of the public in the ordinary course of a trade'.

Virtually identical wording is now contained in *Sec 81*, and so the case is still important in defining a motor car, for the purpose, for example, of deciding whether or not a vehicle should be included within the general plant and machinery pool.

It was held that a car fitted with dual controls was not of a type commonly used as a private vehicle and was unsuitable to be so used. Of wider import is the implication that one must look at the car in its current state, including any adaptations.

Cyril Lord Carpets Ltd v Schofield (1966) 42 TC 637

The taxpayer company traded as a textile and carpet manufacturer in Northern Ireland. In 1958–60, it incurred capital expenditure of £272,419, towards which it subsequently received government subsidies or grants of £84,555. The company claimed capital allowances in respect of the whole of its expenditure, i.e. ignoring the grants received, on the grounds that mere reimbursement by discretionary grant of expenditure already incurred did not mean that expenditure had been 'met directly or indirectly, by [a public body] etc', as provided for by the predecessor of *Sec 532*. The Court of Appeal held that the expenditure had in fact been 'met' by the grants. The word 'met' was held to be used with its everyday meaning.

Kilmarnock Equitable Co-operative Society v IRC (1966) 42 TC 675

The case dealt with whether the screening, sorting and packing of coal constituted a 'process' qualifying for IBAs. In the building in question, coal was fed down a chute through a vibratory screen in order to remove dross. Thereafter, the coal was passed by conveyor belt to a weighing point, where it was packed into 28lb bags. It was held that this did constitute the subjection of goods or materials to a process, despite the fact that the coal itself did not change form.

It was also held that the process described above did not amount to use 'for a purpose ancillary to the purposes of a retail shop'. Customers did not resort to the coal depot to make purchases. Lord Guthrie described 'ancillary' as meaning 'subservient', and the purpose of the process outlined was 'a bigger and broader conception than the mere furtherance of the purposes of a retail shop'.

Bourne v Norwich Crematorium Ltd (1967) 44 TC 164

The taxpayer company claimed IBAs under a predecessor of *Sec 274, Table A, item 2*. The basis of the claim was that a crematorium was used for the destruction of human remains, i.e. the 'subjection of goods or materials to a process'. The claim was not allowed, neither the 'goods or materials' point nor the 'subject to a process' point being accepted by the courts. This case therefore limited the meaning of those phrases, but of perhaps greater import was the comment of Stamp J regarding the construction or interpretation of statute:

'English words derive colour from those which surround them. Sentences are not mere collections of words to be taken out of the sentence, defined separately ... , and then put back into the sentence with the meaning which you have assigned to them as separate words so as to give the sentence or phrase a meaning which as a sentence or phrase it cannot bear without a distortion of the English language.'

Rose & Co (Wallpaper & Paints) Ltd v Campbell (1967) 44 TC 500

The taxpayer company incurred expenditure on bound books of wallpaper designs used as a selling aid, and claimed these were plant for capital allowance purposes. This claim was turned down. Pennycuick J was of the clear opinion that the books, having a life expectancy of two years, did not represent capital expenditure. Following this, consideration of the 'plant' question was unnecessary.

Saxone, Lilley & Skinner (Holdings) Ltd v IRC (1967) 44 TC 122

IBAs were claimed in respect of a central warehouse used for the storage of shoes by a number of group companies. Some of the goods stored had been manufactured by group companies and had not yet been delivered to any purchaser. Others had been purchased from third parties for resale. It was common ground that only the storage of the former would qualify for IBAs under the predecessor of *Sec 274, Table A, item 3(c)*. Shoes from both sources (i.e. manufactured and purchased) were stored together. It was not the case, for example, that shoes purchased from third parties were stored in particular, identifiable parts of the building. The Lord President (Clyde) said: 'a building may be an industrial building or structure if it is used for the purpose of a trade for storing qualified goods, even though it is in addition used for the purpose of a trade of storing unqualified goods as well ... There is nothing in the section about exclusive use ... Merely because it is also used for another purpose it does not cease to be used for the qualifying purpose.'

Abbot Laboratories Ltd v Carmody (1968) 44 TC 569

This case concerned the question of whether capital allowances were available for expenditure on a building used for administration functions. The administration building was one of four buildings on a site, and although separate and complete in itself, was connected to another block 25 yards away by a covered passage. If, by virtue of the covered passage and connecting pipework, the administration building and the other building (which did qualify for IBAs) could be considered to be a single unit, allowances would be given on the whole cost, as expenditure on the non-qualifying part (the administration block) did not exceed 10% of the total.

The case reached the courts first in 1966, but was remitted to the Special Commissioners to decide whether or not the layout of buildings described above could be regarded as 'an industrial building or structure'. The Special Commissioners decided that it could not. The administration block was not sufficiently physically integrated with the other structural units within the layout. The various units, including the administration block, were regarded as separate entities, though sharing the facilities provided by a common boiler-house and connected by made-up roads and pathways.

McVeigh v Arthur Sanderson & Sons Ltd (1968) 45 TC 273

The taxpayer company incurred expenditure on wallpaper designs which it retained for a number of years. It was claimed that these constituted items of plant. The claim was rejected, but only because Cross J felt himself unable to overturn the decision of Rowlatt J in *Daphne v Shaw* (qv) which dealt with a law library. However, Cross J did express dissatisfaction with the earlier decision, but said that if any extension of the meaning of the word 'plant' beyond a purely physical object was to be made, it must be made by a higher court. Two decades later it was, in the case of *Munby v Furlong* (qv).

Wood (t/a A Wood & Co) v Provan (1968) 44 TC 701

The taxpayer purchased machinery and plant along with other assets. In the purchase contract, a specific amount of consideration was stated to be in respect of the various items of plant. Subsequently the General Commissioners made a different apportionment of the consideration under the predecessor of *Sec 562*. The taxpayer then claimed that the transaction was one to which the precursor of *Sec 563* applied, and that therefore it was not within the jurisdiction of the original Commissioners. It was held that:

(*a*) the Commissioners were entitled to make an apportionment, notwithstanding the fact that a separate price for the plant was shown on the purchase contract;

(*b*) *Sec 563* did not apply — although the apportionment was material to the tax liabilities of more than one person, one of the persons was not party to the original sale and purchase.

This case preceded the introduction of *Sec 198*, which provides for a joint (and binding) election fixing the amount allocated to fixtures (see 4.22–4.24).

CIR v Barclay Curle & Co Ltd (1969) 45 TC 221

The taxpayer company, which carried on a trade of shipbuilding and repairing on the River Clyde, constructed a dry dock. It claimed as plant not only the attendant machinery, but also the cost of excavation and concrete work. The House of Lords ruled (by a majority of three to two) that the whole qualified as plant. The Crown contended that the basin forming the dock should be regarded as the setting in which the trade was carried on. However, it was observed that a simple 'hole in the ground' would be of no use to the taxpayer in his trade.

Lord Reid noted two stages in the operations undertaken: 'Firstly, the ship must be isolated from the water and then the inspection and necessary repairs must be carried out.' The dry dock was perhaps merely the setting for the second stage, but the same could not be said with regard to the first stage, which was equally important. In this first stage, the dry dock did perform an essential function in the trade, leading Lord Reid to conclude: 'The whole dock is, I think, the means by which, or plant with which, the operation is performed.' The fact that the dock might also be a structure did not preclude it from being plant. Lord Reid again commented:

> 'I do not say that every structure which fulfils the function of plant must be regarded as plant, but I think that one would have to find some good reason for excluding such a structure. And I do not think that mere size is sufficient.'

Woods v RM Mallen (Engineering) Ltd (1969) 45 TC 619

This case dealt with the question of the 'relevant interest' in an industrial building, and whether the relevant interests were transferred upon the creation of a lease. Mr Hodgkinson was the lessee of a plot of land, under a lease having a term of 99 years from 25 June 1950. He constructed an industrial building, his 'relevant interest', of course, being the 99-year lease. In 1962, Mr Hodgkinson granted a sub-lease in favour of Mallen (Engineering) Ltd, for a term of 99 years from 25 June 1950, less three days. Mallen claimed that it had acquired Hodgkinson's 'relevant interest' in the property, and was therefore entitled to industrial buildings allowances.

Plowman J looked at the respective interests of Hodgkinson and Mallen to determine whether they were, in fact, the same. He decided that they were not: one was for 99 years, whilst the other was for 99 years less three days. Although similar, they were not the same. The important point, twice quoted by Plowman J, was that contained in the predecessor of *Sec 288*: 'An interest shall not cease to be the relevant interest ... by reason of the creation of any lease or other interest to which that interest is subject.'

ICI Australia and New Zealand v Taxation Comr (1970) 120 CLR 396

This Australian case was quoted with approval in *Cole Brothers* (qv). It dealt primarily with acoustic ceilings and electrical wiring. Special sound-absorbing ceiling tiles were added to an open-plan office. Kitto J noted the use of such tiles was standard practice in modern office buildings and that the tiles were therefore 'no more than part of the shelter' in which the taxpayer chose to carry on its activities. He continued:

'Every part of a building makes some contribution to the comfort and efficiency of those who work in it. To take it notionally to bits and describe as "plant" any bit that has a function which is useful in connection with the business carried on there seems to me indefensible.'

Regarding electric wiring, together with conduits, switchboards etc., Kitto J thought it formed no more than the reticulation system without which the building would be incomplete. Neither the ceilings nor the electrics were plant.

Bridge House (Reigate Hill) Ltd v Hinder (1971) 47 TC 182

The taxpayer company, which operated a hotel, contributed a capital sum towards the extension of a public sewer so that the sewer now served the hotel. Its claim for capital allowances was rejected on the grounds that the sewer itself was merely a conduit for effluent, and not plant used in the treatment of that effluent. Lord Denning stated that sewage or drainage pipes were an essential ancillary to the building. Salmon LJ, though agreeing with Lord Denning, did not completely rule out the fact that sewers carrying trade effluent from a factory or a large hotel could be plant.

Odeon Associated Theatres Ltd v Jones (1971) 48 TC 257

The taxpayer's company's sole activity was the showing of films. After World War II, it incurred expenditure on the purchase and repair of cinemas. During and immediately after World War II, the building of theatres and cinemas was prohibited, as was any expenditure on repairs and maintenance, other than that which was essential. Two effects of this were:

(*a*)   a company wishing to expand was forced to buy existing cinemas, rather than build new ones, and

(*b*)   cinemas were invariably in a poor state of repair.

In contrast to the facts in the *Law Shipping* case (qv), the poor state of repair of cinemas acquired did not affect their purchase price nor did it render them useless for their intended purpose. Attendances at the cinemas would not be adversely affected as a result of the disrepair, because all cinemas were in the same state. The Revenue, following the *Law Shipping* case, considered that the expenditure on repairs was properly regarded as capital, to the extent that it related to repairs which became necessary prior to the company's acquisition of the relevant cinemas.

Cooke v Beach Station Caravans Ltd (1974) 49 TC 514

The taxpayer company, which owned and operated a caravan site, incurred expenditure on the construction of heated swimming pools. A claim for capital allowances was accepted in respect of the complex system of filtration, heating and recirculation. However the Inspector refused to accept that the cost of excavating and constructing the pools, together with the surrounding terraces, constituted expenditure on plant for capital allowances purposes. On appeal, Megarry J held that the whole expenditure did qualify as plant, basing his conclusion on three factors.

(i)   The pools could be considered as a unit, together with all the attendant apparatus for purifying and heating the water and so on.

(ii) The pools had to be considered not on their own, but in relation to the business carried on. The function and purpose of the pools was to attract custom to the caravan site.

(iii) The pools could not be regarded as merely passive, but instead per formed an active function and were part of the means whereby the trade was carried on.

To conclude, Megarry J resorted to a 'relatively modern slang expression': 'The pools are not merely "where it's at", they are part of the apparatus used by the company for carrying on its business as caravan park operators.'

St John's School (Mountford & Knibbs) v Ward (HMIT) [1974] STC 69, 49 TC 524; affd [1975] STC 7n

The taxpayers operated a school from leased premises. They incurred expenditure on two prefabricated buildings; one a laboratory, the other a gymnasium. Both buildings had special features — the laboratory had fitted workbenches and sinks, while the gymnasium had a special floor, and walls and roof capable of supporting climbing equipment. The Commissioners held that neither building was an item of plant, and that (in the absence of supporting evidence) it was not possible to apportion the expenditure so as to determine that part incurred in connection with items of plant. Their decision was upheld by the courts. It was appropriate to look at the assets (i.e. the buildings) as whole entities, rather than on a piecemeal basis.

Dixon v Fitch's Garage Ltd (1975) 50 TC 509

The taxpayer incurred expenditure on a canopy over its petrol pumps, and claimed capital allowances. It was contended that the canopy was plant, not in isolation, but because it formed part of an integral complex (the filling station), the whole of which was plant. Brightman J held that the canopy was not plant. Although sales had increased since construction of the canopy, petrol could nonetheless be supplied with a covering canopy. The comfort of customers was not a relevant consideration.

The correctness of this decision was doubted by Lord Hailsham LC in *Cole Bros Ltd v Philips* (qv) and by Lord Cameron in the *Scottish & Newcastle Breweries* case (qv). Furthermore, a garage canopy was held to be plant in the Irish case, *O'Culachain v McMullan Bros* (qv).

Schofield v R & H Hall [1975] STC 353, 49 TC 538

Dockside silos were held to be plant. The primary purpose of the silos was not storage (grain was expected to be held there for only seven days) but was rather to hold the grain in a position from which it could be easily delivered into tankers. The silo housing was also considered part of the plant.

Munby v Furlong [1977] STC 232, 50 TC 491

A practising barrister incurred capital expenditure on his law library, and claimed that allowances were due because the library, or the books that made it up, constituted plant for this purpose. The claim was upheld, ultimately, by the Court of Appeal, reversing the decision in *Daphne v Shaw* (qv). A key argument was that, contrary to dicta in the earlier case, the meaning of 'plant' for tax purposes was something more than its everyday meaning, as the man in the street would have understood it. Lord Denning MR said that various sources show quite conclusively that:

> 'in this taxing statute the courts do not apply the meaning to the word "plant" as the ordinary Englishman understands it. It has acquired by the course of decisions a special meaning in tax cases'.

Lord Denning used this 'special meaning' to include books within the definition of plant. The fact that the books were used intellectually, and not physically, was of no consequence. Sir John Pennycuick agreed with Lord Denning, and commented that *Yarmouth v France* had not been considered in the case of *Daphne v Shaw*.

Ben-Odeco Ltd v Powlson (1978) 52 TC 459

The taxpayer company acquired an oil drilling rig for use in its trade. Whilst the eligibility of direct expenditure on the rig itself for plant allowances was not doubted, the company had also capitalised the interest on borrowings taken out to finance the acquisition. The question put to the courts (ultimately to the House of Lords) was whether the interest could be regarded as expenditure incurred on the provision of machinery or plant, in accordance with the legislation, or whether it was in fact too remote to be so regarded. The courts took the latter view, i.e. that the incurring of the interest was too remote from the acquisition of the rig to be considered as part of the cost qualifying for allowances. Lord Wilberforce put it that: 'the interest and commitment were expenditure on the provision of money to be used on the provision of plant, but not expenditure on the provision of plant'.

Benson v Yard Arm Club Ltd (1979) 53 TC 67

The taxpayer operated a floating restaurant on the *Hispaniola*, moored at Victoria Embankment. It was claimed that the 'ship' constituted plant for capital allowance purposes. The case contained a significant review of decided cases in this area, with the emphasis on the question of whether the ship performed some 'function' in the trade, or whether it was merely the setting for a trade. Buckley LJ acknowledged that patrons came to the restaurant 'to get good food, somewhere different with views of the river etc and a shipboard feeling'. This did not mean, however, that the floating restaurant was plant, any more than a restaurant on land would be plant because its location offered attractive views. Templeman LJ agreed and referred to the restaurant atop the Post Office Tower:

'premises do not become plant merely because they float in the Thames or are suspended in the sky or are to be found on top of the Matterhorn. For the present purposes I can see no distinction between a restaurant in the Thames and a fish and chip shop in Bethnal Green. Premises only become plant if they perform the function of plant'.

Shaw LJ also in agreement, said: 'A characteristic of plant appears ... to be that it is an adjunct to the carrying on of a business and not the essential site or core of the business itself.'

Buckingham v Securitas Properties Ltd (1979) 53 TC 292

The taxpayer was the lessor of a building used by Group 4 Total Security Ltd. Group 4 used the building for the storage of cash and making up wage packets, and it was claimed that this constituted 'the subjection of goods or materials to any process' within the meaning of what is now *Sec 274, Table A, item 2*. The claim was rejected, on the grounds that the notes and coins were not in this instance held as goods but as currency or 'valuable tokens'. Coins and notes could still be 'goods' in certain circumstances. For example, in the trade of a person printing bank notes.

Crusabridge Investments Ltd v Casings International Ltd (1979) 54 TC 246

Under the lease of a building the lessee covenanted to use it only as a ware-house within the meaning of *Class X* of the *Town and Country Planning (Use Classes) Order 1972* and also within the meaning of 'industrial building or structure' as defined by the *Capital Allowances Act*. The lessee's business consisted for the greater part of purchasing used tyre casings, examining and grading them, and re-selling to remoulders. It also sold remoulds on a com-mission basis. The Revenue refused the lessor's claim for industrial buildings allowances, on the grounds that that did not constitute a qualifying use, under the predecessor of *Sec 274*. The lessor therefore proceeded against the lessee for damages for breach of covenant.

It was held that the examination and grading of the casings did not amount to subjecting goods or materials to a process within the meaning of *Sec 274, Table A, item 2*. Finlay J distinguished the case from *Kilmarnock Equitable Co-operative Society v CIR* (qv). He did not believe that the examination and grading of tyres constituted a process: 'It is the very same tyre before the examination and after the examination. Nothing has happened to it that alters its nature or effects any kind of change in the tyre.'

However, the building did qualify as an industrial building by virtue of *Sec 274, Table A, item 3(b)* — the storage of goods or materials 'which are to be subjected, in the course of a trade, to a process' — in respect of the used cas-ings and also by virtue of *item 3(c)* of that Act — the storage of goods or materials 'which, having been manufactured or produced or subjected, in the course of a trade, to a process, have not yet been delivered to any purchaser' — in respect of remoulds held for sale.

Finlay J held also that the person carrying on the process and the person effecting the storage need not be the same: 'In my view it matters not that the trade in which they are to be so subjected to a process is the trade of someone other than the company which is storing the casings with a view to that being eventually done.'

Brown v Burnley Football & Athletic Co Ltd (1980) 53 TC 357

The taxpayer company constructed a new stand, replacing one which had become unsafe. It claimed that the cost of this was properly chargeable to repairs. A second claim held that if the expenditure were not in respect of repairs, then the stand constituted an item of plant. Vinelott J quoted the words of Buckley LJ in *Lurcott v Wakeley & Wheeler [1911] 1 KB 905*:

'Repair is restoration by renewal or replacement of subsidiary parts of a whole. Renewal, as distinguished from repair, is reconstruction of the entirety, meaning by the entirety not the whole but substantially the whole subject-matter under discussion.'

In this case it was found that it was the stand, and not the football ground as a whole, that constituted the 'entirety'. Expenditure on the new stand was not, therefore, allowed as a repair.

On the second question of whether the stand was plant, it was held that it was not. Football matches took place and spectators came to watch within, rather than by means of, the stadium. The stand did not therefore function, either actively or passively in the trade.

Hampton v Forte Autogrill Ltd [1980] STC 80, 53 TC 691

The operator of a number of restaurants installed, in public areas of those restaurants, false ceilings. The primary purpose of these ceilings was to act as cladding for pipes etc. in the sense that the ceilings covered and connected the pipes. The Commissioners held that the ceilings were 'part and parcel' of the equipment which they supported and covered, and were therefore themselves 'plant'. This finding was overturned by the courts where Fox J laid emphasis on the 'function' test, and found no evidence that the ceilings performed any function in the trade. (NB suspended ceilings may qualify as plant under special circumstances, for example, where they form part of an air-conditioning or extraction system.)

Mason v Tyson [1980] STC 284, 53 TC 333

Mr Mason, a chartered surveyor, furnished a flat above his office so that he could sleep there when he was required to work late. He claimed capital allowances on part of the amount expended. The court held, however, that no allowances were due, as the expenditure had not been incurred 'wholly and exclusively' for the purposes of the trade, as required (with slight amendment) by *Sec 11(4)*. The greatest application of this case is perhaps in connection with the licensed trade, where public houses etc. include accommodation for tenants or managers.

Vibroplant Ltd v Holland (1981) 54 TC 658

The taxpayer company carried on a business of hiring out plant and machinery. It owned a number of depots used for storing the equipment between hirings and for cleaning, servicing and, if necessary, repairing the said equipment. It claimed industrial buildings allowances in respect of these depots, but without success. The claim was made under what is now *Sec 274, Table A, item 2* — the subjection of 'goods or materials to any process'. It was held in the first instance that premises used for servicing and repair were not a 'factory ... or similar premises', because, in essence, nothing was made or manufactured. Secondly, it was held that the repair and maintenance of items of plant according to their individual merits and requirements did not amount to a 'process'. Dillon J commented that, in his view, 'process' connotes a substantial measure of uniformity of treatment or a system of treatment.

CIR v Scottish & Newcastle Breweries Ltd [1982] STC 296, 55 TC 252

The taxpayer company operated a chain of hotels and licensed premises, either purpose-built or purchased as a shell and fitted out to the company's specification. It was claimed that one element of the company's trade was the provision of a certain type of atmosphere, or ambience, conducive to attracting custom. This argument proved attractive to the courts, and consequently allowances were given in respect of items used to create this 'ambience', such as decor, murals and sculptures. In the Court of Session, Lord Cameron thought that the terms 'plant' and 'setting' could overlap, and also stated:

> '... the question of what is properly to be regarded as "plant" can only be answered in the context of the particular industry concerned and, possibly, in light also of the particular circumstances of the individual taxpayer's own trade.'

Similar thoughts were expressed by Lord Wilberforce in the House of Lords: 'In the end each case must be resolved in my opinion by considering carefully the nature of the particular trade being carried on.'

Cole Bros Ltd v Phillips [1982] STC 307, 55 TC 188

John Lewis Properties Ltd incurred expenditure on an entire electrical system installed in a store at the Brent Cross shopping centre, leased to Cole Bros Ltd. It was accepted that certain items were plant. These included:

* wiring to heaters, alarms, clocks, cash registers;

* telephone trunking;

* wiring to lifts and escalators;

* emergency lighting system;

* standby supply system.

Other items were disputed by the Revenue, being mainly lighting and wiring, some of it specially designed, and also transformers and switch gear.

The case eventually reached the House of Lords. It was held that the 'multiplicity of elements' in the installation and the differing purposes to which they were put precluded one from regarding the entire electrical installation as a single entity. The claim therefore had to be approached on a piecemeal basis. The transformers and switch gear were held to be plant, other items were not, being a necessary part of the building or 'setting'. The judgment of Stephenson LJ in the Court of Appeal contains the well-known statement:

> 'The philosopher-statesman, Balfour, is reported to have said it was unnecessary to define a great power because, like an elephant, you recognised it when you met it. Unhappily, plant in taxing and other statutes is no elephant (though I suppose an elephant might be plant).'

In an unrecorded decision of the Special Commissioners in 1992, another retailer's claim to treat an entire electrical system as plant was allowed, once it could be shown that certain conditions had been met. These conditions were that:

(*a*)　the electrical system is designed and built as a whole, it is a fully integrated system;

(*b*)　the electrical system is designed to meet the requirements of the trade, it is not a general purpose or standard system designed to meet the needs of a range of occupants;

(*c*)　the end user items of the installation function as apparatus in the trader's business;

(*d*)　the electrical installation is essential for the functioning of the business.

Leeds Permanent Building Society v Proctor (1982) 56 TC 293

A building society installed in its windows variously designed screens. This was part of an ongoing process of making the branches look more like retail shops, the aim being to attract the attention of customers or potential customers. The screens were demountable, but because they were designed to be of local interest, they were not often moved in practice. In addition to their advertising function, the screens served to provide privacy for customers inside the branch, and had a minor security function. It was held that the screens were plant, not setting. Goulding J stated:

> 'They were an adjunct to the carrying on of the business and not the essential site or core of the business itself. They were not used as premises but were part of the means by which the relevant trade was carried out.'

O'Conaill v Waterford Glass Ltd (1982) TL(I) 122

This Irish case considered whether a computer building which served an industrial complex could by virtue of that fact itself be regarded as an industrial building. The taxpayer company carried on a trade consisting of the manufacture of crystal glass. On one site it occupied a number of buildings, the majority of which were used directly for the manufacturing process. One building, however, housed a computer, together with offices and showrooms. Ideally, the computer should have been located in the middle of the factory but could not be sited there owing to noise, dirt and vibration. The fact that it was housed in a separate building did not alter the fact that the computer's primary purpose was to assist in the manufacturing process. McWilliam J summed up that the computer building was 'a vital nerve centre for the whole industrial complex, and forms part of it'.

White v Higginbottom (1982) 57 TC 283

A vicar purchased audio-visual equipment for use in church — there was no private use. He claimed capital allowances on the basis that the machines in question were *necessarily* provided for use in the performance of the duties of his office. This is now dealt with in *Sec 36(2)*. It was held that, although the machines were used wholly and exclusively for the office, they were not strictly necessary. Other vicars carried out their duties without the aid of such equipment, and its purchase was therefore a matter of personal choice. Allowances were not, therefore, given.

Bolton v International Drilling Co Ltd [1983] STC 70, 86 TC 449

The company (IDC) acquired a drilling barge in 1965, and entered into a contract with Amoco to drill for oil in the North Sea. At the same time, IDC granted Amoco an option to purchase the barge in 1969. In that year, the barge in question was the only one owned by IDC (another one was in construction) and so IDC, anxious to stay in business, paid Amoco some £500,000 for cancellation of the option. The two questions put to the courts were as follows:

(*a*)   Did the £500,000 constitute expenditure on plant qualifying for allowances?

(*b*)   Was the expenditure incurred in 1969 (therefore qualifying for an initial allowance)?

It was held that the answer to both questions was yes. IDC did already own the asset, but would have ceased to do so if the option cancellation payment had not been made. The payment was therefore made in connection with the provision (albeit the continued provision) of plant. Also, IDC continued to enjoy possession of the plant after 1969 in consequence of the expenditure, which therefore qualified for the initial allowance available in that year.

Copol Clothing Co Ltd v Hindmarch (1983) 57 TC 575

The taxpayer had for some years traded as a clothing wholesaler and distributor. About 90% of its purchases were imported. These goods were stored in a warehouse in Manchester. IBAs were claimed on the warehouse by virtue of what is now *Sec 274, Table A, item 3(d)* — 'a trade consisting of storing goods or materials on their arrival in the United Kingdom from a place outside the United Kingdom'. Fox LJ agreed that 'on arrival' was not construed so narrowly that the allowance would only be given to buildings in the 'recognised dock area'. 'There may well be cases where a warehouse is situated some considerable distance from the coast but where it can conveniently serve a number of ports.' Fox LJ further concluded that the purpose of the allowance was to encourage the provision of storage for goods which have just arrived in the United Kingdom and before their onward transit. This was held not to apply to the Manchester warehouse, which simply provided the storage which any wholesaler might need for his goods. Consequently, the claim for IBAs was refused.

Van Arkadie v Sterling Coated Materials Ltd [1983] STC 95, 56 TC 479

The taxpayer company (SCM) entered into an agreement to purchase plant from a Swiss company on deferred payment terms. The Swiss company, however, could not afford to fund construction of the plant, and so an arrangement was made with a Swiss bank. Under this arrangement, the bank paid the purchase price over to the Swiss supplier, and SCM was to repay the bank in instalments after installation of the plant. In effect, SCM was making payments as originally envisaged, albeit to the bank, rather than the supplier. Due to currency fluctuations, the price had effectively increased by the time payment was made, and SCM claimed allowances on this exchange loss. In contrast to the *Ben-Odeco* case (qv), it was held that this 'extra cost' did qualify for allowances. It was not in truth a 'loan', but was inextricably tied in with the purchase contract. However, it was also held that the extra amount was only incurred when repayment was made, and not on the date of the original contract.

O'Srianain v Lakeview Ltd (1984) TL(I) 125

An Irish case considered whether a deep-pit poultry house was an item of plant. On the facts of the case, the claim for plant allowances succeeded. The entire design of the house was so made up as to create the most conducive and efficient environment in which hens would lay eggs, and without this design the hens would not lay so many eggs. A key feature pointed out by Murphy J was that the environment was designed for the benefit of the hens (and not the humans) and for the purpose of increasing egg production which was in fact the business carried on by the taxpayer.

Stokes v Costain Property Investments Ltd (1984) 57 TC 688

A company installed various items of plant (principally lifts and central heating) in two buildings. At the time this was done, the company was neither freeholder nor leaseholder of the building. However, upon completion of the works, it was to be entitled to the grant of a lease. Capital allowances were denied on the grounds that the plant in question did not 'belong' to the company, as required by what is now *Sec 11(4)(b)*. The word 'belong' must be given its ordinary meaning, and is not a term of art. In the High Court, Harmon J said it would not be true to say that he owned a Rolls Royce car if he were only renting it for the day, and the case here, though less extreme, was in essence the same: 'It seems to me plain and obvious as a matter of language that property of which the taxpayer has no right of disposition does not belong to him.' This view was supported by Fox LJ in the Court of Appeal, adding:

> 'Nor do I think it is an apt use of language to say that landlords' fixtures "belong" to the leaseholder. He cannot remove them from the building. He cannot dispose of them except as part of the hereditament and subject to the provision of the lease and for the term of the lease.'

However, Fox LJ thought the state of the law very unsatisfactory. The purpose of the statutory provisions was to encourage investment in machinery and plant, yet in this case no relief was given. The landlord could not claim allowances because he had not incurred any expenditure, and the (prospective) tenant could not because the plant did not belong to him. As a result of this unsatisfactory state of the law, 1985 saw the introduction of the provisions now contained with *CAA 2001, Chap 14* enabling the tenant to claim allowances.

Elliss v BP Oil Northern Refinery Ltd; Elliss v BP Tyne Tanker Co Ltd (1986) 59 TC 474

These related cases dealt with the question of whether full capital allowances must be deducted for corporation tax purposes. The taxpayer companies were oil companies. Particular circumstances relating to oil companies at that time did not permit the carry-forward of losses. The companies contended that it was open to them not to claim part of the capital allowances to which they were entitled. The effect of this was to increase the tax written-down values of the assets carried forward, so that greater allowances were available in subsequent years when the companies were able to make use of them. The Revenue contended that in each accounting period the companies' profits should be reduced by the full amount of the allowances to which they were entitled. The effect of this would have been that allowances would have been wasted in earlier years (as taxable profits cannot be reduced below nil) and taxable profits would be increased in subsequent years. The companies' contention was accepted by the Special Commissioner, and upheld by the High Court and the Court of Appeal.

Since the introduction of the modern capital allowances system to encourage post-war reconstruction the taxpayer could choose whether to take the allowances to which he was entitled. Walton J in the High Court applied the maxim that everyone is entitled to renounce any right intended for his benefit. *Sec 3* confirms that allowances will only be given if claimed. A taxpayer can choose not to claim.]

Gaspet Ltd v Elliss [1987] STC 362, 60 TC 91

This case dealt with the question of whether scientific research (now research and development) had been undertaken on behalf of the taxpayer (as required by *Sec 439*). It was held that in order to qualify there must be a link between the taxpayer and the research. Mere funding of the research was not sufficient.

Patrick Monahan (Drogheda) Ltd v O'Connell [1987] IR 661

This Irish case considered whether bonded transit sheds used as a clearing house for goods unloaded from ships were industrial buildings in use for the purposes of a 'dock undertaking' (current English counterpart: *Sec 274, Table B, item 10*). It was held that they were. The storage of goods free of charge for short periods was not a separate trade but merely ancillary to the business of a dock undertaking.

Thomas v Reynolds & Broomhead (1987) 59 TC 502

In this 'unfortunate little case', as Walton J called it, it was held that an inflatable tennis court cover was not plant. The taxpayers appeared in person, and supplied the court with certain facts which tended to show 'that the cover did have a function to play in the business of coaching ... other than that of merely providing shelter from the weather'. However, these facts were not included in the case stated, and no judicial attention could therefore be paid to them. The decision was made with regret, and it is not inconceivable that subsequent similar claims have been resolved in the taxpayer's favour, without having reached the courts.

Wimpey International Ltd v Warland (1988); Associated Restaurants Ltd v Warland [1989] STC 273, 61 TC 51

Both taxpayers were members of the same group and operated restaurants under the names 'Wimpy' and 'Pizzaland'. Each refurbished their restaurants and claimed that various items should be treated as plant. The majority of the relevant items served, it was claimed, to attract custom and provide an atmosphere conducive to the enjoyment of meals. The claim in respect of most items was dismissed. Allowances were given in respect of special lighting which served a business purpose, namely to 'create an atmosphere of brightness and efficiency, suitable to the service and consumption of fast food meals and attractive to potential customers looking in from outside'. Also allowed as plant was expenditure on one very special suspended ceiling also designed for purposes of 'atmosphere'. The items not allowed as plant included:

(*a*)   shop fronts;

(*b*)   floor and wall tiles;

(*c*)   some suspended ceilings;

(*d*)   mezzanine floor;

(*e*)   trapdoor and ladder;

(*f*)   decorative brickwork.

O'Culachain v McMullan Bros [1991] 1 IR 363

This Irish case dealt with the question of whether a petrol station canopy could be regarded as plant. Although similar in this respect to *Dixon v Fitch's Garage* (qv), the outcome was different. It was held that the canopy was plant by virtue of the fact that it fulfilled a function in the trade, namely:

> 'the provision of an attractive setting for the sale of ... products, the advertisement and promotion of those products, the creation of an overall impression of efficiency and financial solidarity in relation to the business of selling petrol and the attraction of customers to stop and purchase those products'.

It was appropriate to take a wider view of the trade carried on, rather than to look merely at whether the canopy assisted in the actual delivery of petrol.

Carr v Sayer [1992] STC 396

The taxpayers carried on the business of providing quarantine facilities for animals entering the United Kingdom. They incurred expenditure on the construction of kennels, both movable and permanent, and claimed that these kennels were plant, or industrial buildings. The General Commissioners held the movable kennels to be plant, and the Revenue did not appeal. The High Court held that the permanent kennels were neither plant nor industrial buildings. As regards the former claim, Sir Donald Nicholls V-C observed:

'... buildings , which I have already noted would not normally be regarded as plant, do not cease to be buildings and become plant simply because they are purpose-built for a trading purpose.'

He also thought it was not possible to apportion the expenditure, so as to give tax relief for that part. The industrial buildings claim was based on what is now *Sec 274, Table A, item 3(d)* — i.e. 'a building or structure in use ... for the purposes of a trade which consists in the storage ... of goods or materials on their arrival by sea or air into any part of the United Kingdom'. The court held this did not apply. Sir Donald Nicholls decided that the taxpayers' service was provided to meet a need which existed, not as part of the ordinary process of physical transportation but because of statutory requirements. The claim for IBAs, like the claim for treatment as plant, was therefore dismissed.

Ensign Tankers (Leasing) Ltd v Stokes [1992] STC 226

The taxpayer, which was not normally involved in film production, purchased into a tax scheme designed to take advantage of the availability of first-year allowances. Of total expenditure on the film (*Escape to Victory*) of $14 million, only $3.25 million was actually incurred by the taxpayer. The balance was lent to a production company on the understanding that it would be repaid out of the proceeds of the film, without recourse to partnership assets. The House of Lords held that an allowance was only due in respect of the $3.25 million, not on the whole $14 million. The fact that the taxpayer only engaged in the film trade for the fiscal purpose of obtaining a first-year allowance was of no import.

Hunt v Henry Quick Ltd; King v Bridisco Ltd [1992] STC 633

The facts in these two cases were practically identical and the appeals were heard together. Each taxpayer had erected a mezzanine platform in a warehouse in order to provide extra space for the storage of goods. These mezzanines comprised free-standing raised platforms on steel pillars with steel beams supporting wooden flooring. They were installed by a specialist firm, and it was admitted that it would have been difficult to buy an 'off the shelf' floor in the market place. The platform was bolted to the floor of the building only to ensure rigidity and safety, not for any reason of structural support. The company had applied for dispensation from building regulations, and in that application the platform was described as 'free-standing and not attached to the building in any way ... will be used exclusively for storage and no person will be resident on it'. The Commissioners had attached great weight to the lack of access by the public. On the grounds that the platforms were movable and temporary structures (they could be dismantled in three to four days if trading requirements changed) it was held that they did constitute plant for the purposes of capital allowances. However, lighting fixed to the underside of the platforms to illuminate the floor space below, did not so qualify, following dicta in *Wimpey International v Warland*, as the lighting was not specific to the trade.

O'Grady v Roscommon Race Committee [1992] IR 425

This Irish case dealt with a new spectator stand at a racecourse. The facts were similar, therefore, to the English case *Brown v Burnley Football & Athletic Co Ltd* (qv). However the findings were different. It was held that expenditure on the new stand did constitute expenditure on plant. In contrast to the *Burnley* case, visitors to the racecourse did not sit in the stand throughout the entire event. Carroll J stated that:

> 'In my view the provision of an improved stand with accommodation which provides shelter from above and at the sides with new and improved viewing steps, must be considered as part of the means to get people to go to that racecourse for viewing horse races. It is very much akin to the swimming-pool provided by the caravan park owners [in *Cooke v Beach Stations Caravans* (qv)].'

Gray v Seymours Garden Centre (Horticulture) [1995] STC 706

The taxpayers incurred expenditure on a 'planteria', effectively a greenhouse used for the nurturing and preserving of plants. Their claim that this constituted 'plant and machinery' for tax purposes was rejected by the Court of Appeal. Nourse LJ re-emphasised the importance of the 'premises test'. Note, however, that some greenhouses, notably those which are fully computer-controlled, have been accepted as plant by the Revenue. The Seymour's planteria did not even have integral heating, so the result should not deter other claimants.

Melluish v Barclays Mercantile Insurance Finance (No 3) Ltd [1995] STC 964

The taxpayer company (BMI) and various associated companies leased items of equipment to local authorities. The court held that the equipment belonged to the lessors where they had the right to remove the equipment at the end of the lease term. Furthermore, it was held that the law of property prevailed to treat as fixtures certain items which the taxpayers had, by written agreement, sought to treat as chattels. The court's decision, however, that an election under what is now *Sec 177* could be made where the lessee was a non-taxpayer, so as to enable the lessor to claim allowances, was reversed (with effect from 23 July 1996) by subsequent amendment of *Sec 177(1)*.

Bradley v London Electricity plc [1996] STC 1054

The taxpayer incurred expenditure on an electricity substation sited beneath Leicester Square, and claimed as plant not only the electrical equipment itself, but also the concrete housing. The latter claim was rejected on the grounds that the housing failed the premises test — other than housing the equipment, it performed no plant-like function. It was observed (at page 1079): 'The fact that the building in which a business is carried on is, by its construction, particularly well-suited to the business ... does not make it plant.' This echoes the conclusion in *Carr v Sayer [1992] STC 396* (see page 280 above).

Decaux (JC) (UK) Ltd v Francis [1996] STC (SCD) 281

The taxpayer company carried on a trade of leasing automatic public conveniences (APCs) to local authorities. It also supplied bus shelters, etc. which were not leased but which were provided on the understanding that Decaux could use them for advertising. The various items were securely fixed to the land and, in the case of the APCs, were connected to mains electricity and plumbing. Allowances were denied both under [*Sec 11*], because the assets, being fixed to the land, no longer belonged to Decaux, and under what is now [*Sec 176*], because Decaux did not have an interest in the land when it incurred the relevant expenditure. It was insufficient that the incurring of the expenditure brought into existence an interest in land. The right to enter in order to maintain the assets was in any case a mere contractural right which fell short of a 'licence to occupy land'. This case also considered the distinction between chattels and fixtures, and laid down principles subsequently enacted in *Sec 179*.

Bestway (Holdings) Ltd v Luff [1998] STC 357

The taxpayer operated wholesale cash-and-carry premises, and claimed industrial buildings allowances on the basis that part of its trade consisted of the storage of goods or materials, or alternatively that repackaging and labelling of products constituted 'the subjection of goods or material to a process'. The claim was rejected. It was held that in order to qualify for IBAs, storage had to be an end in itself — it was not sufficient that goods were stored for some other purpose, in this case sale to customers. Secondly, it was held that the repacking, labelling, etc. did not constitute a 'process', but were 'mere preliminaries' to sale. Lightman, J observed: '... the activities in question were limited, mundane and of no substantial significance'. Lightman J also observed that in order to qualify for IBAs by virtue of what is now *Sec 276* in respect of part of a trade, 'the activities in question must be a significant, separate and identifiable part of the trade'.

Girobank plc v Clarke [1998] STC 182

The bank claimed IBAs on a building in which information-bearing documents were subjected to a process consisting, *inter alia*, of sorting and batching the documents, and reading the information contained thereon. Some documents were then marked to indicate that they had been processed. The claim was rejected by the Court of Appeal on the grounds that the documents were not 'goods or materials'. The Court of Appeal, in contrast to the High Court, held that the term 'goods or materials' should be interpreted in the restricted sense of 'merchandise or wares' previously favoured in *Buckingham v Securitas Properties Ltd* (qv). The Court of Appeal said little about whether the activities constituted a process, but broadly supported Lindsay J in the High Court, who had found no authority for limiting the scope of the term 'any process' to indicate only those processes having an 'industrial character'. A qualifying process for IBA purposes certainly did not have to be a step in or towards the manufacture or sale of something.

The case also includes a useful debate on the meaning of the word 'office'. This was narrowly defined as 'the place where the central management emanates and where the manager and his staff do their work' (following a Canadian case, *Carter v Standard Ltd (1915) 30 DLR 492*).

Sarsfield v Dixons Group plc [1998] STC 938

One company within the Dixons Group used a warehouse for the purposes of a trade which consisted of receiving, storing and delivering goods purchased by Dixons for sale in its retail shops. Industrial buildings allowances were claimed, on the basis that the warehouse was in use for the purposes of a transport undertaking. This claim was rejected by the Court of Appeal on the grounds that any transport was merely ancillary to the purposes of a retail shop. It was stated in the High Court:

> 'A building is used for a purpose which is ancillary to the purposes of a retail shop if its user is confined to furthering the purposes of the retail shop, ie subservient and subordinate to retail selling.'

The transport undertaking was of a substantial size in terms of investment, number of employees and turnover, and made a taxable profit. However, the corporate relationship between the transport undertaking and its customers was a key consideration. The 'transport' company had no external customers, and the use of the warehouse was held to be 'subservient and subordinate and therefore ancillary to the purposes of the retail shops'.

ABC Ltd v M (Inspector of Taxes) (SpC 300)

A taxpayer company entered into complex arrangements whereby a payment for plant and machinery was paid to the vendor, but was then (via a number of group companies) placed on deposit elsewhere within the purchaser's group.

Even though the individual taxpayer company was ignorant of the circular nature of the payment viewed from a group perspective, its claim for allowances was rejected on the basis that the transaction had no commercial reality, and that, in effect, no expenditure had been incurred on plant and machinery.

Barclays Mercantile Business Finance Ltd v Mawson [2002] EWHC 2466 (Ch), [2003] STC 66

Sale and leaseback arrangements were unsuccessfully challenged by the Inland Revenue. In essence, it was held that a finance lessor may obtain allowances on plant, even though the availability of those allowances is a fundamental reason for the acquisition of the plant.

The Court of Appeal confirmed that provided the expenditure was incurred on the provision of machinery or plant wholly and exclusively for the purposes of the trade, it was irrelevant whether or not the trader's objective was or included the obtaining of capital allowances, and the *Ramsay* principle could not be applied.

It was also irrelevant how the trader acquired the funds to incur the expenditure. Whilst the cost of finance will not itself qualify for allowances, the fact that finance has to be obtained by way of loan does not preclude allowances being claimed on the asset itself.

Anchor International Ltd v IRC [2003] STC (SCD) 115

The taxpayer successfully claimed plant allowances on artificial football pitches, which consisted of a 'carpet' of synthetic turf, on a specially prepared base. The carpet was held not to be a structure (*inter alia*, it was not fixed, and could be replaced without disturbing the base or foundation works). Furthermore, although the carpet could be regarded as the setting for the business, that did not prevent it from also being regarded as plant used in the trade.

It was also held that the relevant item for consideration was the carpet alone, rather than the whole asset consisting of carpet and base. As a result, the base for the carpet also qualified for plant allowances. Although it was a structure, it fell within the exemption of what is now *CAA 2001, Item 22, List C, Sec 23* – 'the alteration of land for the purpose only of installing plant or machinery'.

Pro forma Elections

FIXTURES: APPORTIONMENT OF CONSIDERATION

Time limit: within two years of the date of the transaction.
(See 4.22)

HM Inspector of Taxes

....
....

We hereby elect, in accordance with the provisions of *CAA 2001, Sec 198* that in connection with the sale and purchase of [description of land, building etc.] on [date] for [total consideration], the amount regarded by both parties as the disposal value attributable to fixtures will be [£ ...].

This represents expenditure in respect of the items shown on the attached schedule.

....
[Vendor]
[Date]

....
[Purchaser]
[Date]

FIXTURES: GRANT OF NEW LEASE OR OTHER QUALIFYING INTEREST IN LAND

Time limit: within two years of the date on which the lease takes effect. (See 10.25)

HM Inspector of Taxes

....
....

This is a claim under *CAA 2001, Sec 183* relating to fixtures at [details of premises]. On [date of lease], a lease of those premises for a period of [x] years was granted by [lessor] to [lessee] for consideration of [£xxx].

We hereby elect, in accordance with *CAA 2001, Sec 183* for the assets specified below to be regarded as belonging to [lessee], and for the capital sum paid to be regarded as qualifying expenditure in respect of those assets.

[Details of fixtures]

....
[Lessor]
[Date]

....
[Lessee]
[Date]

Appendix 5

FIXTURES: EXPENDITURE INCURRED BY EQUIPMENT LESSOR

Time limit: within two years of the end of the chargeable period in which the expenditure is incurred (by the lessor).
(See 17.15)

HM Inspector of Taxes

....
....

We hereby elect, in accordance with *CAA 2001, Sec 177* for the assets specified below to be regarded as belonging to [equipment lessor].

These assets are fixtures at [details of premises].

[Details of fixtures] [Date expenditure incurred]

....
[Lessor]
[Date]

....
[Lessee]
[Date]

ACQUISITION OF KNOW-HOW WITH A TRADE

Time limit: within two years of the date of the transaction.
(See 18.49)

HM Inspector of Taxes

....
....

On [date], the trade of [description] carried on by [transferor] was transferred to [transferee].

We hereby elect, in accordance with the provisions of *TA 1988, Sec 531(3)* for expenditure amounting to [£ ...] arising on that transfer to be regarded as relating to the know-how described below.

[Description of know-how]

....
[Transferor]   [Transferee]
[Date]   [Date]

GRANT OF LONG LEASE OF INDUSTRIAL BUILDING TO BE TREATED AS SALE OF RELEVANT INTEREST BY LESSOR

Time limit: two years from date that lease takes effect. (See 10.6)

HM Inspector of Taxes

....
....

We hereby elect that the provisions of *CAA 2001, Sec 290* shall apply to the grant dated .... of the long lease of the building [address] by .... (the lessor) to .... (the lessee).

For and on behalf of the lessor ....

....
Secretary

For and on behalf of the lessee ....

....
Secretary

Dated ....

TRANSFER OF ASSETS AT TAX WRITTEN-DOWN VALUE

**Time limit: within two years of the disposal.
(See 12.13)**

HM Inspector of Taxes

....

....

We hereby elect that the provisions of *CAA 2001, Sec 569* shall apply to the transfer of the undernoted assets which took place in the accounting period ended ....

Description of assets transferred   Tax WDV

....   £

....   £

For and on behalf of the transferor ....

....
Secretary

For and on behalf of the transferee company............................

....
Secretary

Dated ....

ELECTION FOR PLANT TO BE TREATED AS SHORT LIFE ASSET

Time limit: within two years of the end of the accounting period of expenditure.
(See 13.74)

HM Inspector of Taxes

....
....

We .... hereby elect to treat the following items of machinery or plant acquired in the accounting period ended .... as short life assets, in accordance with the provisions of *CAA 2001, Sec 83*.

Asset description	Date of expenditure	Expenditure
....	....	£
....	....	£

....
Secretary

Dated ....

TRANSFER OF ASSETS ON SUCCESSION TO A TRADE

**Time limit: within two years after the succession.
(See 12.6)**

HM Inspector of Taxes

....

....

.... plc/Ltd (the successor) succeeded to the trade of ....
plc/Ltd (the predecessor) on [date]. We .... plc/Ltd and
.... plc/Ltd who are connected persons for this purpose hereby elect
under *CAA 2001, Sec 266* that the provisions of *CAA 2001, Sec 267* shall
apply to the undernoted assets which were used for the purposes of the trade
of .... plc/Ltd prior to the succession and which were transferred to
.... plc/Ltd on the succession.

Description of the assets transferred

....

....

For and on behalf of the predecessor ....

....

Secretary

For and on behalf of the successor ....

....

Secretary

Dated ....

CAPITAL EXPENDITURE ON LAND REMEDIATION

Time limit: within two years of the end of the accounting period in which expenditure is incurred
(See 23.3)

HM Inspector of Taxes

....
....

We hereby elect under *FA 2001, Sch 22* for capital expenditure incurred on land remediation to be deducted in computing the profits of the trade.

Details of the expenditure incurred, setting out the nature of the work undertaken and relevant dates, are attached.

....
Secretary

Dated ....

INTANGIBLE FIXED ASSETS: ELECTION FOR FIXED RATE DEPRECIATION

Time limit: within two years of the end of the accounting period in which expenditure is incurred
(See 24.8)

HM Inspector of Taxes

....
....

We hereby elect under *FA 2002, Sch 29, para 10* to write down the cost of certain intangible assets at a fixed rate of 4% per annum. The assets are/are not written down for accounting purposes.

Details of the assets acquired and the expenditure incurred are attached.

....
Secretary

Dated ....

COMPUTER SOFTWARE: EXEMPTION FROM *FA 2002, SCH 29*

Time limit: within two years of the end of the accounting period in which expenditure is incurred
(See 24.14)

HM Inspector of Taxes

....
....

The Company has incurred expenditure on computer software, as attached. We hereby elect under *FA 2002, Sch 29, para 83* for that expenditure to be exempted from the provisions of *Sch 29*.

....
Secretary

Dated ....

INTANGIBLE FIXED ASSETS: ELECTION FOR ROLL-OVER RELIEF

Time limit: within two years of the end of the accounting period in which expenditure is incurred
(See 24.23)

HM Inspector of Taxes

....
....

The company has realised intangible fixed assets and reinvested the proceeds in new intangible fixed assets. We hereby claim relief under *FA 2002, Sch 29, Part 7*.

Details of the assets realised and acquired are as follows:

Description	Assets realised	Assets realised	New assets
	Cost	Accounting value	Cost
xxxxxxxx	xx	xx	xx
yyyyyyyy	xx	xx	xx

....
Secretary

Dated ....

CAPITAL EXPENDITURE ON LAND REMEDIATION STAFF PROVIDERS: ELECTION FOR CONNECTED PERSON TREATMENT

Time limit: within two years of the end of the accounting period in which expenditure is incurred. (The accounting period referred to is that of the company paying for the research and development, not the staff provider)
(See 18.6)

HM Inspector of Taxes

……………….

……………….

[The company] has incurred expenditure of [£xx,xxx] on research and development, this being expenditure payable to [staff provider] for the provision of staff.

We hereby elect under *FA 2000, Sch 20, para 8D* for that expenditure to be treated in accordance with *para 8C* of that Schedule. Consequently, expenditure of [£xx,xxx] will qualify for relief under Schedule 20.

………………..
Company Secretary

Dated …………

………………..
Staff Provider

Dated …………

Transaction Checklists

The following checklists indicate *some* of the issues which should be considered for the more common transactions involving capital allowances. They are not exhaustive, and the taxpayer constructing a new building, for example, should read Chapter 2 in its entirety. Depending on the precise facts of the transaction, this may then point to the relevance of, say, Chapter 7 (industrial buildings), Chapter 8 (hotels), Chapter 9 (enterprise zones), Chapters 13 to 15 (plant), and so on. General principles outlined in, *inter alia*, Chapters 1 and 20 are also likely to be relevant.

This highlights the interaction of the different types of allowances, and the benefit of an approach to capital allowances issues which is driven, not by the allowances themselves, but by the nature of the transaction.

Construction of new building

• Is it an industrial building?	7.22 et seq.
• Will it be used for research and development?	18.4 et seq.
• Is it in an enterprise zone?	9.2 et seq. App 3
• Is there a system to identify and record relevant facts and decisions?	1.29 et seq.
• Has the date been established when the expenditure is incurred?	1.39 et seq.
• Are any contributions or subsidies due?	1.42 et seq.
• Has integral plant been identified?	Ch 15 App 2
• Does any of the plant qualify for first year allowances, being energy efficient?	13.14
• Will any of the plant be a long life asset?	13.54
• Have fees and other similar costs been identified?	2.45
• Has the tax impact of planning agreements, etc. been assessed?	2.41 et seq.

•	Is there any expenditure on 'land remediation'?	Ch 23
•	Is a documentation manual being compiled?	2.45
•	If industrial, will part of the building be non-qualifying?	7.65 et seq. 7.80 et seq.
•	Is there a single building, or more than one?	7.83 et seq.
•	When is the building first used?	7.22 et seq.

Purchase of new building

•	Is it an industrial building?	7.22 et seq.
•	Is it in an enterprise zone?	9.2 et seq. App 3
•	Will it be used for research and development?	18.4 et seq.
•	Is the vendor a genuine property developer?	3.8 et seq.
•	Does part of the purchase price reflect rental guarantees, etc.?	3.14
•	Has integral plant been identified?	3.16
•	Is any of the plant a long life asset?	13.54
•	If the building is industrial, what part is non-qualifying?	7.65 et seq. 7.80 et seq.
•	Has the date been established when the expenditure is incurred?	1.39 et seq.
•	Are any contributions or subsidies due?	1.42 et seq.
•	Have fees and other similar costs been identified?	2.45
•	When is the building first used?	7.22 et seq.

Purchase of second-hand building

•	Have IBAs or research and development allowances previously been claimed?	4.19 20.13
•	Has the vendor provided an IBAs history?	4.5 et seq.
•	What was the original cost?	4.5 et seq.
•	When was it constructed?	4.5 et seq.
•	If relevant, do tenants' trades qualify for IBAs?	7.22 et seq.
•	Has integral plant been identified?	Ch 15 App 2
•	Is any of the plant a long life asset?	13.54
•	Has a joint election been made regarding the value of fixtures?	4.22 et seq.

- Is the cost of fixtures restricted? 4.17 et seq.
  10.42

- Has the land value been identified? 2.6 et seq.
  14.36 et seq.

- Have relevant warranties been sought from the vendor? 4.40 et seq.
  9.39

- Have fees and other similar costs been identified? 2.45

- Is just part of the building being used for non-qualifying 7.65 et seq.
  purposes? 7.80 et seq.
  7.91

- When is/was the building first used? 7.22 et seq.

Renting premises (landlord)

- Will the lessee's trade qualify for IBAs? 7.22 et seq.

- Can commencement of the lease be accelerated to fall 10.3 et seq.
  within the current accounting period?

- If industrial, is the building actually *in use* at the year end? 7.22 et seq.

- Has a *Sec 290* election been made? 10.6 et seq.

- Have fixtures been identified? 10.13
  Ch 15
  App 2

- On a sale, does *Sec 325* limit a balancing allowance? 11.19 et seq.

- Has a capital value been realised? 11.26 et seq.

Renting premises (tenant)

- Has a *Sec 290* election been made? 10.6 et seq.

- Is any sum payable in respect of fixtures? 10.23 et seq.

- Does the landlord require proof of qualifying 7.22 et seq.
  industrial use?

- Are you required to install your own fixtures? 10.19 et seq.

- What will happen to such fixtures at the end of the lease? 10.35

Acquiring plant

- Were building alterations required? 13.24 et seq.

- Were there any installation costs? 2.26

- Do any specific needs of the business influence the choice of plant? — 14.11 et seq. / 14.30 et seq.
- Can the acquisition be timed to take advantage of FYAs? — 1.39 et seq. / 13.5 ct scq.
- What is the expected useful economic life of the plant (>25 years)? — 13.53
- Has a short life asset election been considered? — 13.70
- Does the company or business qualify as 'small' for FYAs purposes? — 13.8
- Have the relevant costs (e.g. transport) been identified? — 13.19 et seq.
- Is there irrecoverable VAT? — 21.2
- Are there any contributions or subsidies towards wear and tear? — 1.42 et seq.
- Is the expenditure specifically allowed by statute? — 14.35
- Is the 'plant' a motor car or another type of vehicle? — 16.1
- Is the plant being acquired on HP? — 17.1
- Is the plant to be leased out? — 17.8 et seq.
- Are the allowances needed — should they be disclaimed or 'sold'? — 17.27 et seq. / 20.1
- Has notification of the acquisition been submitted? — 20.46

Index

Index

Property investors *cont.*
generally, 10.1–10.2
plant, expenditure on,
fixtures,
basic problem and its solution, 10.13
deemed disposal of, 10.33–10.36
disposal value of, 10.37–10.41
equipment lessor, expenditure
incurred by, 10.24
nature of, 10.14–10.21
new, expenditure on, 10.22–10.23
qualifying expenditure, restriction of,
10.42
second-hand,
acquisition of existing interest in
land, 10.25–10.26
creation of new interest in land,
10.27–10.32
generally, 10.10–10.12
Public authority
meaning, 1.72
Purchase of new building. *See* **New
buildings**
Purchase of second-hand building. *See*
Second-hand buildings

Q
Quality control
buildings used for, industrial buildings
allowance, 7.44

R
Refurbishment
generally, 1.13–1.14
improvements, 1.14, 1.19–1.20
like-for-like expenditure, 1.14, 1.18
motive for incurring expenditure, 1.14
nature of asset, 1.13, 1.15–1.17
nearest modern equivalent, 1.14, 1.21–1.22
Relevant interest
industrial buildings allowance, claim for,
2.45, 7.18–7.21
Renewals basis
availability of, 1.25, 1.26
Rental guarantees
pricing, artificial effect on, 3.14–3.15
Repairs
goods or materials, 7.45
improvements obviating, 1.23–1.24
industrial property, to, 7.6
Replacement
improvement, element of, 1.14, 1.19–1.20
like-for-like, 1.14, 1.18
nearest modern equivalent, 1.14, 1.21–1.22
Research and development
balancing charge, avoiding, 18.25–18.26
capital expenditure, 18.7–18.9
change of use, 18.27
disposal, 18.24
employee costs, 18.6

Research and development *cont.*
exclusion from allowances,
18.12–18.15
generally, 18.1–18.4
groups, 18.10
Inland Revenue approach, 18.20–18.21
meaning, 18.16–18.19
practicalities, 18.22–18.23
property companies, 18.11
relief for expenditure on, 1.5, 18.5
revenue expenditure, 18.5–18.6
SME tax credit, 18.5
Reservation of title to goods
date expenditure incurred, 1.51
writing-down allowances, 13.49
Restrictive covenants
know-how, relating to, 18.52
Retail property
electrical systems, 6.10
flats, part converted into, 6.11
industrial buildings allowances, not
qualifying for, 7.71–7.74
repair work, 6.3
roundsmen as retail outlets, 6.6
special features,
generally, 6.1–6.9
plant, 6.10
trade customers, 6.2
Retail shops. *See* **Retail property**
Retentions
date expenditure incurred, 1.52
Revenue
capital distinguished from, 1.6–1.11
deduction, 1.6–1.11
Ring-fence trade
expenditure on, 13.5, 13.54
Roads
industrial estate, on, 7.9–7.10
Roller shutters
plant, as, 15.42–15.44
Royalties
use of intangible asset, in respect of use,
24.17

S
Safety
fire safety, 14.47–14.50
sports grounds, at, 14.51
Sale of property
ascertainment of proceeds, 11.2–11.3
generally, 11.1
industrial buildings,
anti-avoidance, 11.19–11.21
balancing adjustments, 11.4–11.9
balancing allowance, restriction of,
11.19–11.21
buildings not only industrial,
11.15–11.18
demolition, 11.11–11.14
use and disuse, 11.10

320

Index

Taxation
capital gains tax. *See* **Capital gains tax**
maximising tax relief, 1.4–1.5
value added tax. *See* **Value added tax**

Thermal insulation
expenditure on, 14.36–14.39

Time limits for claims
amendments to claims, 20.7–20.8
generally, 20.4–20.6

Trade
acquisition of,
  assets other than plant, 12.10–12.12
  election by connected persons, 12.7, 12.13
  generally, 12.3
  inheritance, succession to trade by, 12.8–12.9
  machinery and plant, 12.4–12.6
change of, 12.22–12.23
discontinuance, sale of property on, 11.8
emigration. *See* **Emigration of trade**
European Union, transfer of UK trade within, 22.16–22.21
immigration. *See* **Immigration of trade**
inheritance, succession by, 12.8–12.9
know-how acquired with, 18.50–18.52, Appendix 5
leasing. *See* **Leasing**
qualifying activity, meaning, 13.18
qualifying activity, purpose of, 13.36–13.41
Schedule A business, 13.75, 22.16
succession to, transfer of assets on, Appendix 5
writing-down allowances. *See* **Writing-down allowances**

Trade mark
intangible fixed asset, as, 24.10

Trading
expenditure prior to commencement of, 1.63–1.64

Trading loss
avoiding, 20.16–20.17
desire to use, 20.18–20.21

Transactions
checklists, Appendix 6
within groups. *See* **Groups**

Transport authority
compulsory transfer of land to, 2.44

Transport undertakings
industrial buildings allowance, 7.31–7.34

U

Unused building
enterprise zone,
  purchase after expiry of, 9.31–9.33

Unused building *cont.*
enterprise zone *cont.*
  purchase before expiry of, 9.26–9.30
purchase of, 3.4–3.7

V

Value added tax
additional liability, 21.11–21.15
capital items scheme, 21.5–21.10
effective date of rebate, 21.11–21.15
generally, 21.1–21.2
partially exempt business, 21.3–21.4

Vehicle fleet
car registration plates, 16.19
cars, generally, 16.3–16.4
electric cars, 13.5, 16.16, 16.20
employees' cars, 16.18
expensive cars,
  generally, 16.6–16.13
  leasing, 16.15
  pooling, 13.3
  restrictions on allowances, 16.14
generally, 16.1–16.2
inexpensive cars, 16.5
low CO_2 emissions, cars with, 13.5, 16.16, 16.20
special treatment, vehicles excluded from, 16.16–16.17

W

Walls
partition, 15.36–15.41

Warranties
enterprise zone building, purchase of, 9.39

Water pollution
land remediation relief, 23.5

Water systems
cold water installations, 15.9–15.10
heating, 14.71
hot water installations, 15.8
plant, as, 15.6–15.10

Wear and tear
furnished living accommodation, 1.26
partial depreciation subsidy, 13.3
subsidies towards, 1.83–1.85, 13.3

Wholly or partly
principle of, 13.30–13.35

Work in progress
sale of, 3.12–3.13

Works
ineligible expenditure, 14.65–14.67

Written-down value
transfer of assets at, Appendix 5

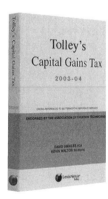